CAPTAIN
DAUNTLESS

CAPTAIN NICHOLAS BIDDLE OF THE CONTINENTAL NAVY. After a portrait by Charles Willson Peale as copied by Christian Schuessele and presented in 1859 to the Historical Society of Pennsylvania. Original portrait hangs in Independence Hall. Courtesy of the Society.

CAPTAIN DAUNTLESS

The Story of

NICHOLAS BIDDLE

of the

CONTINENTAL

NAVY

By

WILLIAM BELL CLARK

Published by the LOUISIANA

STATE UNIVERSITY PRESS

1949

"I FEAR NOTHING but what I ought to fear. I am Much more afraid of doing a foolish Action than of loosing My Life   I aim for a Character of Conduct as well as courage And hope never to throw away the Vessel and Crew merely to Convince the world I have Courage   No one has dared to impeach it yet. If any should I will not leave them a moment of doubt."

NICHOLAS BIDDLE TO HIS BROTHER CHARLES,

JUNE 16, 1776.

Preface

NICHOLAS BIDDLE'S NAME STANDS IMPERISHABLE IN the annals of the American navy. Yet the fact that he died heroically in the frigate *Randolph* seems to sum up the general knowledge about him. One or two pieces of fiction, based upon the fatal engagement in which he lost his life, and certain legends arising from the same disaster, have confused matters by substituting fancy for fact.

In his youth Biddle's life was exciting, colorful, and frequently dangerous. In the Revolution, until death removed him prematurely from the scene, his experiences were varied and unusual. His contributions to the first American naval efforts were of inestimable value. Among his fellow captains he was outstanding for courage, initiative, and ability. Wherever he moved he inspired confidence. With it all he was modest and unassuming, won friends quickly, and held them lastingly.

His deeds deserve better public appreciation than ever has been accorded them, and entitle him to greater recognition in American naval history. To accomplish these aims has been the purpose of this biography.

The author takes full responsibility for the resultant text, even to admitting the deliberate use of the antiquated spelling of "Charlestown" or "Charles Town." As all letters or documents of the Revolutionary period used the old style, it seemed less confusing to adopt it also for general text purposes. Sources are listed in an appended bibliography, which has been expanded to identify some of the more important materials.

Acknowledgments are in order to a number of people who have extended willing and useful aid. Among them special appreciation goes to the late Mrs. John Drayton Grimke and her son, Glen Drayton Grimke, of Charleston, South Carolina, who provided much information about Archdale Hall and the family of Elizabeth Elliott Baker; to Lieutenant Commander M. V. Brewington, U.S.N.R., of Washington, D.C., who ran down many rare manuscripts, and his wife, Dorothy, who transcribed them for me; to the late Cedric V. Merrill, of Evanston, Illinois, who read the text and saved the author from some embarrassing errors; to L. Richard Hawley, Jr., of Evanston, Illinois, who redrew, for use as illustrations, the hull plan of the *Randolph* and a map of Charlestown Harbor; to Joseph C. Wolf, of the Newberry Library, Chicago, who made accessible much in the way of genealogy and local history pertaining to Rhode Island and South Carolina; to Mr. Nicholas B. Wainwright, research librarian of the Historical Society of Pennsylvania, who persisted in his search until he located for me a long-missing collection of Nicholas Biddle letters; to Miss Catharine H. Miller, and the entire staff of the Manuscript Division of the Historical Society of Pennsylvania; to Dr. St. George L. Sioussat, former Chief of the Manuscript Division of the Library of Congress; to Captain Harry A. Baldridge, U.S.N. (retired), director of the Museum of the United States Naval Academy at Annapolis, and to all the librarians of the historical societies listed in the bibliography.

WILLIAM BELL CLARK

Evanston, Ill.

Contents

x

Contents

Illustrations

I

Education of a Sea-Fighter

Chapter I
The Ann and Almack

SECRETLY YOUNG NICHOLAS BIDDLE CONSIDERED THE *Ann and Almack* a most unromantic name for so fine a vessel. He had suggested as much to his portly brother-in-law at first sight of the newly built snow lying in the Delaware off John Wharton's shipyard. But Captain William McFunn, who was not steeped, as was Nicholas, in Smollett's *Roderick Random,* had merely sniffed and remarked there could be no more worthy names bestowed upon any craft than those of Captain McFunn's own beloved sister and said sister's husband, the celebrated London tavern keeper.

Whereupon Nicholas had held his peace. The captain owned one-third interest in the *Ann and Almack,* and Nicholas none. Arousing the testy McFunn's ire might spell disaster for his cherished hope of going to sea in her. Upon that he was determined, regardless of her name. It would be difficult enough to win his widowed mother's approval, even with Captain McFunn as an ally.[1] With the formidable, blustering brother-in-law against him, instead of sailing for Jamaica, he would be doomed to a year at Master Dove's academy, wherein the youth of Philadelphia were schooled in the art of becoming gentlemen.

Nicholas had no desire to become a gentleman in the pattern prescribed by Master Dove.[2] Having learned to read with tolerable fluency, to spell with fair accuracy, to write with some legibility, and to master more arithmetic than might be expected in a lad of fourteen, he had only the burning desire to embark finally upon the profession he had long ago selected—the sea.[3]

There had been a delectable taste of it in the summer just ended. When the academy had closed in April, he had wheedled reluctant consent from his mother to ship as cabin boy for a voyage to Quebec in the brig *Lark*. He had departed, his head filled with fanciful notions of life on the bounding main. The long passage to the city wrested but five years before from the French, and the still longer return had dispelled much of the glamor. But the bracing smell of fresh salt air, the wind whistling aloft through taut rigging, the creaking groans of tall spars under a press of sail, even the odor of bilge water drifting upwards from the hold, had worked a greater charm upon him. By the time the *Lark* had picked up a pilot off Cape Henlopen and poked her homeward way up the Delaware, the sea had entered the lad's soul.[4]

Mary Biddle, who had already seen another son forsake the land to go a voyaging, had hoped the summer would cure Nicholas of his nonsense, make him amenable, even willing, to continue with a year or more of schooling. It was with that idea in mind she had given her consent. Yet her heart sank when he came ashore, rolling a bit on his sea legs, and she saw how healthy, brown, rugged, and supremely happy he was. Ever a boy old for his years, he had matured markedly in the brief four months of absence. About him there was an unspoken assurance which boded ill for her planning. Because she feared the worst, she was content to listen to his enthusiasm and refrain from voicing her desires until a more propitious time. Perhaps an interval at home might wear away the spell of the sea and convince him of the need for that better education she so desired for him.

Alas for hopes! The *Ann and Almack,* Captain McFunn, and even her son Charles, just returned from shipwreck off Fayal, seemed to conspire against her. The home on Front Street resounded day and night to conversations about the new snow, whose outfitting, supposed sailing merits, or promised cargo were sole topics at every meal. Sometimes it was Captain McFunn who held forth, his lusty voice reverberating through the house in a mixture of the polite profanity of His Majesty's quarter-deck and the Billingsgate picked up in long years as master attendant of the navy yard at Antigua. Sometimes it was Charles Biddle, profoundly seawise at the age of nineteen after two voyages to the Azores, and already assured a second-mate's berth on the new vessel. Or, occasionally, it was John Lockhart Naesmith, half-pay lieutenant in the British navy, a strangely taciturn and handsome man who had come from London the previous spring, and who owned the other two thirds of the *Ann and Almack* and would be in command on her maiden voyage.[5]

So Mary Biddle listened—perforce she could do nothing else—and watched sadly the effect upon young Nicholas. It was he, one night, who read aloud the advertisement placed by the agents for the owners of the snow in the *Pennsylvania Gazette,* first exhibiting the page whereon a woodcut of a two-master was supposed to depict the vessel.

"For Kingston in Jamaica," he read, "the snow Ann and Almack, John Lockhart Naesmith, master; a new vessel, with good accommodations for passengers, and will sail with all convenient speed, part of her cargo being already engaged. For freight or passage apply to Stewart Duncan and Company, or said master on board, or at the Coffee House." [6]

"A proper announcement," commented Captain McFunn, "and, egad, it makes me wish I were sailing in her myself. Doesn't it you, Nick, my lad?"

Nicholas nodded in eager-eyed agreement.

After that Mary Biddle knew her cause was lost. When Nicholas, as a dutiful son, a few days later asked her permission to ship for the voyage, she sensed his determination and demurred but little; just enough to show him how reluctant she was to see him go. There was some reward in the bear hug he gave her, ere he dashed from the house to see Captain Naesmith and sign the shipping articles.[7]

Permission for Nicholas to go to sea, while hard for Mary Biddle to grant, filled a practical necessity. It meant one mouth less to feed, one more child self-supporting. Ever since her husband's death some eight years earlier, the valiant widow had struggled to maintain her large family. It had been a bitter battle. Bred to a life akin to luxury in colonial Philadelphia, drudgery had never before been her portion. Yet, when William Biddle died, a disappointed, well-nigh penniless business failure, she had buckled to her task with a stamina surprising even to herself. Boarders were taken into the Biddle home. Catering jobs were sought, and in her spare hours she attended at the Fountain Tavern and sold the maps and plans which had made famous her late father, the celebrated Nicholas Scull, onetime surveyor general of Pennsylvania.[8]

Pride prevented accepting help from friends or relatives. In this gentle lady's veins flowed the blood of pioneering ancestors who had been forced to rely upon themselves for success. Not that she longer expected success, save through her offspring. They were her principal, almost sole, interest, and to raise them to be honest, God-fearing, and able men and women was her abiding ambition. By the fall of 1764, when Nicholas won his cherished desire, she could look back over the years and feel she had accomplished much of her self-imposed duty. All but three of her brood were "on their own," and some of the older ones had reached a station in life where they were able to contribute somewhat to the support of their mother and the younger children still at home.

Best of all, those she had raised until they were able to fend for themselves were willing and eager to help her now. In that admirable trait, she saw the high sense of honor inherent in her late husband. In the estimation of those who measure success by the size of a ledger balance, William Biddle had been a failure. But Mary Biddle knew that his character was a more lasting heritage to his children than a fortune in pounds sterling. His merits had provided them a better patrimony than would have the proceeds of the farm he sold in West Jersey and lost in business ventures in Philadelphia. Of her own merits she thought but little. That she had kept her brood with her and given them schooling, she attributed rather "to the mercy of God." As she was a deeply religious woman, their filial devotion had made her, "in the language of the Scripture, sing for joy." [9]

On the paternal side, young Nicholas had a sturdy line of forebears stemming from a certain William Biddle, onetime officer under Cromwell in the Parliamentary army. This ancestor had fought valiantly during the Civil War but, with English liberties won and King Charles's head severed at the chopping block, had experienced revulsion against war and its cruelties. He forsook the army to unite with the Society of Friends. Then came the Restoration and persecution of the Quakers. William Biddle, after suffering one imprisonment in Newgate and years of abuse and vituperation, embarked for the colonies about 1680 with his wife and two young children. He settled in West Jersey, selecting the banks of the Delaware for his homestead and bestowing upon the plantation the restful title of Mount Hope. His holdings embraced 500 acres on the mainland about midway between Burlington and Bordentown, and 278 acres on an adjacent island. Within a few years he had become a guiding influence in provincial affairs, serving at various times upon the Governor's Council, the Board of Commissioners for Laying out Land, the General Assembly, and the Council of the Proprietors of West Jersey. Almost until his death, in 1712, the Burlington Quarterly Meeting of the Society of Friends convened at Mount Hope.[10]

The merits of William, the emigrant, were early evidenced in his only surviving son. The second William, while not so active in provincial matters, was a man of parts. Under his shrewd Quaker judgment the estate grew to greater proportions, his name being oftener on a real-estate transfer than a public document. When he died intestate in 1743, the broad acres of Mount Hope were divided equally among his six children. One of them —William, the oldest—had already departed from West Jersey to try his fortune down the river in Philadelphia. This third William, restive under the placid life of a young country gentleman, had large ambitions to enter business. His father had acquiesced and, having influential connections in the city, had placed him with a reputable commercial house: that of a Mr. Griffiths, recognized as "one of the first merchants in America." [11]

Within a few years William had acquired a liberal business education and a wife. The good-looking young squire from West Jersey had put to rout all Philadelphia beaux and won— in the spring of 1730—one of the prize beauties of the city; none other than demure Mary Scull. She was of the "world's people," and her influence shortly transferred her husband's allegiance from Quaker Meeting House to Christ Church. Intoxicated by his success in love, William bade farewell to his employer and launched out confidently to be just as successful in commerce. Mild of manner, trusting of disposition, and, despite Griffiths' training, naïve in business matters, he proved a lamb among human wolves. They sheared him at every turn. Each commercial venture cost him money. Misplaced confidence in his fellow men cost him more. The requirements of a growing family sank him deeper and deeper into debt. Too proud to turn to his aging father for financial assistance, he struggled against fate, growing sour of temper and despondent. An end to worry seemed to come with the settlement of his father's estate in 1743. William's sixth was a tidy sum. It enabled him to retire his debts, to provide better for his family, and, ill-advisedly, to launch into a new business venture. A few years of prosperity followed, and then disaster.[12]

"I had nine children, one at my breast," recorded Mary Biddle, "when Mr. Biddle informed me one morning [in 1752] that he had involved himself and ruined me and his children. I was much shocked, but begged he would settle his affairs, and hoped he would be better off than he expected. We had an estate in Jersey, which he sold for two thousand pounds. He could not see his children without tears. We paid all our debts and Mr. Biddle entered into partnership with one Jacobs, a man supposed to be possessed of a great fortune. In one year he broke, and we had to pay fourteen hundred pounds for him. This quite sunk Mr. Biddle. We had very little left. My dear Mr. Biddle was taken with a lingering disorder. For six months before he died, I never slept with my clothes off." [13]

When they laid him to rest, in 1756, the little family was practically penniless. Mary's own money had been swept away in the last enterprise, but at least all debts had been paid. Of the nine children three were provided for. The eldest son, James, born in 1731, had just begun the practice of law in the back counties of Pennsylvania. Lydia, the oldest daughter, born in 1734, was in Antigua in the West Indies, the wife of Captain William McFunn. John, the second son, born in 1736, had employment with a Philadelphia merchant. Before another year

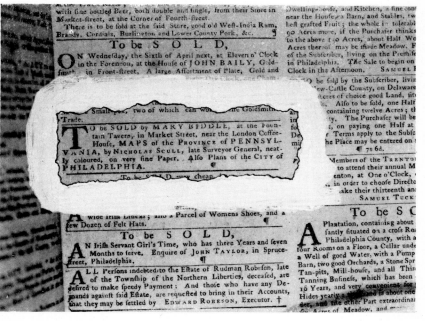

MARY BIDDLE'S ADVERTISEMENT AS A MAP PUR-
VEYOR. From the Pennsylvania *Gazette* of March 10, 1763. From
copy in Historical Society of Pennsylvania.

had elapsed Edward, the third son, born in 1738, was commissioned ensign in the Second Pennsylvania regiment of the Provincial army, and was off for three years of service in the French and Indian War. So was John, who had become a deputy quartermaster in Brigadier General John Forbes's force.[14]

Upon Mary Biddle devolved the care of the remaining five —Charles, born in 1745; Abigail, in 1747; Mary, in 1749; Nicholas, on September 10, 1750; and Thomas, in 1752. From 1757 to 1764, her struggle had gone on unsparingly, determinedly. By the latter year, James had returned to Philadelphia and was deputy prothonotary of the county court. Lydia and her husband were back from Antigua, the redoubtable McFunn on half pay. John and Edward, with land grants for their army service, were establishing themselves in Berks County; the former again in mercantile pursuits, the latter studying law. Charles was going out as second mate on the *Ann and Almack*. Nicholas had just gained his mother's consent to ship on that little vessel. Abigail was engaged to be married, her nuptials set for the following spring. Mary, aged fifteen, and Thomas, the baby of the family and just turned twelve, alone of her precious brood remained at home.

"I am a happy mother," she wrote, "and my soul is rejoicing in the Almighty, who has blessed me in my children." [15]

Captains Naesmith and McFunn registered the *Ann and Almack* at the customhouse on September 24, 1764, and McFunn swelled with indignation when the clerk misunderstood and first inscribed her as the *Almanack*. She was, they attested, once the error was corrected, a square-sterned vessel of sixty-six tons burthen, and snow rigged.[16] Nicholas had heard the pair of them argue the merits of "snow-rigging" almost nightly across the dinner board. Between Naesmith's clipped sentences and McFunn's picturesque oratory, he gathered that a snow differed from a brig only in a trysail mast set a foot or thereabouts abaft the mainmast, and secured aloft to the trestletrees of that mast. Its purpose was to make possible the setting of a fore-and-aft mainsail, which was difficult, even impractical, with ordinary brig rigging. From John Wharton, Nicholas learned that snow rigging was gaining popularity. The shipbuilder recalled eighteen such vessels registered in Philadelphia in the last several years. None of them, however, Wharton admitted with pardonable pride, could hold a candle to his own creation, the *Ann and Almack*.[17]

The trim little snow was really worthy of her builder's enthusiasm. She had a deck length of almost sixty feet, a breadth of eighteen, and a depth in hold of about eight. Her mainmast reared a good sixty feet aloft; her foremast, slightly lower. Every line of her rigging had been lately spun, and her canvas, fresh from the sail loft, was new from jib to spanker, with spare sheets stowed away for future emergency. Nicholas, the last to sign on, whose designation on the shipping articles was "cabin boy," thought her the finest vessel he had ever seen. From accounts of her, as they have come down through the years, his appraisal seems justified.

There were ten in the crew, including Captain Naesmith, Arthur Campbell, a deaf Scotsman who was first mate, and Charles Biddle, second mate. Nicholas had been assigned to his brother's watch, a kindly gesture on the part of the captain. Naesmith also had assured him that a little more experience and the first vacancy would procure him a seaman's rating. For watchmates he had Armstrong, an old salt; Peters, a Scot; and Scull, a distant cousin on his mother's side. With the first two he struck up immediate friendship. Scull he had long known and never liked.[18]

Despite the advertisement in the *Pennsylvania Gazette* and the original outward entry at the customhouse, the destination of the *Ann and Almack* for her maiden voyage had been changed. Instead of Jamaica, she was to clear for Antigua, in the Leeward Islands at the far eastern rim of the Caribbean Sea.[19] Thereafter the owners planned a series of trading ventures in the West Indies, which might conclude with a cargo of mahogany and logwood from the Bay of Honduras for London. Why plans were altered is not clear. Possibly the hoped-for passengers to Jamaica failed to materialize, and McFunn, with his knowledge of the Leeward Islands market, felt a better penny could be turned by shipping barrel staves and pig iron to Antigua.

What with stowing cargo, provisions, and ship's stores, setting up rigging, caulking seams, holystoning decks, and painting the hull, young Nicholas found few opportunities to visit his family. During the week preceding departure he never left the snow. Even when, just before sailing, he was paid for the work he had done and given a month's advance, there was no time to go home. He had pictured the enjoyment of turning his wages over to his mother in person, and was sorely disappointed. Charles, who was in the same predicament, consoled him with assurances they could send the money up from the capes.

The *Ann and Almack* sailed from Philadelphia on October 1, and next day came to off Reedy Island. Winds turned contrary and progress was slow. They dropped down the bay by easy stages : one day to Bombay Hook ; the next, only as far as Deep Water Point ; and the third, to Whorekiln Road, where they cast sheltered anchorage northwest of Cape Henlopen. A stiff breeze from the east held them there until the middle of the month. While they waited, Nicholas and Charles found means of forwarding their wages to the address of Mrs. Mary Biddle on Front Street, the older brother remarking :

"I never disposed of any money that gave me so much pleasure."

Nicholas echoed his sentiments. Their mother's soul could well rejoice in her children.[20]

With a bracing offshore wind over her stern, the *Ann and Almack* passed out between the Delaware capes on October 15, 1764. By nightfall Cape Henlopen was far astern and the snow was ploughing through a choppy sea, her head to the southeast on the favorite course of mariners bound from the capes to the islands in the Leeward group. After two days of pleasant weather, the wind hauled around to the southward, blowing so hard that Captain Naesmith decided to heave to. When Nicholas turned in after dark, the gale was increasing. The vessel pitched and tossed, but he was too dog-tired to be kept awake by timbers groaning under impact of waves and blasts of wind. A wild hail down the steerage hatchway brought him out of his bunk. It was Naesmith's voice, shaken from its accustomed modulation.

"Jump up, my brave lads," he was bawling. "Make haste up, my good fellows, or we all perish."

The watch below piled on deck in the darkness to find an embarrassed and bewildered skipper listening to an apologetic first mate.

" 'Tis no danger we're in, sir," Campbell was explaining in his loud voice—the habit of years of trying to hear his own words. "With the gale growing worse, I had but gone down to 'rouse ye, and suggest we had best take in the foresail."

For days afterwards the crew gleefully quoted Naesmith's agitated remarks; not, of course, within his hearing. Nicholas shared in the general impression that their captain had shown himself a coward. They learned differently later. When the true story of the incident was disclosed, it continued humorous, but with no implication of craven conduct. Naesmith had been dreaming—a horrible nightmare of a foundering ship—when Campbell awakened him. At that moment the snow had given a lee-lurch, and the cabin table had broken loose and crashed to the floor. The dream seemed reality amid the thundering noise, and the startled captain's reaction had been to catapult to the deck and call the crew.[21]

Barring this episode, the voyage proved uneventful but tedious. Usually the passage from the Delaware capes to Antigua took about twenty days. Many a vessel, with favoring winds, had negotiated it in two weeks. But the *Ann and Almack,* with the wind persistently adverse, and with occasional calms, consumed thirty days before she dropped her small bower anchor in St. John harbor, on the rocky northeastern end of the island. For Nicholas, however, the lengthy voyage had been invaluable. How a skilled mariner like Naesmith could tack to get the last ounce of benefit from a vagrant breeze, or turn a contrary wind to his advantage by adroit use of the proper sails were lessons in good seamanship he never forgot.

Appraisal of the Antigua market, as made by McFunn in

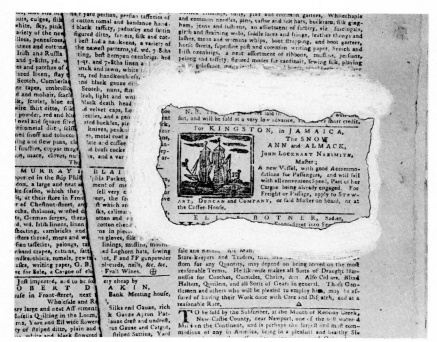

FIRST SAILING OF THE *ANN AND ALMACK*. An advertisement from the Pennsylvania *Gazette* of August 23, 1764. From copy in Historical Society of Pennsylvania.

Philadelphia, proved accurate. Captain Naesmith found immediate purchasers for staves and pig iron, and with some of the proceeds began to lay in a cargo for the Bay of Honduras. It consisted of rum and dry goods with sufficient ballast added to assure the snow's trim for the run westward through the Caribbean Sea.

No chance was given Nicholas or any of the hands to go sight-seeing on the island. Unloading one cargo and taking in another kept them employed daily. The one visit a number of them made one evening to St. John almost terminated in tragedy. Charles Biddle had elected to remain in the longboat while the rest, including Nicholas and Captain Naesmith, went along to the city. Returning, they found their shipmate struggling with a drunken brute, who was rapidly beating him into insensibility. They hurled themselves upon the assailant and hove him overboard. Charles, bleeding and dazed, mumbled an explanation as they rowed out to the snow. The fellow, who commanded a coaster, had demanded to be put on board his vessel and, being refused, had attacked in drunken fury. Being far more powerful, he probably would have murdered the second mate save for the opportune arrival of the crew.

Dressing his brother's wounds, Nicholas wondered how life in such a beautiful port as St. John could be so raw and brutal. Later he would learn that Antigua was peaceful and law-abiding when compared to the region for which they sailed at dawn the following morning. From Armstrong, who had visited the Bay previously, he heard numerous tales of the uncouth men who dwelt in "His Majesty's Settlement in the Bay of Honduras." They were a lawless lot, the logwood cutters, constantly at odds with the Spaniards from whom the colony had been wrested more than a century before.

"They're bad, them Baymen," Armstrong said, with a solemn wag of his head. "Most of 'em are old seamen or merchants who couldn't turn an honest penny anywhere else. You'll find 'em hospitable enough, lad, and generous, too. They'll share their liquor and provisions with you any time you visit 'em, but they expects the same treatment when they come on board ship. It pays to treat 'em kindly, or they'll never sell you no wood, and

insult you every time you go ashore. And you got to watch 'em,
too, or they'll resell the wood you just bought to some one else
before you can load it. Once they get your money in their jeans,
all hell can't pry it loose."

About the tenth day out of Antigua, Naesmith picked up the
Mosquito Coast, and hove to. Nicholas watched a dozen canoes
put off from the low-lying shore and make for them. Paddles
came to rest a few yards away, while from each frail craft arose
a voluble chatter of broken English. The captain picked out an
Indian—the basis of the selection being beyond Nicholas—who
climbed aboard, and the snow stood off to the westward. Armstrong previously had explained this practice. All vessels hired
a native, when bound for the Bay. He was called a "striker,"
and it was his duty to supply the crew with fish and turtle.

"And you'll get so sick of fish and turtle," Armstrong had
warned, "that you'll be begging for a good mess of salt pork." [22]

Threading a perilous course past coral reefs and tiny isles, the
Ann and Almack anchored around December 1, off St. George's
Key, and Nicholas marveled that anyone would choose to live in
such a country. The air was steaming with heat and heavy with
rain. The settlement on the key looked dismal and drenched;
the shore of the mainland to the west appeared low and swampy
with a tangle of mangroves and tropical jungle right down to
the water's edge, save at one point where the village of Belize
squatted at the mouth of a river. Occasionally, when the clouds
opened, tall mountains were visible off beyond the swamps. To
the lad it was oppressive and depressing—far different from
what his imagination had pictured. The only consolation was to
learn that the rainy season was almost over.

Heat and torrential rains were no deterrents to Naesmith.
Within the next few days, he located customers at St. George's
for the rum and dry goods. The crew, naked to the waist, toiled
in the heat of the hold passing kegs, boxes, and bales to the deck,
or sweltered in the beating rain to roll the cumbersome goods
into a lighter, while the captain set off for Belize to locate a
cargo of mahogany and logwood. He returned, having contracted for the wood, and brought back with him a young negro
who answered to the imposing name of Marlborough—a really

handsome lad who had been raised in Bristol, England, and who proved an excellent gentleman's valet, as well as a willing handy man and a general favorite of the crew. Naesmith had hired him from his owner, a settler named Cook, who lived some miles up the river. The captain's enjoyment of the refinements of being shaved and dressed by Marlborough was short-lived. Within a month, Cook arrived on board and demanded his black boy. Both Nicholas and Charles hated to see the likable negro depart.

By then the rains had ceased and the heat had grown a trifle less oppressive. The dry season was setting in, and the cargo was beginning to arrive. One shallop, with a load of logwood came alongside while Naesmith was up the river on a visit. A few tons had been taken from her when a Captain Wright, commanding a brig from New York, boarded the snow.

"That's my wood you're loading," he informed the first mate on a truculent note. "That shallop was intended for me, and I want it."

Campbell scratched his head. Wright was an old privateersman and had a reputation as a bully. Perhaps it would be better to placate him.

"Now, maybe you're right," the mate admitted, "but Captain Naesmith ain't on board, and I wouldn't dare release it without his permission."

"Then, by God, I'll take it," Wright shouted, and attempted to cast off the shallop. Campbell grappled with him and was hurled to the deck. Wright's boat crew climbed on board, and Nicholas was in the midst of his first melee. The fight was vicious. The New Yorkers outnumbered the crew of the *Ann and Almack* and were burlier fellows. Charles and Nicholas, battling to the best of their abilities, were beaten down. George Peters, the Scotch seaman in Nicholas' watch, was knocked from the gunwale into the shallop, sustaining a broken arm, and lay seemingly lifeless. The first mate was pummeled into unconsciousness; and Wright and his crew, bearing numerous scars from the encounter, carried off the shallop.

When Naesmith returned that night, he heard the story and went pale with rage. At dawn, arming them with cudgels, barrel staves—anything resembling a weapon—he embarked his crew, and set off for the New York brig. This was a different Naesmith from the captain who had amused them during the storm off the Atlantic coast.

"I'll have that shallop or lose my life," he told them, as they rowed across the sunlit water, and Nicholas, nursing his bruises, envisioned another bloody encounter. It turned out otherwise. Wright had been so used up the previous day that he was unable to get out of bed. Without leadership, his crew would not fight, and Naesmith brought the shallop back in triumph.

Thereafter, the loading went on without opposition, and by the beginning of March the snow was ready to sail. Her destination was the Dutch island of Curaçao, off the South American coast, where a good market for logwood was reported to exist.[23]

More than 1,300 miles of water lie between the Bay of Honduras and Curaçao, but once beyond the Mosquito Coast it is open sea, with only a few keys and banks to be avoided. Also, in March the weather on the Caribbean is generally fair, and so it proved that March of 1765. Naesmith beat for several days after leaving St. George's to get beyond the dangerous shoals surrounding the island of Bonaco. From then on it was clear sailing through pleasant days and nights.

Barring one single eerie incident, the voyage was uneventful. It was in mid-March, a starlit, balmy evening. Nicholas lay curled up asleep on deck beside the helm, with Charles at the tiller. Suddenly the elder brother shook him awake.

"Nick!" he gasped. "Nick! Something extraordinary has just happened. I was standing right here, when the apparition of our sister Abigail appeared before me. I'm sure of it! I could see her as clearly as though she were in a lighted room. What do you suppose it means?"

Nicholas was too sleepy to be interested.

"Something you ate, perhaps," he yawned, and turned over to resume his interrupted nap.

But Charles, disturbed by the experience, set the whole curious matter down in his journal.

If the Curaçao market for logwood was as good as reported,

Naesmith was not destined to enjoy it. Somehow they passed the island about ten o'clock one morning, mistaking it for one of those further to windward. The error was not discovered until late afternoon when they spoke a schooner. Her skipper informed them they were standing for the island of Aruba. The *Ann and Almack* hauled her wind, and Naesmith again hailed the schooner, asking if he could be furnished with a pilot. There was some delay before an assent came back, and this, coupled with the large number of men on board her, aroused suspicion. Nevertheless, Naesmith sent Charles Biddle off in the longboat.

"They may be wreckers or some ruffians who would like to plunder us," he cautioned. "Bring off the pilot, but don't let anyone else get in your boat."

As he drew near the schooner, Charles observed some thirty or forty men on deck. He had with him three hands, including Nicholas, and his sole armament was a boat hook. If they were determined to board him, he knew it could not be prevented, but he would try to bluff it through. The longboat slid alongside and the pilot descended. Two ill-looking fellows sought to follow, but Charles raised his boat hook.

"My orders are to receive the pilot only," he called, "and I'll drive this into anybody else who attempts to come aboard."

They desisted, and the crew pulled back to the snow, the pilot informing them the schooner was loaded with wreckers who had sailed from Curaçao to a vessel ashore near Aruba.

For several days the *Ann and Almack* beat toward Curaçao, but daily lost ground. As provisions were getting low, Naesmith decided to forego any further effort and turned her bow toward Jamaica. His decision delighted all hands save the pilot, who was to have been married on his return to the island, and was inconsolable.

The wind that had baffled their efforts to reach Curaçao wafted them right speedily on their course to Jamaica. They made the island on the fourth day and anchored in Kingston Harbor. Shortly thereafter, three of the crew, all from the first mate's watch, deserted. The defections served Nicholas a good turn, for, true to promises, he received the coveted rating of seaman, and replaced one of the deserters. The other two berths were filled without difficulty, and Nicholas' duties as cabin boy were assumed by John Phillips, an English lad.

Naesmith's early good fortune seemed to desert him. The cargo of mahogany and logwood found no purchasers in Jamaica, at least for a price that would suit the captain. Days were spent in fruitless negotiations, with Naesmith growing angrier after each trip ashore. His final decision was to store it —a costly procedure. April was nearing an end when the *Ann and Almack,* in ballast, cleared Kingston for the Bay of Honduras. The captain had determined to take in another cargo of logwood there, and head for London, rather than trust again to the uncertainties of the West India markets.[24]

The month of May was well advanced before the snow, successfully negotiating the treacherous approaches, anchored once more off St. George's Key. Then came delay in contracting with the woodcutters, and a long wait for delivery of the first loads. Nothing disturbed the monotony of the days. The only diversion was when Naesmith would take it into his head to visit an up-river settler, and the longboat crew would row him to his destination. He was off on such a visit, in mid-July, when word came from St. George's that the negro slaves along the New River had revolted. A band of them had waylaid and killed the crew of a flat taking off wood to the ship *Sally,* of London. Naesmith returned with a story which brought the matter closer home to Nicholas and the others on the snow.

Marlborough, the black boy of whom they had grown so fond during the previous visit to the Bay, had killed his master and fled. There had been provocation enough. Cook, the settler, had charged the unfortunate negro with a petty crime of which he was guiltless, and had cut off one of his ears in punishment. Marlborough had seized a gun, shot Cook to death, and sought refuge in the woods. Other negroes were fleeing their masters, and an expedition was set on foot to recapture them.

The settlement seethed, and a number of captains loading wood volunteered their boats to join in the search for the runaways. Among them was Naesmith, who sent off his longboat with young Scull in command. Coming down the river a few days later, a forlorn negro emerged from the brush and hailed Scull's boat. It was Marlborough, driven from hiding by hunger. He had recognized his former shipmates and asked only for food. Scull urged him to come on board and promised not to deliver him to the authorities. The trusting lad obeyed. They fed him, and as he ate overpowered him. Then they continued down the river and turned him over to the magistrates at St. George's. Scull, who had never been popular, was roundly cursed for his treachery.

A few days later, in St. George's, Naesmith and Charles Biddle witnessed the inhuman action of the magistrates in dealing with the black boy. Marlborough had been given the semblance of a trial, convicted, and sentenced to be burned at the stake. The unfortunate negro was bound to a heavy pole set in the ground. Around him were piled empty barrels and brushwood until he was almost covered. The executioner applied the torch, and a brutal crowd howled its delight at the torture.

"No man ever suffered with more fortitude," Charles told the crew in relating the fate of the negro. "Once, when a barrel was blazing close to his head, Captain Naesmith kicked it away. Marlborough knew the act was intended to relieve him from some pain. He was unable to speak, but he bowed his head in thanks."

After that recital, Scull was in constant fear of the wrath of his shipmates. To the very end of the voyage he was detested by every man on board.[25]

The *Ann and Almack,* deep-laden with logwood, was about to up anchor and begin the long voyage to London, when a vessel arrived from the Delaware. It bore letters for Naesmith, among them one from Captain McFunn urging the return of the snow and promising a good market for her cargo. As a majority of the crew hailed from Philadelphia, the captain's announcement that they were sailing for home was greeted with cheers. They cleared the Bay of Honduras during the first week of August, and made the passage in less than thirty days, speaking only two vessels en route—a schooner off Cape Anthony, at the western tip of Cuba, on August 11, and another a few days later as they were entering the Gulf of Florida.

About ten o'clock on the night of September 2, 1765, the snow anchored off Philadelphia,[26] and by special dispensation Charles and Nicholas were the first ashore. They were hurrying home when they overtook their young sister Mary. After the first greeting, Charles, with the strange vision in his mind, asked anxiously:

"How is our sister?"

"She is well," Mary replied, "and has a fine boy."

"No! No! Not Lydia—not sister McFunn," Charles interposed, "but Abigail?"

"Oh boys, hadn't you heard?" Mary's voice was subdued. "We have lost her. It is upwards of six months since she died."

They told her then of Charles's uncanny experience, and compared dates. The apparition of Abigail had appeared before him, far down in the Caribbean, on the very day of her death!

A saddened trio entered the house on Front Street, where Mary Biddle gathered her two big lads to her heart and sobbed over them, in joy at their return and in sorrow over the renewed memories of the lost daughter.

It was Captain McFunn who relieved the tension. He came booming in with a surprised:

"What's this? Where's the snow? Why haven't we heard from you?"

They explained that upon every occasion they had forwarded word of their whereabouts. A great light dawned in McFunn's red face, and he grew almost apoplectic with anger.

"Why damme," he thundered. "I see what's happened. The dunderhead skippers you spoke, blast their dirty hides, reported you as the Almanack. I never coupled the two. The scurvy swine have sullied the fair names of my sister and her husband. Almanack! Damn 'em. It's Ann and Almack, and I'll keel-haul the filthy blighter who calls her otherwise!" [27]

Chapter II
Shipwreck

PLANS FOR THE NEXT VOYAGE OF THE *ANN AND ALMACK*
were under way even before her cargo was unladen. This time
she was definitely Jamaica bound, as Captain McFunn had
found shippers who would stow her hold with flour, staves, and
pig iron for Kingston. From thence, she would proceed to the
Bay of Honduras. He announced her outward entry at the
customhouse, on September 26, under Captain Naesmith, only
to find to his embarrassment that the latter had other ideas.[1]

What Naesmith proposed was incomprehensible to McFunn,
and to Nicholas and Charles when they heard about it. The
handsome and quiet Englishman said briefly he had bought a
shallop in which he intended to sail to the Bay and trade up the
rivers. He was willing to retain his two-thirds interest in the
Ann and Almack and to provide her a cargo in anticipation of
her arrival there, but they must look elsewhere for a master.
After that he drew his cloak of taciturnity close about him, and
even the doughty McFunn had not the temerity to question him
further. Nicholas, recalling the numerous visits paid to upriver
settlers while the snow had lain at St. George's, conjectured
that Naesmith's decision had been under consideration for
some time.

Only after the shallop had departed, slipping out at night,
did light dawn. A certain elderly Philadelphia gentleman had
been alarmed the following morning at the disappearance of a
beautiful young wife. When he found that her possessions had
disappeared with her, alarm had turned to chagrin. If we can
read between the lines, McFunn and his two young brothers-in-
law, while not condoning Naesmith's cutting-out enterprise,

had no sympathy for the deserted husband. Also, they kept their peace, and the matter never became a public scandal.[2]

Actually, the public that fall had little time for a minor bit of moral turpitude. It was, instead, in Philadelphia and elsewhere throughout the Continent, railing against the King and a Parliament which would impose upon it a stamp tax without allowing it a voice in the matter and threatening the newly appointed stamp officers with fire, sword, and brimstone if they did not resign. Liberty was raising its infant head to the accompaniment of a new idea—"taxation without representation is tyranny"—and Naesmith probably could have eloped even with the Governor's wife and caused no more than a ripple of excitement.[3]

The Stamp Act aroused no comment from the various Biddles (at least, none has been preserved) largely because the affairs of the *Ann and Almack* had their entire attention. Captain McFunn had decided to go out as master of the snow in person, and that decision had resulted in much commotion. While the first voyage was in progress, the McFunns had moved into their own home on Third Street above Arch, and Lydia Biddle McFunn objected seriously to being left alone with an infant son in so large a house. Troubles had been smoothed out by Mary Biddle's agreement to close her home and, with Mary and Thomas, now aged sixteen and thirteen respectively, to take up residence with her married daughter. James, her eldest son, then obligingly obviated the necessity of closing the homestead by moving into it with his own growing brood.[4]

Then there had been the matter of a crew. Deaf Campbell and Charles Biddle had shipped again as first and second mates, and four of the former crew had signed on, namely Nicholas, old Armstrong, Peters, and the English lad, John Phillips. Young Scull was deliberately dropped; two other hands were unwilling to reship. It was early October before they were replaced. What with other delays, the *Ann and Almack,* deep laden, did not clear for Jamaica until about October 20.[5]

A figure to wield a tremendous fascination upon an impressionable youth was Captain McFunn. He might, thought

Nicholas, have stepped from the pages of *Roderick Random*— a picturesque, irascible, lovable sea dog, whose very presence seemed to exude salt air. He was, to quote Charles Biddle, "one of the stoutest, most resolute and passionate men in the world." And on the voyage, which commenced that fall of 1765, the captain demonstrated the many facets of his character. On the run to Jamaica he soon convinced them he was as good a navigator as Captain Naesmith, if not a better one. They reached the island early in November after a remarkably short passage during which he sailed a course that made the most of every favorable wind.

At Kingston he bullied and bantered the blacks on the harbor lighters into laboring far beyond their wont. The *Ann and Almack*'s cargo consequently was discharged in record time. After one day of visiting the Jamaica trade he announced his future plans.

"We'll take in ballast for the Bay," he said. "These Kingston merchants, dad rat 'em, think I'll ship their wares for a song. Egad, I'll show 'em. Their rum can rot in their warehouses, the dirty swabs, before I'll take their stingy commission. I've ordered the ballast, Mr. Campbell, and lighters will be alongside in the morning. You'll oversee its proper stowing."

True to promise, the first lighter arrived at dawn, and the crew went to work with a will transferring the ballast to the snow. Midway in the work, the captain of a London ship came on board. Campbell was in the hold, McFunn in his quarters below, and Charles Biddle the only officer on deck. To him the Londoner strode, voice and manner belligerent.

"What in hell are you doing with my ballast?" he roared, chin thrust forward and fists clenched.

Charles stiffened. "How about keeping a civil tongue in your head, Mister. This is our ballast."

"Why, you thieving scoundrel," and the words rose to a bellow. "You know damned well the ballast belongs to my ship, and I'm going to have it."

From below came McFunn's voice: "What's the matter up there, Charles?"

The second mate told him, and the captain erupted on deck,

one side of his face shaved, the other coated with lather. He stalked down upon the Londoner.

"How dare you board my vessel in this manner?" he demanded.

The reply was a filthy epithet. McFunn's right arm swung out in a backhanded buffet that knocked the other over the gunwale and into the water, close by his waiting boat. His oarsmen hauled him in. Dripping and bedraggled, he rose unsteadily and shouted a furious challenge:

"Come ashore, you lout, and I'll fix you for this!"

McFunn turned to the crew.

"Swing out the long-boat, lads. I'll give the rotten blighter a chance to prove his words."

Nicholas, hauling on an oar, was half amused by the lather drying on the captain's face, and giving him a most ferocious appearance, and half alarmed over what serious consequences might result. He could have spared himself the latter worry. The London captain was rowed back to his ship and stayed there. McFunn landed, fumed for awhile on the stepping stones to the pier, and then reluctantly ordered a return to the snow.

Several days later, the *Ann and Almack* dropped down the harbor to Port Royal, and the captain had another encounter from which he emerged without laurels. In his sea chest he carried a King's Jack—a cherished memento of his earlier days in the service. During McFunn's absence at Kingston one Sunday in early December, Charles Biddle conceived the idea of hoisting it. Scarcely had it mounted the halyards when a near-by sloop of war sent aboard a midshipman, accompanied by a boat crew, who seized it with the comment that no merchantman had any right to fly a Jack.

When McFunn returned, he surmised that a visit to the sloop of war and an explanation that the flag was hoisted in his absence and without his permission would suffice to have it restored to him. He acted on the surmise and received a shock. The commander of the war vessel told him in no uncertain terms that being an old naval officer made the offense even more inexcusable, and flatly refused to hand over the Jack. Highly mortified, McFunn was rowed back to the *Ann and Almack*.

Nicholas, at an oar, heard him mumbling that if "the snob of a tailor's dummy in uniform" came ashore, he'd have satisfaction for the insult. Fortunately, there was no subsequent encounter, as the snow sailed for the Bay of Honduras a day later.[6]

When the *Ann and Almack* moored off St. George's, Captain Naesmith was the first visitor. He came to announce he had engaged a cargo of logwood and mahogany for Antigua. Expeditiously, ballast was discharged and hardwood taken in. McFunn was all energy, setting a pace the rest were hard put to follow. Within two weeks the snow was laden and ready for sea. Farewells were said to Naesmith (his Philadelphia lady fair had not put in appearance), and on December 28 they cleared the Bay.

The course was north by east to avoid the numerous reefs, before veering eastward into the Caribbean. With light airs and variable breezes, they made little headway. By January 2, 1766, the *Ann and Almack* had only reached a point about midway between the Yucatan mainland and the Northern Triangles, a particularly dangerous reef chain. That day it fell calm. Toward dusk compass bearings were taken which placed the southernmost end of the reef to the southeast of their position. When, after dark, a light breeze sprang up from the northwest, McFunn ordered all sail set, and steered a course to the southwest. Toward eleven o'clock the wind increased, and the captain had all canvas taken in save the foresail and close-reefed maintopsail. A half hour later he expended a gusty sigh of relief and turned to the second mate:

"Damme, Charles, don't ever go to sea without insurance. That's what I've done, for the first time in my life. I've been uneasy ever since. But we're past the reef and out of danger. I feel as if a mountain were off my chest."

Hard on his words, the wind grew to gale proportions, and he swung from musings to action.

"Call all hands, and take in the maintopsail," he shouted; then, in an aside to Charles, "I'll stand to the eastward under the foresail."

As the crew swarmed aloft, Campbell took the tiller. Just

when the maintopsail was being hauled in, a wild shout rose from George Peters, on lookout at the end of the bowsprit:

"Starboard! Starboard for God's sake, or we are all lost!"

Whereupon deaf Campbell put the helm aport. Again came Peters' cry of warning, and Charles Biddle, racing aft, grabbed the tiller from the first mate and swung it to starboard. Forward at an eight-knot speed in the howling storm leaped the *Ann and Almack,* to rise on a great, cresting sea and come down with a splintering impact on the reef they had sought to avoid. Then a second tremendous wave picked up the snow, carried her within the outer barrier, and tossed her broadside to the sea.

McFunn's hoarse bellow brought order out of chaos.

"Hoist the boats out to leeward," he commanded. "Quick, for your lives!"

The longboat was first, but was torn loose as it hit the water and vanished in the black night. That taught them caution. They lowered the yawl, with Nicholas in it, and veered it away from the snow with a hawser. Charles paid his brother a tribute for his courage.

"He did everything he was ordered with as much coolness as he would have done alongside a wharf," he said.

Once satisfied the yawl would not break away, McFunn ordered the masts cut by the board. One fell to starboard, the other to port, easing a bit the strain upon the wreck.

"Thank God for mahogany and logwood," the captain ejaculated. "An ordinary cargo, and we'd gone to pieces when we hit the reef. Stiff upper lips, lads, and we'll sail another day."

Not all shared his optimism. Campbell followed Charles Biddle down into the cabin with the dire prediction that none of them would live to see daylight. Charles had gone below to make fast any loose gear. The first mate's forebodings caused him to desist, but as he was drenched he decided he might as well drown in dry clothes and took time to change. Water was rising in the cabin as he went on deck. McFunn herded the ten of them (Nicholas having come aboard from the yawl) into the steerage, hoping the snow might hold together through the night, and knowing nothing further could be done. Within an hour they felt the deck settling and each made his precarious way to the after part of the quarter-deck, the only part of the wreck the sea was not breaking over. There they clung, waiting helplessly for dawn.

Daylight disclosed a low, distant island about eight miles to the northwest. They had struck on the southernmost part of the reef, and Campbell aggrievedly protested in his loud voice that if the helm had been left aport they would have cleared it, passing between it and the island.

"I didn't hear what Peters called out," he admitted, "but a hearin' him yell, and knowin' the reef was to eastward, I shifted to port."

"Small use to know that now," McFunn commented sourly. "Here we are. There's the island, and no blasted boat will live in such a storm. We've got to sit tight till it blows over."

All that day and through a second dismal night the gale raged. Toward morning it abated, and the wind hauled around to the northward. McFunn eyed the little yawl dubiously. It might accommodate six men. To crowd in ten was to take grave chances. But he was none too sure the wreck could hold together another twenty-four hours. They would have to chance it, and carry some provisions as well. Sheltered in the lee of the snow, the yawl was boarded without difficulty. Five of the crew were at the oars; Nicholas and John Phillips lay in the bottom, and McFunn and Campbell crouched fore and aft to bail, with Charles Biddle steering. They took along a small cask of water, a bag of bread, a compass, and a few other necessaries. Ere they cast off, little Phillips, lying in the stern, gazed up piteously at the second mate.

"I can't swim," he whimpered. "If the boat sinks please try to save me."

"Aye, lad, there's no danger," Charles Biddle said encouragingly, but thought to himself it was doubtful they would ever reach shore.

Once clear of the protection afforded by the wreck, the yawl was buffeted by heavy seas. She rode so low that with every wave they shipped more water than McFunn and Campbell could bail out. Nicholas and Phillips were nearly submerged and well-nigh drowned. Within a few minutes they discovered the boat was too deep in the water to row. McFunn ordered the water cask tossed overboard. That lightened them a little, so that the oars began to make some headway. Charles Biddle watched the distant shore anxiously. Were they gaining on it, or were they being swept astern? He knew that in the latter case they were lost. For four long hours, while the men toiled, captain and first mate bailed, and the two on the bottom alternately breathed or half strangled, he could perceive no progress. Then the land suddenly seemed just a little closer.

"We're making it," he called in encouragement. "Keep it up, boys, we're gaining!"

Slowly but surely the yawl forged landward, but it was after dark, and after more than ten hours of toil, before the boat ran through the last line of surf and grounded in shallow water. Weak from hunger and exhaustion, the ten staggered ashore, dragging the heavy craft with them. Even McFunn lost his poise. Every man jack of them ran up and down the beach shouting for joy. Then, too fatigued to bother with any more food than some dry bread, they threw themselves on the sand and slept.

The next day was spent in contriving two rude huts from underbrush and driftwood. The next, it having grown calm, Charles and four hands embarked in the yawl and rowed out to the wreck for flour and other provisions. They were gone the better part of the day, but could report the snow still perched safely on the reef. As the weather continued moderate, daily trips were made and more food and clothing brought ashore. Also they equipped the yawl with a makeshift mast, and with washboards to keep out spray and make her more seaworthy. McFunn directed these steps, knowing that some of them must venture in her in an effort to reach St. George's and return with a larger craft to rescue the others and salvage as much as possible from the *Ann and Almack*.

"We've got to stir our stumps, my lads, or we'll never get off this blasted island," he put it up to them one evening. "The yawl is sound enough to sail to St. George's, which I reckon can be made in a couple of days, with a little luck. But she won't hold more than six. There's greater danger in going in her than staying here. I propose we draw lots—six to go and four to stay. What say you?"

There was general agreement. McFunn broke up ten sticks, four shorter than the others and placed them in a pot. Each man drew in turn, and the four short ones fell to Nicholas, old Armstrong, George Peters, and the cabin boy, Phillips. The others prepared for departure the following morning, January 15. Just before boarding the yawl, Charles drew his brother aside:

"Nick, if we don't return in two weeks you can conclude we've been lost."

They shook hands solemnly. McFunn blustered to avoid a show of feeling.

"Avast there, and step lively. We'll make a sweet run of it, and be back for you lads in no time."

Four forlorn castaways stood on the beach and watched, misty-eyed, until the yawl became a tiny spot and faded from sight beyond the horizon.

Once placed upon their own resources, Nicholas found the others turning to him for guidance. That the little cabin boy should rely upon him was understandable, but he was surprised to have Peters, a mature man, and Armstrong, well past fifty, tacitly awaiting his directions. He was then but four months beyond fifteen years of age—certainly a youngster in years, if not in experience, to assume the role of leader. Appearance and temperament, however, well qualified him for the responsibility. Here was no fledgling, but a youth old for his years, of good height, full of demonstrated courage, and with the ability to win confidence by soundness of judgment, clarity of expression, and cheerfulness of disposition.

The island—the Spaniards, they learned later, called it the "Devil's Nut"—had been explored thoroughly a day or two after their arrival. It was about two miles in circumference, with no traces of habitation. It boasted some cocoanut trees, much scrub pine and palmetto, and a sandy soil with one or two brackish springs. The water was practically unfit for drinking.

Of wild life they found only iguanas—lizard-like animals about the size of a squirrel—which were easily caught, as when chased they ran to their holes and buried their heads. Roasted iguana proved a delectable variation from ship's bread, salt pork, and peas.

Taking stock of their situation, resources, and prospects, Nicholas laid out a simple routine. They must maintain constant vigilance to be sure no possible rescue craft passed the island unaware of their presence upon it. At the same time, they must be prepared, he pointed out, for a chance visit from unfriendly Indians or still more unfriendly Spaniards. During daylight hours a lookout was posted in the tallest cocoanut tree and spelled at intervals. At night the fire was kept burning, with the four dividing themselves into three-hour watches. Each man had cut himself a good, stout cudgel. Meanwhile the habitation had to be made more livable, driftwood and dry underbrush gathered, and enough iguanas killed to provide a good roast once a day, thus supplementing the fast-dwindling provisions. Water was the big problem. One cask, it will be recalled, had been tossed into the sea. Another had gone with the yawl, and the third was already half emptied. Unpalatable as the spring water was, it had to be drunk. A mild dysentery resulted, so that by the time the second week was nearing an end all four were weak, haggard, and gaunt. But they maintained their tree-top vigil by day, and fire watch by night, looking and hoping in vain for rescuers.

Some thirteen days after the yawl had departed, Nicholas, taking his turn in the cocoanut tree, espied a boat approaching the shore from the direction of the wreck. He slid to the ground, informed the others, and, armed with their homemade war clubs, they concealed themselves in scrub growth along the beach. They crouched there watching the boat draw nearer until they could make out six occupants.

"Spaniards!" whispered Nicholas, as he observed the swarthy-visaged boatmen. To all of them that word conjured up potential enemies, for during more than a century the Spaniards had fought the Baymen as interlopers. Then the boat reached the outer line of surf, and a new figure arose from the bottom, hailing in an English voice they recognized:

"Ahoy, the island! Ahoy, Nicholas! Come out of hiding, lads. All's well."

They broke from cover, Nicholas and Armstrong in the lead, dashed out waist-deep to meet the boat, and to enfold Charles Biddle in hungry arms. The Spaniards grinned and jabbered as they beached their craft, while the castaways jubilantly carried the second mate ashore.

" 'Twas a cruel joke to play on you," Charles admitted. "We anchored near the wreck last night and saw your fire. So this morning I put off in the boat, and thought I'd have a little fun at your expense." He looked at the four haggard men. "I'm sorry I did it," he added contritely. "I didn't realize what you'd been through."

He told them of his own experiences. Five days after leaving the snow they had reached St. George's, where McFunn had hired a shallop in which Charles, Campbell, and three hands had started to the rescue. Twice adverse winds drove them back. On the third attempt, Naesmith had volunteered his shallop and accompanied them. Off Turneffe Island, east of St. George's, they encountered some English turtle hunters, who informed them a party of Spaniards had been on the Northern Triangles and murdered all the people left there. The murderers, according to the turtle hunters, were four miles down the shore of Turneffe.

"I went to the Spaniards," Charles concluded, "who denied the story, and six of them volunteered to accompany us. We made the reef in three days, and Naesmith and Campbell are in the shallop over at the wreck awaiting word of you."

For more than three weeks the reunited party remained on the Devil's Nut, using boat and shallop to save what they could out of the snow. The Spaniards in that time salvaged a quantity of old iron from the wreck and were well satisfied that they had joined the rescuers. They sailed from the island on February 22, and as the shallop passed the reef, Nicholas waved farewell to what remained of the once stanch *Ann and Almack*.

Winds were favorable; in two days they made St. George's. McFunn came aboard, face wreathed in smiles but hiding his relief behind bluster.

"Dod rat me," he said, holding Nicholas at arm's length and eyeing him from head to foot. "It took a wreck to make a proper sailor out of you."

Back safely at the Bay of Honduras the two Biddles looked for employment, and found it on a ship belonging to Boston, Charles as second mate, and Nicholas as an able seaman. Just before they were ready to sail, McFunn sent word he had chartered a sloop to take a cargo for Charlestown, South Carolina, and asked them to join him. They left the Boston ship with reluctance, but as the elder brother expressed it they "could not refuse to comply with any request this worthy man could make, especially as he had been unfortunate." Then, too, Mc-Funn offered Charles the berth of skipper.[7]

The sloop was called the *Kingston*. She was owned at Jamaica, and had been built there on the plan of the famous Bermuda sloops. She sat well upon the water but, again to quote Charles, "was one of the worst barks that ever went to sea." They cleared St. George's on June 3, and the *Kingston* lived up to his appraisal of her. A few days out they were compelled to throw overboard a considerable part of the cargo to prevent her foundering. After that, between storms and calms, they made slow going of it. Provisions and water ran low. A leak developed which the carpenter could not completely plug, so one pump had to be kept going constantly. They were on half rations and water was being doled out by the time they reached the South Carolina coast in late July. Charlestown was gained July 29, and the youthful master breathed a sigh of relief when he got the sloop across the bar and dropped anchor in the Cooper River opposite the customhouse.[8]

Once the cargo was discharged, Captain McFunn announced his intention of taking passage in a packet for Philadelphia. Nicholas elected to join him. Before they started homeward, Charles sailed the *Kingston* out on August 22, bound again for the Bay. Nicholas watched her depart with no regret. He had, he vowed, seen enough of His Majesty's settlement in the Bay of Honduras.[9]

Just when Nicholas and Captain McFunn reached Philadelphia is not in the record; it was probably well toward the end of September, 1766. At any rate, they found the family in health—Mary Biddle as industrious as ever in her valiant effort to supplement the money received from her sons. She had abandoned the Fountain Inn as a place to sell her father's maps, now advertising her whereabouts as "the House of Capt. M'Funn, in Third Street, about Arch." Likewise, she had augmented her wares and could also offer not only plans but "Prospects of the City of Philadelphia." [10] It is hard to say how lucrative this business was. Alone it would have been insufficient to support her and the two youngest children, and she spoke appreciatively of the way James, Edward, John, Charles, and Nicholas "all were happy in rendering me every assistance in their power." [11]

Of Nicholas and his whereabouts for the ensuing four years we have precious little information. Apparently he left home either late in 1766 or early in 1767 to pursue his chosen vocation. Charles, who had kept close tabs on him during the voyages of the *Ann and Almack,* was no longer on hand to report his goings and comings. For the years 1767 to 1770, inclusive, Charles seems to have had little knowledge of Nicholas' movements, and what he knew is embraced in a single sentence: "After he returned home, he made several European voyages, in which he acquired a thorough knowledge of seamanship." Two of these voyages were to Rotterdam as a mate in the ship *Crawford,* Charles Smith, master. The *Crawford,* of 200 tons burden, was engaged in bringing emigrants from the German Palatinate.[12]

Barring one trifling incident, the four years are vague; this incident only proves that on May 10, 1769, he was home from one of his voyages. On that day he ran an errand for his mother to the provision store of John Lawrence and purchased some salad dressing, five bottles of wine, four bowls of punch, and five bottles of beer. He receipted for the four items, at a cost of

£5 8s. 10d. and took them home. They may have been the good
cheer attendant upon a home-coming dinner.[13] If so, that part
of the festivity could have been of little interest to Nicholas, for
those who knew him best remarked years later, "He never
drank a quart of liquor in his life." [14]

However frequent or infrequent his arrivals in Philadelphia,
each visit would disclose some change in the family picture.
Upon one occasion he was saddened to learn that his doughty
brother-in-law was no more. William McFunn had departed
this life, leaving a widow, two small children, and, if we inter-
pret the vague record correctly, a rather sadly depleted estate.
Nicholas mourned for the stout old mariner and consoled his
sister Lydia as best he could.

Upon another visit, the Pennsylvania Assembly was in session in the city, and he had opportunity to spend many hours
with his brother Edward, now not only a flourishing lawyer
in Reading, but representing Berks County in the provincial
legislature. Nor did he neglect his brother James, still living
in the old homestead and now boasting a total of thirteen offspring, living and dead. James, like Edward, was prospering
and was then serving as deputy Judge of Admiralty under the
royal government.[15]

Perhaps, too, he became better acquainted, during these
home-comings, with two cousins who would play rather important parts in the Revolution, which was then years away
and undreamed of. They were Owen and Clement Biddle, sons
of his uncle John, and both considerably older than Nicholas.
Clement was in the dry-goods business with his father in a shop
two doors below the Indian King Tavern, on Market Street,
and Owen was a clock and watchmaker near by.[16]

But he gave most of his brief time at home to his mother.
Mary Biddle had pride in her eye at every sight of this stal-
wart son of hers. She was devoted to her entire brood, but
seemed to idolize Nicholas a bit more than the others. He was
certainly developing in a way that would give joy to any mother.
A pen portrait of him, which would relate to this period—about
1770, when he was twenty years of age and had attained his
full growth—limns him through the eyes of a brother.

"His temper was uniformly cheerful, and his conversation sprightly and entertaining," the description runs. "In his person he was about five feet nine inches high, remarkably handsome, strong and active, with the most amiable mildness and modesty of manner. A sincere Christian, his religious impressions had a decided and powerful influence upon his conduct." [17]

While this brotherly enthusiasm depicts him almost as a paragon, contemporaries also attest to his charm. He had flashing dark-brown eyes, a strong, aquiline nose, lips that denoted firmness, a high forehead, and dark-brown hair cropped above the ears and showing a comb-defying unruliness.[18]

Neither painting nor pen portrait, however, discloses one of his outstanding traits, and that was his restless, adventuresome disposition. The years in plodding cargo ships had begun to pall upon him, and his spirit was craving new excitement. By the fall of 1770, he had just about determined to abandon the mercantile marine. He was in Philadelphia that November, and purchased two hundred acres of land in Berks County. Not that he intended to settle ashore. The land acquisition was an investment made at the suggestion of his brother Edward, who knew property values in that section of the province.[19] It was a good way to put some hard-earned sea pay to work. As for Nicholas himself; well, he was toying right seriously with the idea of service in the British navy.[20]

Chapter III
Mr. Midshipman Biddle, R.N.

THERE WAS MUCH TALK IN PHILADELPHIA OF WAR with Spain over a little group of unimportant islands in the South Atlantic—the Falklands. Each issue of the weekly *Pennsylvania Gazette* contained news which Nicholas read avidly. One story reported that English settlers on these remote islands were being driven out by the Spaniards; another, that a hot press to man the fleet was on in British ports. Later came an account of the arrival at Cadiz of the dispossessed English and a glowing description of Britain's war preparations. Then appeared the usual unconfirmed rumors. . . . two of His Majesty's frigates had been taken. . . . the Spanish ambassador was about to leave London. . . . five ships of the line had joined the British Mediterranean fleet on a secret mission.[1]

Certainly the war pot was boiling with just the kind of news to fire the imagination of an eager and restless youth. Towards the end of March, 1771, Charles Biddle brought a new command of his, the ship *Lark,* in from Port-au-Prince, to report the West India islands in constant dread of hostilities.[2]

That was enough for Nicholas. If there was to be a scrap with the Dons, he was going to get into it. A peacetime naval career might not be overly exciting, but, with fighting thrown in, the Royal Navy was just the place for high adventure and sure advancement. And if the war clouds blew over by the time he reached England, there was the East India Company to fall back upon for a lucrative berth and steady employment.

Nor were the necessary steps difficult of accomplishment. Thomas Willing, senior partner in the great mercantile house

of Willing & Morris, had a brother-in-law who was a captain in
the British navy. Joseph Galloway, speaker of the Pennsylvania
House of Assembly, was a close friend of Benjamin Franklin,
then in England as the colony's agent. Nicholas knew neither
Willing nor Galloway, but his brother Edward did and paved
the way for the necessary meetings. Both gentlemen obliged, as
did several others with influential friends in London. Willing
gave him a letter to the brother-in-law, Captain Walter
Sterling,[3] and Galloway supplied a most kindly recommendation
to Franklin. The letter from Galloway to Franklin has been
preserved:

This will be delivered to you by Mr. Nicholas Biddle to whom I wish to
render acceptable Service, not so much from a personal Acquaintance with
him, as from the general Good Character and Esteem he has deservedly
acquired among all those who have any knowledge or Experience with
him. He is warmly recommended to me, as an Active, Sensible, prudent,
enterprizing young Gentlemen. The Merchant Service has hitherto engaged his Attention. But, not content in that Sphere of Action, where his
Friends wou'd immediately promote him, his laudable Ambition leads him
to pursue some Thing more honorable. The Navy, under the prospect of
war, is the first Object of his wishes. But shoudt the Peace continue his
next view is to obtain a Birth in the East-India Company Service. He
brings letters from several Gentlemen here to others in London. Permit
me also to recommend him to your Advice and Assistance, assuring you
that I am confident he will never dishonor any Favor he may receive from
your Friendship.[4]

Armed with this and similar endorsements of his character,
spirit, and enterprise, Nicholas boarded the ship *Britannia,*
Nathaniel Falconer commander, "a new Cedar Ship and a
prime Sailer," with "extraordinary Accommodations for Passengers." She cleared the Delaware around the beginning of
May and made an expeditious passage of about a month.
Nicholas was in London early in June, presenting the Galloway
letter to Dr. Franklin, at the latter's Craven Street lodgings,
where that sage and statesman made "a long speech full of
good advice and encouragement." But what struck Nicholas
most, as he wrote to his brother James, "was the kind and free
manner with which he delivered it." Influence from many

sources produced the desired results. By mid-June Nicholas had a midshipman's warrant and orders to report to Captain Sterling on board His Majesty's ship *Seaford* at Sheerness.[5]

Nicholas went down to the *Seaford* on June 22, 1771. He found her a smart little ship, a sixth rater of twenty guns. She lay just off Sheerness with her hands busily engaged raising her rigging. He boarded her from the shallop which had brought him down the Thames and reported to the officer of the deck. Captain Sterling had been expecting him, he was informed. Meanwhile, here was the clerk with the ship's articles. Nicholas signed: "Nichs Biddle, Mid." [6]

Later in the day he met his commander. Captain Sterling had the character of an excellent officer and the reputation of a humane man who ruled a ship's company with a firm but kindly hand. Moreover, he made Nicholas feel immediately at ease by his eager inquiries about relatives and friends in Philadelphia. Nicholas knew the captain's story—a romantic one in which, as a penniless adventurer, he eloped with one of the richest heiresses in the colonies, the sister of Thomas Willing. They sat, the captain and his newest midshipman, for a long hour of conversation in the cabin, and Nicholas was quite won by Sterling's charm. That first favorable impression would last and intensify throughout their association.[7]

The *Seaford* had been recommissioned the previous fall, and Captain Sterling had been assigned to her in November. Since then, lying off Sheerness, she had been much neglected by the Lords of the Admiralty, who had been more intent upon outfitting the Grand Fleet. At the time Nicholas arrived, the *Seaford* had but two thirds of her complement of 130, and lacked a full quota of officers. In the warrant officers' mess, presided over by George Hair, the ship's surgeon, were three other midshipmen, John France, Erasmus Orrock, and Charles Sterling, the captain's son. With them he struck up an immediate friendship which was to endure through more than a year of subsequent service together.

Barring the novelty of the experience, Nicholas found life on the *Seaford* monotonous and aimless. His chief duty was to walk the quarter-deck, which, as he remarked, meant "I must always keep myself Clean." He described his quarters on board as a "Room which is Square about 8 feet by twelve   chests are placed round a Table in the Middle   Our Partitions and curtains are the same viz Spare Hammocks   In a word I never was so well of[f] for Room [and] for time." [8] In early July, they changed their berth, running into the Little Nore and anchoring about three miles off the Kentish coast. Occasionally he had opportunity to go ashore in the longboat or yawl, but these visits would be for an hour or two at the most. Even then, duty would keep him on the wharf with the boat crew, while Captain Sterling wended his way on some errand to the office of the commissioner of naval stores.

From one such visit, on the morning of August 1, the captain returned with good news.

"Sailing orders, Mr. Biddle," he told Nicholas. But, as the latter's face brightened, he added, "Not of any moment. Just instructions to run around into Spithead."

A pilot came on board that afternoon, and the *Seaford* weighed a few hours after midnight. With a fair breeze and under a modest spread of canvas she sailed eastward, bringing to some hours after dawn almost abreast of Margate. Unfavorable winds held her there for several days, but on August 5, with a breeze from the right quarter, she rounded the North Foreland and stood southward into the Strait of Dover. Nicholas marked her progress by the headlands on the English shore —South Foreland, Dunge Ness, Beachy Head, and, on the morning of August 7, Selsey Bill. Straight over the bow loomed the Isle of Wight and, to starboard, the waters of The Solent opened to view. An offshore breeze brought them to until late in the afternoon. Then, under main and foresail, the *Seaford* ran into Spithead, where Nicholas saw the vaunted British Channel Fleet at anchor, an imposing spectacle of mighty ships of the line, many frigates, and innumerable other craft from sleek sloops of war to small cutters.

As the *Seaford* sailed nearer, her gunport lids lifted, six-pounders tucked their squat noses through the apertures, and, in well-timed sequence, thirteen guns roared—a salute to Sir Thomas Pye, Admiral of the Red. Pye's flagship, the *Barfleur,* thundered an eleven-gun return. Naval amenities concluded, the *Seaford* dropped anchor. Captain Sterling went on board the *Barfleur* to report his official presence in Spithead, and Nicholas from the *Seaford*'s quarter-deck drank in the might of England's sea power.[9]

Rumor ran from quarter-deck to forecastle next morning. The Dons had given in! There would be no war! The captain was to be promoted! Who would succeed him, and who would be fortunate enough to be transferred with him? An air of uneasiness permeated the ship, and Nicholas shared the general gloom. Had he come all the way from America to be disappointed in his desire for action? It looked that way. A summons to the captain's cabin interrupted his brooding. Captain Sterling greeted him in friendly fashion.

"I understand the ship is buzzing with rumor, Mr. Biddle," he began, "and not without reason. It has been my good fortune to be appointed to command the Portland and convey the new Governor in Chief of the Leeward Islands to his station. The war threat with Spain has blown over, but, if you wish to continue in the service, I would be delighted to have you transferred with me."

Nicholas spoke right from the heart; "Nothing would please me more, sir. When do we transfer?"

The other laughed.

"You have five days to get ready. I leave the Seaford on August 13, and take command next day on the Portland. Surgeon Hair, Mr. Orrock, and of course my son Charles have elected to follow me also. I think I can promise you a more interesting experience than you have had to date in his Majesty's navy." [10]

His Majesty's ship *Portland* was in dock at the Portsmouth navy yard. She carried fifty guns on two decks and was a fourth rater with a complement of three hundred officers and men. Nicholas, who had gone ashore from the *Seaford* the night before with Captain Sterling, came on board in a pelting rain, which in no way interfered with the work of swarming shipwrights and riggers. For three days he watched the outfitting until order appeared out of chaos and the *Portland* was towed from the dock to be lashed alongside the old ship of the line *Dreadnaught* in the basin.[11]

But, as he discovered, much remained to be done, with the crew taking over where the navy-yard riggers had left off. Three days alongside the *Dreadnaught,* and the frigate was towed to the jetty. Here the outfitting was completed, and on September 1 she was moved to a berth alongside the supply ship *Phoenix.* Daily thereafter stores came on board—provisions; surgical supplies; canvas; spare spars; carpenters', coopers', boatswains', and gunners' stores; and finally powder and ball. Later in the month, the clerk of the cheque came from the navy yard and mustered the crew. With rare disregard for spelling, he recorded Nicholas as Midshipman "Beadle." [12]

In the commissioned and warrant personnel of the *Portland,* meanwhile, Nicholas had found nobody to dislike. Captain Sterling's reputation had attracted a desirable group of midshipmen; the other officers, appointed by the Admiralty, were of the same caliber as the commander. Today they are merely names on a soiled muster roll, but to Nicholas they were real personalities among whom he established friendships, and with whom he left a lasting memory of his own worth. There is no better evidence of this than the experience of Charles Biddle years afterward when a prisoner in Jamaica. His lot was made easier by an officer who had served as a midshipman on the *Portland* with Nicholas, and "had a great affection for him." Charles, unfortunately, did not name his benefactor, and there were ten midshipmen on board, including young Sterling and Erasmus Orrock.[13]

Fully outfitted, the *Portland* slipped her moorings on the morning of September 26, 1771, and stood forth from the harbor. As she passed the *Barfleur* her nine-pounders spoke in a thirteen-gun salute, and Admiral Pye returned the customary eleven. Thereafter, the best bower was dropped, and the frigate came to anchor in Spithead. She awaited only the arrival of the Governor in Chief of the Leeward Islands, but what a wait that proved to be! [14]

Days passed; weeks passed; still the distinguished passenger failed to arrive. Nicholas, who daily made his own copy of the captain's journal, found little of interest to record. Other ships of the fleet arrived, or departed, or went into dock, or came out of dock. The *Portland*'s longboat overset at her moorings in a gust of wind. Two men were punished for quarreling and another for drunkenness. One stormy night the buoys were torn from the anchors and had to be found and restored. The clerk of the cheque came on board for another muster. On November 5, thirteen guns were fired commemorating the anniversary of the Gunpowder Plot. Several drafts of seamen were received to fill out the ship's complement. Then the navy commissioner came out and paid the crew for two months' service. Bumboats scented money and surrounded the frigate with wares to entice pence or shillings from the hands. Pleasant fall days gave way to November winds and leadened skies, but still no colonial governor.

"Moored at Spithead." "Moored at Spithead." So read the monotonous opening line of the daily log. Nicholas again began to doubt the wisdom of his course. The East India service would certainly have provided more interest and excitement than the dreary routine on the *Portland*. A break to monotony came on November 1, but not a pleasant one. An order was received from the Admiral. Two men were to be hanged from the yardarm of the *Royal Oak* for desertion. Each ship in the fleet would send a boat with an officer and six seamen to witness the execution. When the boat returned the following morning, laughter rang through the after cockpit where the midshipmen were housed. The two deserters had been given a last-minute reprieve, and three of the *Portland*'s boat crew had run away at night while alongside the *Royal Oak*.[15]

Finally, on the morning of November 24, almost two months after they had anchored at Spithead, the long-awaited colonial governor arrived. He came off from shore in a lugger piled high with baggage, accompanied by an entourage that amused Nicholas and his fellow midshipmen no end.

With side boys flanking the gangway, marines in close file, seamen in serried ranks behind them, and Captain Sterling and his officers in full uniform to receive him, Sir Ralph Payne,

Knight of the Bath and Captain General and Governor in Chief of His Majesty's Leeward Islands, was piped on board. He was followed, if not by "his sisters and his cousins and his aunts," at least by his secretary, his private valet, his cook, and twelve other servants—fifteen in all, including one woman.[16]

Only for this had the *Portland* been delaying. By noon Captain Sterling had the frigate "laying short on the Small Bower Waiting for the Tide." At two o'clock that afternoon they weighed and came to sail—outward bound at last.[17]

Out into the English Channel the *Portland* sailed, the wooded shores of the Isle of Wight to starboard. South, then south by west lay her course through the afternoon and night. Dawn saw the coast line receding, and at noon the jutting head of The Needles, four leagues off to the northward, was Nicholas' last glimpse of England for many a day. A following wind drove them steadily down channel; fresh gales and a cross sea greeted them as the frigate poked her nose into the Atlantic. Here winter came suddenly on them with cold, piercing winds, ice forming on yards and rigging, and occasional snow flurries lacing the deck with white paths that gyrated to each blast of frigid air.

Sterling knew how to handle the *Portland,* and within a week after leaving Spithead had much necessity for exhibiting his seamanship. As November ended, the wind tore at the frigate with fresh force. One gusty blast caught them as the topsails and staysails were being lowered. It tore three cloths from the after leech, reducing them to rags. Ten hours later, in the continuing gale, the fore steering yard broke and tore the sail. Thereafter, for a week, there was a continuous battle with the elements, as the log recorded frequent damage to rigging and sails. But the storms had all come out of the north, driving them along at a merry pace south by west. The temperature rose as the latitude dropped. Snow gave way to rain, and finally the sun peeped out and glowed warmly. That day, December 10, the lookout sighted the island of Madeira off to the southward. They had come better than 1,500 miles in fifteen days.

Sir Ralph Payne wanted to stretch his legs and pay a formal

visit to Madeira. So the *Portland* rounded Brazen Head late that afternoon and came to anchor in Funchal Road. As she moored, her nine-pounders saluted the Portuguese fort with thirteen guns and received a like response. Then the guns spoke again an hour later as the Governor in Chief, his secretary, and his valet went ashore. Sir Ralph was a stayer, and from his biographer we gather he was an extremely verbose and tiresome gentleman as well. No doubt they entertained him royally at Funchal, but the stay there was no fun for the crew of the *Portland*. Nicholas' opportunities to visit the island were few. When he went ashore it was in command of one of the boats plying between ship and pier with water casks.[18]

Ten days they rode at anchor, the only break to monotony being the arrival of the French frigate *Flora* on a voyage of discovery. Her captain and six officers visited the *Portland* and told of their mission.

"They were going out to try Observations having on Board five Watches and some Gentlemen of Experience in Astronomy," Captain Sterling entered in his journal. ". . . these time Pieces were kept in a Room fixt Amid Ships Abaft the Mizen Mast and was Lock'd up under three Keys, They Sailed from Brest to Cadiz from thence to Madeira and intended for Teneriffe Martinico Saint Domingo, The Island of Saint Peters, Iceland Coppenhagen [*sic*] and to Brest."

Nicholas found it most interesting and alluring. It was his first experience with a scientific expedition, and undoubtedly an impression was made upon him which influenced him subsequently.[19]

Finally, on December 26 the dilatory Governor in Chief returned on board, greeted as usual with thirteen guns. After him came the governor of Madeira, who was received with fifteen guns, and upon his departure saluted with fifteen more. Followed the British consul and factor, who perforce must also have thirteen guns, coming and going. That evening, with the last guest safely thundered ashore, the *Portland* weighed and stood to sea.[20]

For more than a month, while they sailed along to the westward across the Atlantic, days were uneventful and hot. There were periods of calm when they baked under a boiling sun, and one brief storm in which the frigate rolled and tumbled with much damage to sails. Late in January, when about thirty leagues west of Antigua, the sailing master entered an interesting incident in his logbook: "At 7 A M Saw a Sloop to the Northw^d which made the Signal of Distress and bore down to us. ½ past 9 Sent the Boat on Board found her to be the Sally Timothy Pike Master belonging to Falmouth Casco Bay in New England Thomas Smith owner from St Croix bound to Casco Bay being drove off the Coast and in Want of every Assistance Supplyed him with Provisions and Water and took him in tow."

To Nicholas it was a moving spectacle—these gaunt New Englanders, whose little sloop had been out for eighty-four days, during the last twenty with nothing to eat but some fish they had caught. The *Sally*'s sails were in rags, her crew too exhausted to bend new ones. The bread, meat, and water from the *Portland* revived them quickly, and two days later, when Antigua appeared above the horizon to the northwest, they thanked Captain Sterling, cast off the towline, and stood around the north side of the island.[21]

Later that day, with the frigate on a larboard tack, Nicholas watched the shore line of Antigua take shape to starboard. More than seven years had elapsed since he had been there in the fall of 1764. Then he had been a cabin boy, getting almost his first taste of the sea. A vast experience had been his in those intervening years.

The *Portland* veered toward the distant coast and picked up a pilot. As they sailed along the shore line, the fort above English Harbor greeted them with seventeen guns. An hour later a similar salute reverberated from the fort on Monk Hill. Each was answered in kind. In the early afternoon of January 29, 1772, they were abreast of Johnston's Point, where fifteen more cannon roared. Antigua was aware its governor was on board the *Portland* and, as he was a native of the colony, was doing itself proud.[22] Long after nightfall, the frigate anchored in the broad harbor of St. John. At sunrise came another salute —this time from Fort James—with a like reply. Sir Ralph

Payne and his retinue went ashore at noon on February 1.

In the meanwhile, Nicholas had gone to English Harbor in the longboat for a new maintopmast and other stores. He came back five days later, and early next morning the new spar was hoisted and fidded into place. The *Portland* weighed shortly thereafter and stood to the southward.

Captain Sterling had orders to proceed to Dominica for water and wood, and then to rendezvous at Barbados with Robert Mann, Rear Admiral of the Red, in the ship of the line *Montague,* and the Leeward Island squadron. It was mid-February when the *Portland* moored in Carlisle Bay, Barbados, after having spent four days in Prince Rupert's Bay, Dominica. On March 6 the *Montague* arrived with several frigates and sloops. Having reported several masts and yards and much rigging in bad shape, Sterling received permission to proceed to Freeman's Bay, Antigua, for repairs.

For ten days the frigate lay in Freeman's Bay and then ran into St. John to receive Sir Ralph Payne for a tour of his Leeward Islands domain. Arrived the Governor in Chief and his entourage, and to Nicholas it was the scene at Spithead all over again. Sir Ralph, his secretary, valet, cook, and servants came aboard to the roar of fifteen guns. The *Portland* weighed and stood out with Fort James banging away in a seventeen-gun salute and the ship returning it gun for gun.

If Nicholas thought a precious lot of powder had been wasted so far on the Governor, he must have revised his estimate upwards as the tour of the various presidencies which comprised Sir Ralph's colonial empire progressed. Cannon banged in salute after salute upon every pretext, at Montserrat, Nevis, and St. Christopher's with the Governor either going ashore or coming on board again. Evidently Captain Sterling grew tired of it also, for, when the *Portland* returned to St. John, Sir Ralph was allowed to go ashore without even the courtesy of a mention in the ship's log. That he landed on May 2 is known only through the discharge on that day of his retinue, carried on the muster roll as "Supernumeries born for Victuals only."

Peacetime activities of His Majesty's Leeward Island squadron Nicholas found to be humdrum once the Governor in Chief was off their hands. The force which had been augmented during the Spanish war scare was much too large for the few duties imposed upon it. As a result the *Portland* spent more time in harbor than at sea, and a midshipman's duties were correspondingly lessened. "I have plenty of time to study and improve my mind," Nicholas wrote his brother James on May 14, "which I think I do not misapply for I somehow or other think Myself much more refin'd Which I think proceeds more from conversing with good Books than good Men." From May to June, barring a brief cruise to Barbados, they lay at Antigua. Caulkers swarmed quarter-deck and main deck for one week. Then came instructions to prepare for the homeward voyage and to take on board a quantity of stores, chiefly hawsers, sails, and blocks, for shipment to England. During this period other vessels of the squadron came and went. The gunner and his crew took the powder ashore for sifting. The King's birthday was observed, on June 5, by a salute of twenty-one guns from each warship in port. Sails were repaired, fireplaces rebricked, and longboat reconditioned.[23]

On June 16, the *Portland* sailed over to Montserrat for water, and anchored in Plymouth Road. Nicholas was bored by inactivity and voiced it four days later in a letter to his brother Charles: "I have little, too little, duty," he complained. "This situation I liked well enough with the expectation of a War. But as that prospect is past I cannot bear to think of murdering more of my time." [24]

Time would hang heavily on his hands. There was nothing the British navy could teach him on seamanship and navigation. He had been proficient in both long before joining the *Seaford*. Discipline, as observed on a man-of-war had been mastered within a few weeks of his entry on board, and the handling of ordnance had been his principal study. His keen mind had absorbed many other things: how to maintain a well-regulated ship, the various responsibilities of the warrant officers, and all the routine inherent in naval life. The knowledge thus gained would stand him in good stead some years later, but just now he had had quite enough of it.

After the frigate returned to Antigua the monotony continued. Provisions came on board—beef, pork, bread, rice, butter, flour—but no orders to sail for England.[25] Nicholas had a talk with Captain Sterling on the subject of said Nicholas' future, and Sterling urged him to continue with the *Portland* to the end of the cruise. Home lay just about twenty days away, and he was sorely tempted to throw up his midshipman's rating and take ship for Philadelphia. The captain's counsel prevailed, because Nicholas had a tremendous regard for this able and understanding officer. The conversation served to renew his interest in His Majesty's navy, as is evidenced by a letter written from Antigua on July 6 to his brother James.

"I shall make a purchase of a sextant if I can meet with one that is cheap," he wrote, "as I know every method yet proposed for finding the Longitude. I will also get a three-foot telescope if I continue in the Navy, in which I intend to be guided by Captain Sterling's advice. I am extremely fond of him, he has not only the character of an excellent commander but that much nobler of an excellent man." [26]

The long delay came to an end early in August. Rear Admiral Mann had been recalled, so the *Montague* and *Portland* were to return in company. Nicholas copied the log entry of August 4 in his own journal with a sigh of relief: "at ½ past 11 The Admiral made the Signall to Weigh at Noon Weighed and Came to Sail." The course was north past the island of Barbuda and then north by east.[27]

Three times during the homeward voyage the admiral sent them in pursuit of suspicious sails. While the brave days of the freebooters had long ago come to an end, there were still occasional piratical craft—particularly from the Barbary ports—marauding in the shipping lanes to Europe, and a function of His Majesty's ships was to hunt them down mercilessly. On the afternoon of August 5, some sixty-five leagues on their voyage, they went after a distant sail to find it a French snow standing for Guadeloupe. Nine days later they set sail after a vessel to the northeast and overhauled her toward dusk. Captain Sterling gave her a warning gun, and she came to in a flutter of descending canvas. But she proved to be a ship from Philadelphia for Barbados. The final pursuit was on September 9, when they were well across the Atlantic. This time the quarry scurried off, and it took four hours to overtake her. She came to meekly enough when the *Portland* got within gunshot. Sterling, a bit suspicious because of the effort to escape, sent a lieutenant off to her in the longboat. The officer returned an hour later and gave her a clean bill of health—the sloop *Sukey,* from Bristol for South Carolina.

Late in the afternoon of September 15, a lookout spotted the St. Agnes lighthouse on the Scilly Islands. Thereafter they passed frequent sails as they made their way upchannel to anchor two days later within the buoys off Spithead. During the night they weighed, the *Montague* in the lead, working toward the main anchorage, and at sunrise saluted the flag at Spithead. Around them was spread a formidable fleet—eight ships of the line and a swarm of attendant vessels.[28]

A week later, on September 22, Nicholas witnessed another lavish expenditure of powder. It was the anniversary of the coronation of George III. Great cannon in the shore batteries, light fieldpieces of the marine corps, and the heavy guns of all the war vessels in the harbor of Portsmouth and at Spithead thundered a twenty-one gun salute.[29]

Three days later and Rear Admiral Mann struck his flag on the *Montague*. Both ships were ordered to Sheerness to be paid off. They came to sail, saluting Admiral Pye with thirteen guns each as they went out. The *Portland* ran into The Downs, spent a day working up the Swinn, and by October 4 was moored in Sheerness Harbor.[30]

For more than a week Nicholas watched and learned how a ship went out of commission. He saw the main yard rigged as a derrick to lift out the guns and deposit them in a lighter; topmasts, topsail yards, and spare spars transferred to another lighter; anchors, cables, and rigging loaded into still another. The stores received at Antigua came next, followed by casks and provisions, gunners', carpenters', and coopers' stores, until by October 13, 1772, the ship was clear of virtually everything movable.[31]

That morning the navy commissioner came out to pay off the ship's company. Before the day was done only a skeleton crew remained.[32] Nicholas was one of the last to leave. Sterling had been ailing for several weeks and had determined to take a rest from sea duty. He urged Nicholas to continue in the service, and the latter, going ashore in the longboat, had no fixed ideas for the future. As he looked back at the *Portland,* forlornly stripped at her moorings, he knew that he really regretted not a day of the fourteen months spent upon her.[33]

Chapter IV
The Polar Expedition

"THE PORTLAND IS PAID OFF AND CAPTN. STERLING being in a bad state of health don't choose to be employed," Nicholas wrote to his sister, Lydia McFunn, from London, on October 20, 1772. "But the case is otherwise with your Most Obedient. I am ready for any service."

Then, in humorous vein, he told of his despair of seeing active service in the British navy, because England, said he, seemed too much involved in suppressing an Indian revolt on the island of St. Vincent to engage in war with any European nation.

"I foresee your curiosity will not be satisfied with what I have already said," he resumed on a playful note, "therefore shall endeavor to do so far as my abilities will let me." Lydia must have been amused at what followed, for, said Nicholas, "I wear my own hair [No powdered, foppish wig nor sailor's queue for him!], black hat, cloth coat, knit breeches, paper colored stockings, leather shoes, metal buckles and linen shirt." And, he concluded, "I lodge in London and sleep in a bed." [1]

Just where he roomed in London is not explained, nor what he did to entertain himself during the fall and winter that followed. Captain Sterling had come up to the city to recuperate, and Nicholas saw his former commander frequently. Their principal discourse had to do with His Majesty's navy. Sterling recognized the merits of this young colonial and tried hard to hold him in the service, promising to use every interest to get him promoted to a lieutenancy. Nicholas was not convinced that a peacetime navy held any inducement. His ardent disposition called for activity, and he toyed again with the idea of entering the East India service. Meanwhile, being in funds and enjoying the delights of a London winter season, he coasted along without reaching a decision. Nominally he was a midshipman awaiting call to duty. It pleased Captain Sterling and it entailed no obligations. If a call came for service, and the lieutenant's commission materialized, then there would be necessity for making up his mind.[2]

So the winter slipped by and early in March he learned of a contemplated voyage of exploration into the polar regions. The Royal Society had laid before the Earl of Sandwich, First Lord of the Admiralty, "a proposal for an expedition to try how far navigation was practicable towards the North Pole." Sandwich had recommended it to the King, and George III was pleased to direct that it should be immediately undertaken, "with every encouragement that could countenance such an enterprise, and every assistance that could contribute to its success."[3] By the time all this reached Nicholas' ears the project had taken shape. Two bomb ketches, the *Racehorse* and *Carcass,* had been selected for their sturdy construction. Captain Constantine John Phipps had been appointed to conduct the expedition and had been commissioned to the command of the *Racehorse,* while Captain Skeffingham Lutwidge was to command the *Carcass.*[4]

Fired with enthusiasm for such an adventure, Nicholas lost no time in seeing Captain Sterling. Here was something that would offer far more excitement than the voyage of the French frigate *Flora,* whose advent at Madeira had so intrigued him more than a year before. But Sterling threw a wet blanket upon his hopes.

"Only officers of long experience and great influence will be chosen," he explained. "I have talked to Phipps, who has authority to recommend all officers, even midshipmen, and every commissioned and warrant post on each vessel has been bespoken for by more applicants than there are places."

Then he launched anew upon the desirability of regular-line service, the advantages that would accrue in sticking by the navy, and not going off on a tangent because of the lure of an expedition in which frozen ears and toes would likely be the only reward. True, the project was being developed by the navy, and naval men only would be accepted; but it was not an enterprise that would lead to promotion. Nicholas remained unconvinced. He could not forget the *Flora* with her learned scientists, her astronomical instruments locked in a carefully guarded room, the enthusiasm of her officers, and the broad area of her proposed voyage.[5]

Daily he heard more about the expedition. The *Racehorse* and *Carcass* had been sent into dry dock to have their sides strengthened to withstand the ice. Four masters of Greenlandmen had been engaged as pilots. The course was to be due north past the Orkney and Shetland Islands and west of Spitsbergen. Who knew but what a passage might be found across the top of the world into the Pacific and thus to the East Indies and fabled Cathay. Nicholas purchased a copy of Hakluyt's *Voyages* and perused every page that dwelt upon the possibilities of a polar passage. He procured other volumes and found accounts of the vain efforts of Henry Hudson in 1607 to penetrate the northern ice fields, and of subsequent futile attempts by ships employed by the Muscovy Company in 1610 and 1611, and Baffin and Fotherby in 1614 and 1615. All of these, however, had been fitted out by private enterprise.

With the Royal Navy conducting this newest exploration everyone was confident of success. Then, too, a very noted scientist was to accompany the expedition, Mr. Israel Lyons of Woolwich, who had agreed with the Board of Longitude to make astronomical observations. For that matter, Captain Phipps was regarded highly by the Royal Society as one of England's foremost navigators. Nicholas heard of special equipment Phipps was procuring—instruments to enable him to make experiments and observations in matters relative to navigation. These included two watch machines for keeping the longitude by difference of time, a special pendulum to determine acceleration in high latitudes, a megameter for marine surveying, a marine dipping needle for observations, and an invention to distill fresh water from the sea.

The complement of each vessel, he learned, had been fixed at ninety. The ordinary establishment would be departed from by appointing additional officers and entering effective men instead of the usual number of boys. Toward the end of April both the *Racehorse* and *Carcass* had come out of dock—the former at Deptford, the latter at Sheerness.[6] By then Nicholas had made up his mind. He intended to go on the expedition even if he had to enroll as a seaman. Too late, he discovered that the complement of the *Racehorse* had been filled. It behooved him to step lively if he hoped to be accepted on the *Carcass*. The crew, all volunteers, was being mustered in at Sheerness. Therefore, to Sheerness went Nicholas posthaste, arriving May 4, 1773. He was twenty-five years old, he informed the officer on duty at the rendezvous; actually, he was not yet twenty-three. However, he had just the experience the lieutenant was looking for, and would have been accepted in any event. Within an hour he was signed up and sent to His Majesty's ship *Resolution* where a dozen fellow crew members were being quartered until the *Carcass* was ready to receive them—a matter, they were assured, of but a few days.[7] Among the volunteers on the *Resolution* was a seaman from the *Portland,* who recognized Nicholas and surmised he had been demoted. This worthy fellow "was greatly affected" until he learned "the true cause of the young officer's disguise," when he was "equally surprised and pleased," and, of course, was sworn to secrecy.[8]

A stanch little vessel was His Majesty's bomb ketch *Carcass*. She was of about 200-ton burden, brig-rigged, and mounted eight 6-pounder carriage guns. She rated in the navy as a sloop of war, but was "no great shakes" as a sailer. Her selection, along with the *Racehorse,* which was her counterpart, had been based upon her durable construction. In equipping her for the polar voyage the Lords of the Admiralty had gone to great pains for the safety and comfort of the crew. Her boats, for example, were of a special design to accommodate the entire complement should the *Carcass* become imprisoned or crushed in the ice. Additional clothing was also put on board to be issued when the arctic latitudes were reached. The usual supply of spirits was augmented to be issued at the discretion of the captain when extraordinary fatigue or severity of weather might make it expedient. Even a quantity of wine was allotted for the use of the sick.[9]

Nicholas heard about all this on May 10, six days after he had signed for the voyage, when the *Carcass*'s launch called for him and his companions on the *Resolution* and deposited them on the ketch's deck. Captain Lutwidge looked them over, and singled out Nicholas and two others for questioning. His inquiries were terse and pointed: they looked like seasoned and experienced mariners; where and when had they served? The answers satisfied him, and he dismissed them. Next morning the captain's clerk notified each of a promotion. One would be rated as a boatswain's mate; another as a carpenter's mate; Nicholas as coxswain of the captain's launch.[10]

It was an auspicious beginning, and Nicholas, for his part, realized its importance as he observed Lutwidge's method of selecting a crew. The captain was analyzing each group of hands, separating the good from the indifferent. Some were tentatively kept on the regular muster roll. Others were temporarily classed as supernumeraries. On May 21 there were on board the *Carcass* 115 officers and men, and her final complement was set at 90. The weeding out took place six days later. Many were discharged and others transferred. When the clerk of the cheque came off from Sheerness, on May 28, he tallied a ship's company of ninety and two supernumeraries—the pilots. Also, the aforesaid clerk listed the new coxswain as "Nich⁸ Beddle." As simple a name as Biddle seemed to puzzle His Majesty's clerks mightily.[11]

Meanwhile Captain Lutwidge, finding the *Carcass* too deep in the water to proceed to sea with safety, had applied to the Admiralty for permission to put two guns on shore, reduce his complement to eighty, and return a quantity of provisions proportionate to the reduction. Permission was received on May 28, right after the clerk of the cheque had departed for Sheerness. Nine able and ordinary seamen were transferred that afternoon, and guns and provisions were sent ashore the following morning.[12]

Officers and men of the *Carcass* impressed young Biddle as the very pick of the Royal Navy, and undoubtedly they were. Lutwidge was one of the finest type of British commander, and his three lieutenants were of similar high caliber. Of all the six midshipmen, the most interesting was a sixteen-year-old lad, who made up for his lack of years by a poise and self-confidence that won the respect of the most hardened seamen. His name was Horatio Nelson, who in the years ahead would become that most famous of all English sea-fighters, the Lord Nelson who died in the moment of victory at Trafalgar. The roster embraced other good men and true, but none of them save Nelson were individually picked out by Nicholas for comment.[13]

As coxswain of the captain's launch, Biddle spent much time during May in conveying Lutwidge back and forth between the *Carcass* and Sheerness. Naturally, the captain and he became better acquainted during these almost daily contacts. While he never expressed the same affection for Lutwidge that he did for Captain Sterling, it is evident there was mutual respect between the commander of the *Carcass* and his coxswain. This is borne out by the fact that Lutwidge granted Nicholas permission to make a copy of the ship's log daily, a privilege seldom extended to anyone below the rating of midshipman.[14]

The final trip ashore, on May 29, brought advice that the *Racehorse* was in The Nore, some seven miles northeast of Sheerness, awaiting them. The *Carcass* weighed the following morning, standing northeast until in the late afternoon she dropped anchor near her consort. The launch was out immediately and Biddle brought it alongside the *Racehorse,* where he tied up while the two commanders conferred.

Phipps and Lutwidge were closeted for several hours during which the former outlined his orders from the Lords of the Admiralty. He was directed, he explained, "to fall down to the Nore in the Racehorse and there taking under my command the Carcass, to make the best of my way to the Northward, and proceed up to the North Pole, or as far towards it as possible, and as nearly upon a meridian as the ice or other obstructions might admit; and, during the course of the voyage, to make such observations of every kind as might be useful to navigation, or tend to the promotion of natural knowledge; in case of arriving at the Pole, and even finding free navigation on the opposite meridian, not to proceed any farther; and at all events to secure my return to the Nore before the winter should set in." [15]

Lutwidge returned to the *Carcass* after nightfall, and Nicholas overheard him direct the sailing master to be prepared for departure at dawn. It was not to be, however. Easterly winds prevailed for nearly a week. There were a few brief hours, on June 2, when they weighed and shook out topsails, but a flood tide retarded them and forced them to anchor between the Warp and The Nore, a few scant miles on their journey. Not until the morning of June 4 did the breeze shift to westerly, and the signal rose on the *Racehorse,* "Make Sail." Captain Phipps's launch came alongside as they began to slip through the water. It bore instructions, "in case of separation to rendezvous at Brassey Sound in Shetland." The voyage toward the North Pole was under way at last! [16]

The east coast of England was unfamiliar to Nicholas, but precious little did he see of it after the first few days. With the *Racehorse* in the lead, the two bomb ketches skirted the Essex and West Suffolk shores, their progress marked by distant spires to port, appearing off the bow, glistening in the bright June sunshine on the quarter, and finally disappearing astern. On the second night they anchored in Hoseley Bay, while Captain Phipps and Mr. Lyons made some test observations with the new instruments. Next morning they were under way, with the wind at south-southwest, and their course seaward to skirt the shoals off the Norfolk coast. Nicholas saw Aldborough church steeple fade in the distance, and caught a glimpse of Spurn Head at the mouth of the Humber the following evening; he sighted Flamborough Head at noon next day, and Scarborough a few hours later. On the morning of June 10 they anchored in Robin Hood Bay, awaiting the turn in the tide to carry them up to Whitby Road. The wind had fallen and it was late afternoon before they worked up abreast of Whitby, where, by order of the Admiralty, livestock and fresh vegetables awaited them. Water casks were refilled also, but the captain's launch was not used, and Nicholas, perforce, remained on board. [17]

From Whitby, Captain Phipps set their course northeast by east "to get so far into the mid-channel as to make the wind fair easterly or westerly, without being too near either shore before we were clear of Shetland and Norway." [18] Three days later came a beautiful sunset, and for hours afterwards the clouds to the northward reflected the sun below the horizon. It was nearly as bright as day, and a lookout on the *Carcass* picked up the Shetland Islands, leagues away to the northwest, at ten o'clock at night. Next day, while they ran northward about three leagues off shore, Shetland boats came off with fish. By June 15 they were almost abreast of the northernmost island in the group, and a fog descended. They lost sight of the *Racehorse,* but half-hourly guns were answered by their consort through the evening and night.[19]

Captain Phipps signaled for a lieutenant when dawn of June 16 disclosed the two vessels only a few miles apart. The launch was used and Biddle took First Lieutenant John Baird over to the *Racehorse* and brought him back an hour later. By Baird came further orders for Captain Lutwidge. Nicholas copied them from the logbook into his own journal. They consisted of detailed instructions as to the procedure in case of separation, with a sealed packet to be opened only at Hakluyt Head, at the northern end of Spitsbergen, if the *Carcass* reached thereabout by July 20, and was not joined within eight days by the *Racehorse.* Phipps was determined that one of the vessels must proceed if the other was delayed or, by greater misfortune, lost.[20]

Due northward was the subsequent course, astride the meridian of Greenwich. On June 18, although the weather was of midsummer mildness, Captain Lutwidge had the purser serve out the heavy clothing. Three days later the *Racehorse* spoke a snow from the seal fishery bound for Hamburg and a packet of letters was sent off southward in her. As they climbed the latitudes the evenings grew chilly, although by now it was scarcely correct to speak of "evenings" as it was "light enough all night to read upon deck." [21]

A break in the summer weather came on June 24. The wind

ORIGINAL DRAWING OF THE POLAR EXPEDITION. From Constantine John Phipps's "A Voyage Towards the North Pole Undertaken by his Majesty's Command, 1773"; Dublin, 1775.

swung around to the northward, and by afternoon the thermometer had dropped to 34 degrees. A fire was lighted in the cabin, and the warmth of the brick oven in the galley was welcome to the seamen. There followed four days of uncertain weather, periods of little wind and some sunshine interspersed with sleet and snow. By then winds and current had carried them some eight degrees steadily northward. In the brightness of the arctic night on June 28, land was sighted some twelve leagues off to the eastward—Spitsbergen, that frozen land known chiefly to the seal fishers of the Scandinavian countries and Holland.[22]

With the wind northerly, the two vessels stood closer in during the rest of the night. In the dancing sunlight of the morning, Biddle was able to study the bleak coast with the naked eye. It was formed of high, barren, black rocks, devoid of vegetation. Higher points were bare and pointed, with an occasional snow-covered peak. The cliffs and valleys between were filled with snow and ice. It was a setting of perpetual winter, save for the complete absence of any ice in the sea. They ought to be fighting floes by now, he reasoned, yet the water was smooth as glass and shimmering in the sun's rays.[23]

All that day and the next they skirted the shore, moving northerly, and, on the last day of June, came upon a Greenland ship, whose master boarded the *Racehorse*. He had just come out of the ice, which lay to the westward about sixteen leagues off, he said. And he added, on an ominous note, that one Dutch and two English ships had been lost in the ice pack so far that season. More sealers were sighted daily thereafter, several of whom were spoken, and agreed that the ice was closing in ahead. Meanwhile they had reached the northern end of Spitsbergen—granite, jutting Hakluyt Head—with not one tiny floe visible on the sunny sea, and the temperature hovering around 40 degrees whether noon or midnight.[24]

Biddle was ordered to get the launch out on the afternoon of July 5, and took Captain Lutwidge over to the *Racehorse* through a dense fog. Both vessels were anchored in a small bay south of Hakluyt Head. Lutwidge and Phipps went ashore in the latter's boat, while Nicholas and his crew visited on the

Racehorse. Hours later the captains returned; on the way back to the *Carcass,* Lutwidge said the decision had been to proceed to the northward until ice was encountered.

The fog rolled down upon them as they weighed. They kept in touch with the *Racehorse* by half-hour guns. At noon Nicholas spied some small floes ahead; a lookout soon afterwards electrified them by announcing a large body of ice off the starboard bow. As the fog lifted it was clearly visible, a quarter mile distant, a compact and heavy mass extending as far as the eye could reach and appearing like rough, craggy land against which a great surf beat.

The *Carcass* hauled her wind to the westward and tacked to the southeast. Later both vessels moved cautiously northward through hazy weather and viewed the great barrier again. Before they realized it, they were in drift ice. All through July 7 the boats were out, towing the *Carcass* up to the *Racehorse,* which had held a more easterly course. When they were within hailing distance Captain Phipps called for a conference of pilots. Biddle's crew paused in the grueling tow to take the two pilots over to the *Racehorse.* On the return they told him the ice pack was solid to the eastward, and an effort would be made to find a passage further to the west. But they were frozen in before they could weigh, and had to get out ice anchors and ice poles to haul clear.[25]

For two days they skirted the great barrier, running westward until, on the afternoon of July 10, Captain Phipps came to the conclusion "that the ice was one compact impenetrable body, having run along it from East to West above ten degrees." [26] Nevertheless, for five more days the two vessels explored every opening, to return finally to Hakluyt Head, baffled at every turn. Much of the work had fallen on the boats which, time after time, had to tow both vessels through floating ice. South of the head they anchored in Vogel Sound amid several Dutch sealers, and on July 15 Captain Lutwidge ordered out the launch and went ashore to where Captain Phipps had fixed a tent for observations. Nicholas stretched his legs along the hard beach while the experiments were being made and the boats were watering.[27]

One more effort was made to the westward, but the ice pack stretched uncompromisingly before them. Finally Captain Phipps gave up and ordered an easterly course. They proceeded to the northward of Hakluyt Head, and to their surprise found open water. They kept close to the ice barrier, venturing further and further eastward. On July 26 they came upon Moffen's Island, a low, flat, circular bit of land about two miles in diameter. Captain Lutwidge sent the master ashore in the launch, and he and the coxswain explored the barren waste. They plodded their way over gravel and stone, disturbing innumerable birds and trampling upon nests. At a distance they sighted three polar bears, and finally they stumbled upon a gravestone with an inscription barely decipherable—the last resting place of a Dutchman who had been buried in 1771.[28]

From Moffen's Island the course was north by east until on July 27 they reached the northernmost point of the voyage— 80° 48′ north latitude—and the ice barrier rose before them. So they turned east by south, skirting it for seventy-two hours until they espied the northernmost of the Seven Islands ahead. They were disappointed as they drew nearer for no open water appeared, the main body of the barrier "seeming to be firmly joined from one island to another." Just to be sure, Captain Lutwidge went ashore.

"I went to one of these Islands about 5 or 6 miles to the N E^t of the Ships," as he described it, "thro narrow Channels, being obliged to hawl the boat over the Ice in several places. [It was Biddle and his crew who hauled the boat, not the captain.] Here I had an extensive view of the Sea to the Eastward which was entirely frozen over, not like the Ice we had hitherto coasted, but a flat even surface as far as the Eye could reach, which was undoubtedly 10 leagues at least, as the Weather was remarkably fine and clear, and the Hill I was upon about 200 yards above the surface of the Sea." [29]

Nicholas judged the island to be three or four miles long and was glad when Lutwidge was through investigating, and they headed back for the launch. Plowing through the deep snow and dislodging driftwood, cask staves, and deer horns was no child's play. Then came the grueling return in the launch with

countless hauls across the ice—more hauls, he noticed, than
when they had been headed the other way. But the journey was
to prove a pleasure jaunt compared to what lay before them.

Captain Phipps had ventured too far northeastward for the
season of the year, and the four pilots, who knew the treachery
of the ice pack from past experiences, were visibly alarmed.
Well they might be, for, when Captain Lutwidge and Biddle
reached the *Carcass* at six o'clock on the morning of July 31,
they found the open water through which the vessels had made
their way eastward narrowing behind them. Not a breath of
air was stirring, and the day was delightfully sunshiny with a
temperature of 48 degrees. Yet the situation was ominous. The
bomb ketches were becalmed in what appeared to be a large bay,
of which an open stretch of smooth water, about a mile long and
a half mile wide, was steadily diminishing as the ice floes closed
in. The *Racehorse* was moored to the edge of the ice, but the
Carcass lay to amid drifting floes.

On the solid ice were great pools of pure, fresh water, surface meltings under the sun's rays, and both captains sent their
casks ashore to be refilled. After that the men frolicked on the
ice during the late afternoon and evening, save for a detail
which measured the solid surfaces and found them to be better
than eight yards thick! More alarming, the *Carcass* was drifting steadily eastward. Late at night the boats were sent out and
towed her to the pack ice where she moored with an ice anchor
not two lengths to the east of her consort.

The ice pressed in fast, and by morning open water had vanished. Solid ice separated the two vessels, and neither had room
to turn. Moreover, the ice pack was no longer a flat surface.
With great crackings the mass was upheaving, being forced by
giant squeezing into huge piles, some higher than the main yard.
The wind had risen but it was blowing out of the west. From the
topmast of the *Carcass* open water could be seen, but it was
eight miles away to the westward, and solid ice lay between.[30]

Phipps's fears for the safety of vessels and crews were confided to Lutwidge only, but the consternation of the pilots could
not be concealed from the men. Nor did thick, foggy weather,

with the wind still in the wrong direction, bring any solace. Biddle observed that while the ice immediately about the bomb ketches was a little looser, the heaving pack around them grew thicker. He wondered what their chances were, but his dauntless spirit was not the kind to brood over the possibilities of death in the Arctic. He had faith in Phipps and Lutwidge, and he rather pitied the pilots for their fears. In that he did them a grave injustice, for the four Greenland skippers had knowledge to justify them. They, of all the 170 men on the expedition, could appreciate the extreme perils surrounding them.

At their insistence Phipps turned all hands out, at five o'clock in the morning of August 3, to try and saw themselves clear. The commander had no confidence in the effort, but considered it a good way to keep the men working and hence not so apt to grow panicky. All that day they sawed down through drift ice from eight to twelve feet thick, and in twelve hours had moved three hundred yards westward. That was how it appeared to the two crews, who could see the actual channel they had made. But Phipps's observations, which he kept to himself, showed that while they were advancing through the ice, wind and current had carried the ice itself, and them in it, far to the northeastward. They had lost five times as much ground as they had gained. In the slow advance, they had stretched a towline from the stern of the *Racehorse* to the bow of the *Carcass*. If it held, it would keep them close together. The situation was no better the next day, with the wind at northwest and the whole ice pack continuing its eastern movement.[31]

Toward nightfall a thick fog descended, and Horatio Nelson and a companion elected to slip off on an unauthorized bear hunt. They were missed from the *Carcass* a few hours later, and Captain Lutwidge was filled with anxiety. In the morning of August 5, the fog lifted, disclosing the doughty hunters far across the piled ice attacking a polar bear. A recall signal was hoisted, and Nelson's companion turned back, but not Horatio. Fortunately, a chasm separated him from the bear, for his musket flashed in the pan. The lad scrambled down the side of the chasm to get at his quarry with the musket butt. Then Lutwidge, seeing his danger, ordered a gun fired to terrify the

animal. It had the desired effect. The bear ambled off, and
Nelson returned to get a severe reprimand. More bears ventured close to the vessels that morning, and three were brought
down by well-aimed musket balls fired from the deck of the
Carcass.[32]

The probability of getting the vessels out appearing slighter
every hour, Captain Phipps realized he had to have a better knowledge of how far westward the ice pack extended.
Twelve miles away was a black pile of rocks, and that afternoon
he sent Midshipman Frederick Walden, of the *Racehorse,* and
two of the pilots off across the ice to it. Walden was to report
how far beyond this point would be clear water. The trio was
gone twenty hours and staggered back, on the morning of
August 6, with the discouraging news that five leagues of solid
ice separated the vessels from open sea. Walden had another
disappointing fact to report. On the rock pile, or island, they
had found the wind very fresh from the eastward. It was a
contrast to the vicinity of the bomb ketches where it had been
calm every minute of their absence.[33]

That afternoon Phipps sent for all officers. The conference
in the cabin of the *Racehorse* was long. Biddle learned about it
later in making his daily copy of the log. Phipps had presented
their dire situation without mincing words. He explained he
had been forced to give up any hope of an easterly breeze. Apparently they were in a sheltered pocket, a fear borne out by
Midshipman Walden's account. They could await the event of
the weather upon the bomb ketches in hopes of getting them out,
or resort to the boats. They had sounded an hour before and
found bottom at fourteen fathoms. Should they, or the ice in
which they were fast, take the ground, they must inevitably be
lost, and probably overset. Having no harbor, it would be impossible to winter the vessels with any probability of their again
being serviceable. Provisions would be very short for such an
undertaking were it otherwise feasible. Even if they could get
to the nearest rocks and make some conveniences for wintering,
they were in a place unfrequented by whalers and would encounter worse difficulties in another year, with fewer resources
at their command. Certainly not more than half the company

could survive the hardships of winter. He would not hastily relinquish the hope of getting the vessels out, but he would not, on
the other hand, obstinately adhere to such a course. He realized
the undertaking of moving 170 men so considerable a distance
by boats was a most serious one. The Dutch whalers stayed at
Hakluyt Head, he understood, until September, provided the
harbor there remained clear. If they could cross the five leagues
of ice, launch the boats in open water, and make the Head before the Dutchmen left, all could be saved. If they delayed, it
might be too late. Therefore, he had decided to prepare all
the boats for going away. That would take some days. Meanwhile, the launches of the *Racehorse* and *Carcass* would be
fitted out first and started across the ice. He hoped, he concluded
gravely, that God might yet send them a strong easterly wind.[34]

During the balance of that day all boats were lowered to the
ice. Some of the hands were engaged in fitting them out; the
others, in making and filling small canvas bread bags and dressing provisions. Everywhere were grave faces. Men realized
the seriousness of their position, and the dangerous step which
was to be taken. Biddle got his orders that night to set out with
the launch in the morning.[35]

Captain Phipps took command of the launch expedition, with
Biddle in charge of an augmented crew from the *Carcass,* and
William Finley, coxswain of the *Racehorse,* in charge of the
latter's crew. The intention was to move both boats a little way
to the westward to see how they would haul over the ice. Before
setting out, Phipps noticed the ice was a little more open around
the bomb ketches, and instructed Lutwidge to keep all sail upon
them on the chance that a vague east wind might strengthen
enough to move them a little toward the west. The launches
hauled much easier than had been anticipated. Not that it was
accomplished without dreary toil. They were big, clumsy craft,
and every jutting ice hill was an impediment that had to be sur-
mounted or, if too high, evaded by a detour. For two miles
they pushed, and hauled, and tugged, and Biddle saw how it
was exhausting himself and his men. After some five hours of
labor, Phipps ordered the two crews to return to the vessels.
They got back at three o'clock in the afternoon to be cheered

by the fact that, during their absence, the wind had strengthened sufficiently to advance the *Racehorse,* with the *Carcass* in tow, about a mile to the westward. The position, however, was still east of the point where they originally had been beset. Within another hour the ice again began to press in and gloom deepened. Nor was optimism restored by a report from the pilots, who went off during the night to discover the condition of the ice to the westward and returned, after sunrise on August 8, to describe it as "very heavy and close, consisting chiefly of large fields." [36]

Biddle had informed Captain Lutwidge that, if any worthwhile progress was to be made, more men were required to haul the launch than the detachment previously given him. As a result, the first and second lieutenants went forward with fifty men, and Phipps headed a similiar contingent from the *Racehorse.* They made four miles that day—four grueling miles— and then trudged wearily back through a rising fog, arriving on board around six o'clock in the evening. Meanwhile, at noon, the ice had opened slightly, and the whole pack, with the bomb ketches in it, moved along slowly to the westward. Fog enfolded them all night. The *Carcass* was cast off and set all sails, as there was now a perceptible easterly wind. Around four o'clock in the morning of August 9 the fog lifted, and a great cheer rose. The launches were visible resting on the ice a short distance ahead to the southwest. Not only had the vessels advanced nearly four miles through the ice during the night, but the pack itself was moving rapidly westward.[37]

All that day they warped their way along, resting the crew occasionally, for it was exhausting work. By late afternoon they were abreast of the launches, and Biddle was sent off with twenty-five men to bring up the *Carcass*'s boat. He hauled her alongside at one o'clock in the morning of August 10.[38]

At daybreak the wind came strong upon them from the northeast. Every sail was set in a desperate effort to break through. It succeeded. Many times they struck hard upon the great floes, but staunch construction saved them from damage. At noon the ice opened, and an hour later they had gained the sea. Men danced on deck in high elation. The countenances of the pilots changed from gloom to joy. Biddle, joining in the jubilation, harkened back a bit regretfully to the unaccomplished purpose of the expedition. He, for one, however, was convinced there was no sea route to the North Pole; no short cut over the top of the world.

So they ran to the westward, the ice pack behind them and to the north. With dawn of August 11, they picked up Hakluyt Head some eight leagues in the southwest. The weather was hazy, but the prevailing wind was still out of the east. Gradually the land took shape—no longer dark and foreboding to them, but a welcome bit of solid ground. In the late afternoon they anchored in Smeerenberg, a well-sheltered bay of which Hakluyt Head formed the western shore. The hands on four Dutch whalers cheered them as the bomb ketches dropped anchor.[39]

For a week they remained "to refresh the people after their fatigues," and to continue with the interminable observations and experiments Captain Phipps and Mr. Lyons were conducting. When they weighed, on August 19, it was to try one last cast to the westward, but the barrier ice rose before them, solid and forbidding.[40] Even Phipps was willing to call it quits, explaining: "The season was so very far advanced, and fogs as well as gales of wind so much to be expected, that nothing more could now have been done, had anything been left untried. The summer appears to have been uncommonly favorable for our purpose, and afforded us the fullest opportunity of ascertaining repeatedly the situation of that wall of ice, extending for more than twenty degrees between the latitudes of eighty and eighty-one, without the smallest appearance of any opening." [41]

The homeward voyage went well until early in September off the Shetland Islands, when heavy gales assailed them. How serious was the plight of the *Carcass,* Biddle realized vividly on the morning of September 11. Added to the roaring wind, a great sea was running. They secured the boats and cleared the decks of empty casks and lumber, as the main deck was being swept by heavy waves. The launch was scuttled and cleared ready to be thrown overboard if the storm increased. That night the *Racehorse* disappeared into the darkness and no answer came to their signal guns. By midnight the stanch little bomb ketch was almost waterlogged by the weight of water on her decks. Somehow she staggered on, and the gale moderated at daybreak.[42]

Five days later they picked up a pilot from a fishing vessel, and, on September 18, dropped anchor in Yarmouth Road.[43] From there Captain Lutwidge sent off an express to London. They had returned, and would proceed to The Nore when the winds permitted. With his letter he sent a copy of his log to show their Lords of the Admiralty that "Captain Phipps has done everything that was possible (tho' without Effect) to accomplish a passage Northwards, and that it is impossible to proceed farther than we did towards the North Pole, on the West Side of Spitzbergen." [44] Meanwhile, the *Racehorse* had made Oxfordness, further down the coast, and both vessels entered The Nore early in October.[45] London newspapers made much of the expedition, as for example: "They were several Times embayed in the Ice, as to find their Situation almost desperate, and were happy to get back into the open Sea, after having made the strongest Efforts, with the utmost Risk, to perform their undertaking." [46]

Biddle chuckled over the encomiums paid them and voiced his amusement in a letter to his sister, Lydia McFunn, on October 18. Written from London, it typifies the carefree, adventurous soul that he was.

" 'Tis three days since we were discharged from the Carcass," he told her. "I suppose I should now give you some small account of our proceedings, or do you not think it would be most proper first to forewarn you not to credit idle tales; for you must know I have been so frightened, so terrified at hearing of the surprising difficulties we encountered, the dreadful dangers we were in, that I am positive my hand shakes while I write, and what astonishes, confounds, and frightens me most of all is that during the whole voyage, I did not apprehend danger. But now good lack-a-daisy perceive it plain as the Ballad in sister Polly's hand!"

He did not intend to go to Greenland again, he continued in the same jocular vein, because it prevented him from writing or

receiving letters. Then he fired several questions at her and
supplied her answers to each:

"Should I tell you of the Suns not setting for two months and
of our observing him when lowest at 12 P M or with Merridian
in order to find the Latt. the same as at 12 Midday   You who
are perfectly well acquainted with those things would be apt to
answer certainly in the Latt: 80 or 81 it will be so

"Should I tell you that all the Valleys Coves &c are fill'd with
What once was snow and is now so on top   But the under part
either warmed by the upper coat or by the Sun when upper
most is Congealed into Ice and from these Coves fall Large
Pieces of Ice which appear higher than any to be met with at
Sea and Places from whence they Part are Perpendicular higher
than Delf[t] Steeples   That all the Ice you meet seems formd
of the Same Matereils Coverd with Snow &c that most of
the Ice you meet with at Sea is her[e] 2 or three feet above the
surface of the water some 4 or 5 and some few hummocks 18
or twenty feet   would you Answer you Supposed so   Whatever you would say   wherever you are   whatever you do May
God of his infinite Mercy Bless and Protect you from all Evils
both now and evermore." [47]

One phrase in that letter provides a graphic key to Nicholas
Biddle's character: "I did not apprehend danger." Actually,
the polar experience had whetted his appetite for more adventure, and several months after his return there was promise of
new fields of exploration. Reports in London were that the
Royal Society was contemplating an expedition into the Southern Ocean. He applied immediately to Sir Joseph Banks, that
eminent naturalist, who was the Society's most enterprising
member. It was by then early in January, 1774, and Sir Joseph
was graciously disposed to employ this young colonial should
the voyage be carried out.[48]

But the Royal Society's plans went into the discard a few days
later when the momentous news of the Boston Tea Party
reached London. To that time, Biddle had not taken provincial
unrest too seriously, or at least had not expressed himself as
even cognizant of the growing tension between the British
ministry and the American colonies. But the implications of the

Tea Party were inescapable. Dumping 340 chests of the East India Company's tea into Boston Harbor may have been a radical act, but the newspaper accounts indicated quite clearly that it was a carefully premeditated one.[49] All thoughts of further maritime explorations, of his continuation in the British naval service, came to an end. Great Britain could not overlook so deliberate a flouting of her authority. Punitive action was inevitable, and, as Biddle knew the temper of his countrymen, he saw that an attempt at punishment would lead inevitably to war.

So he did what would be expected of him—returned his midshipman's warrant to the British Admiralty and embarked for Philadelphia.[50] That action which he had been craving and which had drawn him to England three years before would, he was positive, be found at home.

Chapter V
The Franklin Galley

OUTWARDLY THE PORT OF PHILADELPHIA APPEARED unchanged to Nicholas Biddle when he returned home in the late spring of 1774. The same bustle and activity were evident on the many docks from Southwark to the Northern Liberties. Hogsheads, tierces, barrels, and bales were being trundled in or out of the warehouses, from or to the vessels alongside the piers—tall-masted ships from Europe, brigs and schooners from the West Indies, shallops from upriver or the Jerseys. Out on the broad Delaware, barges, scows, and bumboats plied their way between ship and shore. In the background, rising on the higher land above the warehouses lay the city of neat and uniform red-brick homes, row after row along the narrow streets. Above the line of their slant roofs rose the stately shafts of Gloria Dei, St. Paul's, St. Peter's, Christ Church, and the State House. "Yes, truly the same as I left it more than three years ago," thought he, as, having arranged for the delivery of his sea chest, he set off for his sister's home on north Third Street.

Only after the home-coming, after he had swept his mother into his arms, given sister Lydia a resounding buss, and been enthusiastically received by his young nephew Billy McFunn, did he perceive that inwardly Philadelphia was different. Whether at home or abroad in the city, his family and friends had but perfunctory interest in his adventures in the British navy or on the polar expedition. After polite attention, the conversation would soon be swung to the tea tax, and what might be expected from the British ministry in the way of re-taliatory measures against Massachusetts for its famous Tea

Party. Philadelphia, too, had had a tea party, he learned, but a minor one compared to the affair at Boston. The other colonial ports had also reacted violently against the tea ships, bundling them back to England unloaded. Upon everyone's lips was that phrase first coined in the days of the Stamp Act, "Taxation without representation," and in everyone's heart was the fear of severe punitive action from England.[1]

From his brother Edward, who, representing the county of Berks, was in Philadelphia attending the Assembly, Nicholas heard in detail of the happenings in America. Edward was no compromiser. From the start he had taken an active, belligerent part in opposing any measures of the ministry or Parliament which he considered inimical to the welfare of the American colonies. His opinions were shared by brother James, who, while holding a deputy judgeship in the Admiralty under the royal government, was also ardent in denouncing the tea tax and justifying the refusal of all the colonies to accept the tea. Their sentiments could not have failed to influence Nicholas had there been any doubts in his mind, though of course there were none. He had not abandoned a naval career in England and taken ship for home on snap judgment. Like Edward and James, he was an exponent of colonial rights. Perforce, however, he became for the time being an observer rather than an actor in the final steps leading up to the American Revolution. The stage was being occupied by the lawyer, the agitator, and the demagogue; the fighting man's entry would come in due course.

It is well, therefore, to summarize the events which Nicholas witnessed during the first year of his return, a year spent part in Philadelphia with his mother, and part in Reading with brother Edward, when the latter was not discharging his duties in the colonial capital.[2]

Parliament acted and the news of this action followed hard on the heels of Nicholas Biddle's arrival in Philadelphia. The port of Boston had been ordered closed from June 1, 1774, until the tea dumped into the harbor should be paid for. Massachusetts had been denied the right of electing a Council, which after August 1 would be named by the King. General Thomas Gage had been appointed governor of Massachusetts and ordered to uphold the new acts with military force if necessary.

On the day the Boston Port Bill had become effective, Philadelphia and other colonial cities went into mourning, with closed shops, flags at half-mast, and radical clergymen denouncing the oppressive measures of a tyrannical Parliament. On June 15, at a rousing meeting at the State House, a general colonial congress was proposed and acclaimed unanimously along with the appointment of a Committee of Correspondence with the other colonies.[3]

When the First Continental Congress convened in Philadelphia, on September 5, 1774, Edward Biddle was one of Pennsylvania's seven representatives. He took an active part in its deliberations, and in the forming of the various measures which it passed—among others the futile address to the King, the Declaration of Rights, and, most drastic of all, the Continental Association with its nonimportation and nonexportation clauses. That fall also Edward was chosen speaker of the Pennsylvania Assembly and in December was elected to the Second Continental Congress, which was to convene in Philadelphia the following May.[4]

Aside from watching political events, Nicholas Biddle's recorded activities in this period consisted of two land purchases, both in Northumberland County. On October 18 he acquired three hundred acres and on December 29 added one hundred acres more. As Edward and James Biddle purchased three hundred acres each in the same county on the same date in October it is likely that investment or speculation was behind the venture. Nevertheless, Nicholas journeyed northwestward to view the land for which he had a warrant. Nor was he pleased with the site, as he reported to his brother James by letter, commenting, "I am not quite so anxious about Clearing that Place as I was,   Every one objects to the situation and I am in great hope of getting a tract more pleasantly situated." [5]

It was after this last land purchase, when Edward Biddle was coming down the Schuylkill River by boat from Reading to Philadelphia in January, 1775, that his active career received a severe check. The boat was crowded, and he fell overboard. They dragged him out, chilled to the bone.

"He went ashore to a tavern," according to his brother Charles, "drank some wine, stood before a fire in his shirt to dry. The Tory landlord antagonized him and he beat him up. With passion and wine Edward Biddle became ungovernable. He lay down in his damp shirt before the fire. He was ill the next day and broke out with blotches on his body. One in the eye deprived him of the sight of that eye. Before that he had never been sick. Afterwards, he had scarcely a day's health until his death."

This illness forced him to resign as speaker of the Pennsylvania Assembly in March, but when the Second Continental Congress met in May he dragged himself to the opening sessions.[6] Events had marched to their inevitable conclusion before this Congress convened. Tom Gage's expedition to seize powder, arms, and two patriots had run into a deadly rebuff at Lexington and Concord. A pox on words and petitions! Action was needed now. The call went forth for men, for guns, for powder—particularly for powder.

On June 3 the seven Pennsylvania delegates were appointed a committee with power to borrow £6,000 for the purchase of that commodity wherever it could be found. That day, ere disease again laid him low, Edward Biddle sent for his brother.[7]

Nicholas Biddle was in Reading when the summons came. He lost no time in repairing to Philadelphia, where Edward from a sick bed directed him to Thomas Mifflin, to whom the committee had delegated the task of securing the powder. Within twenty-four hours, in command of a small schooner which nominally served as a pilot boat at the Delaware capes, he was outward bound for the French island of Santo Domingo, armed with letters of introduction, negotiable drafts, and authorization to purchase up to ten thousand pounds of gunpowder.[8] How sanguine of success the committee felt was disclosed in a letter Sam Adams wrote to a friend in Massachusetts, on June 10: "Mr. Mifflin assures me that large quantities

of powder are expected in a few Weeks in this place. . . .
Every step is taking [*sic*] here for the procuring of Gunpowder
from abroad." [9]

Of Biddle's quick and successful voyage to Santo Domingo
we have no detailed information. While he was gone His Majesty's sloop of war *Nautilus,* Captain John Collins, armed with
sixteen guns and manned by one hundred men, turned up off
New Castle, in the Delaware below Philadelphia. She was lying
there, stated a Pennsylvania newspaper, "for the 'Protection
of our trade' in the courtly style, but in plain English to pick our
pockets, and try to enslave us." [10]

The *Nautilus* was still off New Castle when Biddle came up
the Delaware, with six and one-half tons of powder stowed carefully under barrels of molasses in the schooner's hold. So he
hoisted French colors—jack, ensign, and pendant—knowing the
British commander would not dare stop and search a vessel of
foreign register. The ruse worked. Captain Collins allowed
the schooner to pass unmolested, and on July 26 John Adams
exulted by letter to James Warren, with the army before Boston: "12 o'clock. This Moment 135 full Bls. making Six Tons
and an half of Powder is brought into the State House yard
in Six Waggons—to be sent off to you." [11]

Other powder shipments came in during the remaining few
days of the month, and on August 1, for a job well done, Congress paid the Pennsylvania delegates $16,000 (the equivalent
in Continental currency of the £6,000 authorized).[12] Biddle,
the cargo delivered and the schooner turned back to its owners,
found his talents in immediate demand by a newly created or-
ganization—the Pennsylvania Committee of Safety—whose
members embraced, among a total of twenty-five, his brother
Edward and his cousin, Owen Biddle.[13]

While Biddle was absent at Santo Domingo, the Pennsylvania Assembly, acutely conscious of how vulnerable Philadelphia lay to the warships of the King, had taken protective measures of vigorous nature. The Committee of Safety had been
appointed on June 30, charged, among other things, to make
provision "for defending this Province, and the City in particu-

lar against the Attacks of Armed Vessels that may be sent to annoy them." [14]

That defense could best be effected, the Committee promptly had concluded, by constructing row galleys capable of mounting a heavy cannon in the bow, and light of draft to negotiate the shallows of the Delaware; by repairing and rearming the old colonial fort on Mud Island, now rechristened Liberty Island, below the mouth of the Schuylkill; and by obstructing the channel south of the city with sharpened logs sunk in the French style of chevaux-de-frise. [15]

By the time Biddle had returned with his cargo of powder much progress had been made. Thirteen row galleys, each about fifty feet long, with a beam of thirteen feet and a depth of four and one-half feet, had been contracted for. Two of them had been launched. From Emanuel Eyre's shipyard in Kensington to that of John Wharton, in Southwark, came fevered activity as the hulls of the remaining eleven took shape. [16] "Dr. Franklin's row-galleys," they called them, rather conclusive evidence that this worthy patriot, who was a member of the Committee of Safety, had proposed them. [17] Their outfitting, however, had been delegated largely to a subcommittee of two, Owen Biddle and Robert White, which was engaged in July in procuring guns, ammunition, and sailcloth. [18]

Primarily the galleys were propelled by oars, sixteen to a side. Each, however, mounted two short masts with a long yard on each for a lateen sail. How they were to be manned had not been settled. The Committee estimated fifty men would be required for each galley and was toying with the idea of using the military companies in the city and county as "Minute Men on Board the Boats when required." [19]

Three captains had been appointed in July—Henry Dougherty, John Rice, and Charles Alexander. Dougherty and Alexander had been shipmasters out of Philadelphia for a decade, and Rice was a shipbuilder, engaged in constructing the galley he was to command. [20] These three were senior to Biddle, who on August 1 was unanimously elected "to the Command of the Boat called the Franklin, now building by Emanuel Eyres." [21]

Inquiry disclosed that Eyre would not be able to launch the

galley before the end of August, and that the form of commission for the captains had not yet been approved. Consequently, Nicholas had little to do but advise the Committee, which set considerable store on his experience in their efforts to perfect the naval armament. Two more galleys took the water ahead of his, on August 23 and August 24, respectively.[22] Owen Biddle had procured thirteen heavy cannon—one 32-pounder, four 24-pounders, and the remainder 18-pounders. Forty rounds of cartridges were being collected for each of these great guns.[23] Necessary medicines were being put up "in convenient Boxes" for the galleys and, with an idea of close fighting, one hundred pikes had been ordered.[24]

No pleasanter afternoon could have been found for the launching of the *Franklin* on August 28. The row galleys were still sufficiently novel to attract a crowd, and Eyre's yard was well filled when the stanch little craft slid down the ways. The builder assured Biddle he would have her ready for delivery, complete with oars, masts, and sails, within two weeks.[25] This included mounting a twenty-four-pound cannon in the bow and two swivels amidships.[26]

By mid-August, meanwhile, the Committee of Safety had abandoned the idea of employing the military companies as minutemen. Regularly enlisted crews would be provided for each galley, but before recruiting them it became necessary to decide upon articles for their government and length of their enlistment. The latter was finally set at two months "and from that time until discharged by orders from Assembly or this Board." The articles, thirty in number, were approved on August 29, but, as they had to be printed, more delay occurred.[27]

Each galley was to provided with a lieutenant, master's mate, gunner, carpenter, boatswain, steward, cook, captain's clerk, and drummer. On September 1, resolving that "there are good reasons to suppose the Armed Boats may very soon be called into action," the Committee set the pay table—graduated from twenty dollars monthly for a captain to six dollars for a private —and determined the weekly allowance of provisions and rum.[28]

The call to action feared by the Committee could not have

been against the *Nautilus*. That sloop toward the end of August intercepted a powder vessel and vacated the Delaware. Captain Collins, "in low obscene language," vented his dislike for all rebels, ere he quitted the capes, by sending word to Philadelphia "that he did not value all their gondolas or Committee of Safety a ———— !" Maybe not! But his departure belied his words.[29]

While the final draft of the officers' commissions was approved in late August, the printing thereof took almost three weeks. Not until September 15 did Dr. Franklin, as president of the Committee of Safety, receive the forms, fill them in and present them to the seven captains who had been selected by that time.[30] Nicholas Biddle's, dated back to August 1 and countersigned by William Govett, secretary of the Committee, was long preserved. It read in part:

> We reposing special trust and confidence in your Patriotism, Valour, conduct and Fidelity, Do by these Presents constitute and appoint you to be Captain of the Provincial Armed Boat, called the Franklin fitted out for the protection of the Province of Pennsylvania, and the Commerce of the River Delaware, against all hostile Enterprises, and for the defence of American Liberty: you are therefore to take the said Boat into your charge, and carefully and diligently to discharge the duty of Captain by doing and performing all manner of things thereunto belonging. . . . And you are to observe and follow such orders and directions from time to time, as you shall receive from the Assembly or Provincial Convention, during their Sessions, or from this or a future Committee of Safety for this Province, or from your Superior Officer, according to the Rules and Discipline of War, pursuant to the trust reposed in you.[31]

Young Thomas Houston, a Philadelphia lad who had been bred to the sea, had been appointed a lieutenant by the Committee on September 2 and assigned to the *Franklin*. Upon him devolved the task of drumming up a crew—no mean task with lieutenants from the other completed galleys competing for men, the pay small, and the service none too popular.[32]

Biddle, meanwhile, had turned his attention to getting his command outfitted. The *Franklin* was neither better nor worse than her sister galleys. She was crank and unwieldy, and would have been swamped in any kind of a heavy sea. For the river she would serve admirably, but he shuddered at the thought of taking her down into the bay, where waves could on occasion roll as viciously as outside the capes. Of course, he knew no such service was contemplated for the galleys. Theirs would be to await the enemy's arrival up the river.

Even such waiting would not be pleasant once a full crew was enrolled, for certainly there was not room for fifty hands on board. The *Franklin* had been decked over, and bulkheads divided her hold into three compartments—a tiny cubbyhole aft for the captain; next, a slightly larger cabin with bunks for the lieutenant and warrant officers; the crew's quarters forward. As headroom was never more than four and one-half feet, only a dwarf could have stood erect below deck.[33]

By the end of September seven of the galleys were sufficiently equipped and manned to warrant pulling away from their outfitting piers. With pardonable pride the Committee of Safety extended an invitation to the members of the Continental Congress and the State Assembly. "Come ride with us up and down the Delaware," they suggested, and set a rendezvous at a wharf at the foot of Arch Street for the morning of September 28. Congress took a holiday that Thursday and the delegates hied themselves to the wharf, where members of the Committee were on hand to help their captains play host.[34] Who of the celebrities sailed with Biddle in the *Franklin,* history sayeth not. John Adams, in whose diary is preserved a brief account of the junket, took passage on the *Bull Dog,* Captain Alexander, and had three committee members, including Owen Biddle, on hand to entertain him.

"We passed down the river by Gloucester," said Adams, "where the vaisseaux de frise are. These are frames of timber to be filled with stones, and sunk in three rows in the channel. . . . Our intention was to have gone down to the fort, but the winds and tide being unfavorable, we returned by the city, and went up the river to Point-no-Point, a pretty place." [35]

He omitted an incident in the junket, which another diarist reported almost with a chuckle.

"About one went down to the wharf to see the gondolas sail

by," wrote Christopher Marshall, "the delegates being on board with a great number of others. Two of them, about Master's wharf, each carried away a mast." [36]

After this demonstration, the Committee dispatched the galleys to Liberty Island as rapidly as their heavy cannon could be mounted. Here each was berthed along a boom extending into the river from the fort. Nine were in commission by early October. Not one of them, however, had better than twenty hands.[37]

The deplorable apathy of seamen and landsmen to the galley service disturbed the Committee. Recruiting efforts of the lieutenants had been woefully lacking in results. So the senior captains were requested to attend the board, and Biddle was among the five or six who presented themselves on October 9. Asked to recommend the best steps to spur enlistments they gave the obvious reply—a bonus in advance for each man who would sign up. The amount of the bounty was, after some discussion, referred to the captains to decide and report back. They later agreed upon fifteen shillings, but not to be paid until one month after entering the service.[38] Meanwhile the captains were charged "to push on with vigour and expedition the fitting and manning their respective Boats, so that they may be in readiness to oppose any Hostile attacks at a moment's warning." [39]

Shortly thereafter the captains put their fingers on another deterrent to recruiting. Among the articles governing the conduct of officers and men was one providing that the disposition of prizes and their cargoes should be as the Provincial Assembly might thereafter direct. Men wanted prize money, not promises, should captures be made—waiting until the Assembly decided what to do about it did not appeal to prospective hands.

At the same time Biddle and the other captains, who had been for some weeks on duty off Liberty Island, had learned to their discomfort that they were forced to stand watch on, watch off, with their lieutenants. So on October 12 they memorialized the Committee of Safety, to the effect:

"That the Officers belonging to the Boats Are too few for the number of men, and think a Second Lieutenant necessary—

"That they find the 15. Article—Relative to Captures, discourages the men from Entering into the Service freely." [40]

The Committee could and did acquiesce in the first request by authorizing the appointment of another lieutenant for each galley. The other matter, however, was beyond its jurisdiction. With the royal Admiralty Courts superseded, only the Assembly could determine what was to be done with prizes. Considering that the galleys were never going to venture out of the river, the question did seem an academic one. [41]

More disturbing, however, was the news that, in selecting a commodore for the fleet, the Committee of Safety had ignored the galley captains and had recommended Captain Thomas Read, of Delaware, to the Assembly. [42] It was an affront the captains could not accept passively. Yet the memorial drawn up on October 30, while strong in its disapproval of the proposed appointment, was couched in diplomatic, almost humble tone. The captains signed in order of seniority, which meant that Biddle was fourth to affix his signature.

Not out of dislike or disaffection to the person, character, or ability of Captain Read were they presenting the memorial. It was rather "to vindicate their own Characters & Honour from any unjust Aspersions." Understanding that the Committee had the sole power to appoint a commodore of its own choosing, they did not want "to presume to dictate" to it, but they did have certain observations they wished to make. These were three in number.

First, in entering the service they had "no lucrative Views," but solely the desire to serve the common cause, and fondly hoped "their Conduct, as yet, had not been blamed or disapproved of." Second, the harmony now existing between officers and men would be at an end once the crews learned of the appointment of a commodore "who had not before belonged to any of the Boats." Third, they believed some of the captains were as well qualified as any one to serve as commodore, and had hoped the eldest captain would have been appointed. This, which they "apprehend to be the general Custom in the Navy," would, they felt sure, "excite a Spirit of Bravery and Emulation among the Officers."

In conclusion they again admitted the "incontestable right"

of the Committee of Safety to appoint a commodore and repeated their desire to give not "the least Umbrage or Offence
. . . but only to pray if it is not already too late, & that it can
be done with Propriety, that you will be pleased to reconsider
our Case." [43]

While the Committee's minutes give no indication that the
memorial was even received, the desired result was attained by
the captains. The Assembly dismissed the recommendation of
Captain Read by stony silence and, for as long as Nicholas Biddle remained with the Pennsylvania fleet, Henry Dougherty, the
senior captain, served as acting commodore.

In anticipation of the coming winter and the discomfort of
trying to house the crews in the galleys in freezing temperatures,
the Committee had ordered the construction, at Fort Island, of
a crude barracks capable of holding two hundred men.[44] By
early November, however, it was agreed such a shed would not
only be inadequate, but an improper place "for defending the
People from the inclemency of the weather." A real building
program was launched including a pier at the upper end of the
island.[45]

It was high time such steps were taken as, thanks to the
bounty, the galleys were filling up fairly rapidly, and thin ice
was forming each morning in the marsh grass along shore. In
fact, as officer of the day on one of those dismal and chilly morn-
ings, Biddle was only too glad to acknowledge receipt of about
ten cords of oak and hickory wood which one Michael Ming-
ham "had delivered on Liberty Island for the use of the fleet." [46]

Scum and riffraff of the water front naturally found their
way among the galleymen, and one of these, William Green,
provided the first case of serious insubordination. He was of
the crew of the galley *Congress,* and bore an unsavory reputation. His offence was a blatant announcement that he would
enter on board a British man-of-war at the first opportunity,
and would "do what Mischief he could, as he was a pilot." The
articles governing the fleet provided for a court-martial for
such a case, but Captain Dougherty, as senior officer, apparently
decided to handle it otherwise. He reported Green's remarks to
the Committee of Safety, which promptly issued an arrest and

clapped the culprit "in the Gaol of Philadelphia County" to await the Committee's future disposition of his case.[47]

As subsequent events showed, Biddle was familiar with Green and his reputation, indicating that Dougherty must have consulted his fellow captains before taking the action he did. The captain of the *Franklin* has left us no appraisal of his own crew, although they probably were no better than the average for the service, which was nothing to boast of. No muster roll of the galley for that period has been found, but there is preserved a return of the military stores and ammunition put on board in November. The latter included fifty 24-pounder round shot, thirty cartridges, eighty pounds of 1¼ grape shot, fifty pounds of partridge shot, seven crossbar shot, and one hundred swivel cartridges. Among the military stores were rammer, sponge, wad hook, ladle, bed, quoin, and match stock for the great gun; two pairs of pistols, fifteen cutlasses, ten pikes, and a miscellaneous assortment of budge barrels, tomkins, horn bitts, crows, handspikes, and matches.[48]

As December approached, Biddle became more and more dissatisfied with the inactivity, almost futility, of the Pennsylvania naval service. Discomfort was to be endured if it would prove a prelude to action, but with the galleys designed solely for defense he could not foresee anything but idleness for many a long month to come. To await the enemy's attack rather than go forth to seek him was entirely foreign to his nature. While he might be able to whip his crew into a fine fighting unit, and train them to the twenty-four-pounder until they could fire it with some precision, he had the feeling that his efforts would bear no fruit in the way of actual combat.[49]

How long he would have remained as a galley captain is hard to say, but fortunately opportunity arose to enable him to find the action he craved. Again it was Edward Biddle, still a member of Congress although seldom in attendance because of illness, who provided the opportunity for expanded activities. In October, after a deal of debate and much protest, the Congress had authorized the arming of a number of vessels, and appointed a Naval Committee to attend to acquiring, outfitting, manning, and directing its proposed fleet. During November that com-

mittee had purchased two ships and two brigs and, dominated
by New England members, was passing out commissions almost
exclusively to fellow New Englanders.[50]

Edward Biddle was not a member of the Naval Committee,
but he was a powerful influence in the halls of Congress. As
Nicholas had confided to him his distaste for the monotonous
galley service, and as he banked largely upon his younger brother's abilities in the naval line, he was emphatic in his demand
that one of the captaincies go to Pennsylvania, and that Nicholas' talents warranted the honor of that command.[51]

Undoubtedly the Naval Committee was influenced by the
pressure exerted by Edward Biddle. However, Nicholas Biddle's reputation and background were not unknown and, as
naval experience was highly desirable, he was a logical ap-
pointee. When the Naval Committee offered him a commission
to command one of the brigs in the Continental fleet he accepted
promptly. On December 9, 1775, he applied to the Committee
of Safety for "Liberty to resign his Commission in order to enter into Continental Service." [52] His resignation was received,
we assume with regrets, and Biddle's four months of service in
the Pennsylvania navy came to a close.[53]

II

The Andrew Doria

Chapter VI

The First Continental Fleet

THE BRIG TO WHICH NICHOLAS BIDDLE HAD BEEN appointed by the Naval Committee of Congress was named the *Andrew Doria,* in honor of the celebrated Genoese admiral.[1] Most generally, however, she was called "the black brig." [2] She had been purchased in mid-November and, for conversion to war purposes, turned over to Joshua Humphreys, master builder in Wharton's and Humphreys' shipyard. Now, after twenty-four days of ship-carpentry work under the supervision of the capable Humphreys, she lay moored to James Cuthbert's wharf, her sides painted black, her low bulwarks pierced for fourteen guns. Most of the gun carriages for her 4-pounders had been delivered, so mounting the cannon was going on apace.[3] Riggers were swarming over her, directed by a tall, redheaded merchant captain named John Barry, whom the Committee had employed to superintend the outfitting of the whole fleet.[4]

Another brig, the *Cabot,* of about the same size and armament, lay along the opposite side of the wharf. She had yellow sides and a small white figurehead to distinguish her from the *Andrew Doria*'s black sides and no head. Her decks too were crowded with riggers.[5]

Further downstream, at Willing and Morris' wharf, were the other vessels of this first Continental fleet. Largest of the converted merchantmen, and the flagship, was the 200-ton ship *Black Prince,* which the Committee had renamed the *Alfred,* in recognition, as John Adams reported, of the "founder of the greatest navy that ever existed." [6] She had a white bottom, a broad band of black along the water line, and bright yellow sides. She had been armed with twenty 9-pounders on the lower

deck, peeping through newly made gunports which cleared the
water line by only eighteen inches, and ten 6-pounders on the
upper deck.[7] At her main floated the new flag of the rebellious
provinces, commonly called the Grand Union. It had thirteen
stripes, alternating red and white for the thirteen colonies, and
the Union Jack in the canton at the staff.[8] The *Alfred* boasted a
striking figurehead—a man in armor drawing a sword. Designed originally to depict the Black Prince, it could just as well,
allegorically, betoken the good King Alfred.[9]

Second in size was the *Columbus,* formerly named the *Sally.*
She boasted eighteen 9-pounders on the lower deck, and ten
6-pounders on the upper. Her bottom was white, but her sides
were entirely black, and she sported no figurehead.[10]

The final vessel was an armed sloop, of twelve 6-pounders,
which had sailed into port from Rhode Island, on December 5.
She was the property of that colony, and had been called the
Katy. The Naval Committee bought her soon after her arrival.
This same committee, which could bestow such historic and
significant names as *Alfred, Andrew Doria, Cabot,* and *Columbus,* had bogged down in rechristening her. It finally had decided upon *Providence;* not because of the divine connotation,
but because the venerable chairman of the Naval Committee,
Stephen Hopkins, hailed from that town and the sloop had been
built there.[11] She too was black sided and had come in fully
armed.[12]

To command this fleet the Naval Committee had pitched
upon Esek Hopkins, brother of its chairman and well-nigh as
venerable. As a privateersman in the French and Indian War
fifteen years before, and a merchant captain since, he had gained
some measure of distinction, but his appointment as commodore could be traced more to influence than to ability. In response to the Naval Committee's invitation written November
5, and a buttressing letter from brother Stephen pointing out
that "Your Pay and Perquisites will be such as you will have no
Reason to complain of," [13] Esek had arrived in Philadelphia
late that same month, an "antiquated figure," who "swore now
and then." [14] When he learned that Congress had set six and
two-thirds dollars per month as a seaman's wage, he considered

returning to Rhode Island, being fearful "that a sufficient number of hands cannot be raised in time to do anything to purpose this season." That had been on the morning of December 2.[15] By afternoon his fears had been dissolved, and the Rhode Island delegates had reported to their governor that Hopkins' acceptance of "the Command of the Fleet gives universal Satisfaction." [16] Five days later the new commodore had stood proudly on the quarter-deck of the *Alfred* while a lieutenant named John Paul Jones had raised the Grand Union flag to the masthead.[17]

The captain of the *Alfred* had not yet arrived. He was another New Englander, a "sleepy gentleman" from New London, one Dudley Saltonstall, brother-in-law of Silas Deane of Connecticut, a member of the Naval Committee. A commission had been proffered Saltonstall on November 27, "as a proper person to take the command," but because of tedious communications his acceptance had not yet been received.[18]

A third New Englander, Abraham Whipple, brother-in-law of Stephen and Esek Hopkins, who had brought the *Katy* (now *Providence*) into port, had been named captain of the *Columbus*. As Whipple's commission was dated December 8, it is apparent that Nicholas Biddle was the third captain to be commissioned.[19] By the next day a fourth New Englander had been added, with the appointment of Commodore Esek's elder son, John Burroughs Hopkins, as captain of the *Cabot*.[20]

Other than Biddle the only officer so far appointed to the *Andrew Doria* was another Philadelphian, Isaac Craig, the lieutenant of marines.[21] For the line lieutenants and the warrant officers, the Naval Committee seemed inclined to consult the captain, and this undoubtedly brought about the selection of twenty-four-year-old James Josiah as first lieutenant. Like Biddle, he had been serving in the Pennsylvania fleet. He resigned as lieutenant of one of the row galleys on December 11 "to enter the Continental service." [22]

A number of prospective officers had arrived in the sloop *Katy,* being assured by Esek Hopkins before he had left Providence in mid-November, that commissions in the fleet awaited them at Philadelphia.[23] One of these Rhode Islanders, Elisha

Warner, was appointed second lieutenant of the *Andrew Doria*. For third lieutenant, the Naval Committee named John Mc-Dougall, a promising young nephew of Colonel Alexander Mc-Dougall of the New York line. The choice for master was Benjamin Dunn, another Philadelphian. Biddle approved them all as well as three master's mates and four midshipmen for whom warrants were issued at that time.[24]

Progress in recruiting hands, however, moved slowly. There was reluctance on the part of able seamen to engage in a service whose term of enlistment ran more than a year to January 1, 1777. Even when Congress, on December 13, increased the wage to eight dollars a month, the response was not satisfactory.[25] The problem was not confined to the *Andrew Doria*; it affected the whole fleet. The commodore placed the matter before the Naval Committee, which looked hungrily at the fairly well-manned Pennsylvania row galleys, and sent its chairman a begging to the Committee of Safety. He bore a resolution desiring permission "to apply to the Seamen on board the Galleys for such as are willing to enter on board the Continental armed Vessels now fitting for sea in this city." [26] The Committee of Safety on December 20 graciously authorized recruiting from the row galleys of "any Number of Seamen not exceeding one hundred." [27] To the galleymen eight dollars a month represented a 33⅓ per cent increase in wages. The Continental provision allowance also offered somewhat better fare by matching the quantities of rum, meat, bread, and vegetables provided by the Provincial fleet, and adding twelve ounces of cheese and two ounces of butter per man weekly. Hence, the hundred additional hands were soon signed up.[28]

To help the shortage of seamen, the Committee of Safety looked over the list of malefactors in the public jail, picking out a few to whom it offered freedom upon condition of entering the Continental service. Among those accepting was the same William Green, who had been the "bad man" of the row galley, *Congress,* and who now shipped on the *Andrew Doria*.[29]

This, however, only partly solved the problem. Upon the suggestion of the commodore, a request was sent to Rhode Island to drum up some likely seamen and dispatch them by a fast sailing vessel for the Delaware.[30] That would take time, and some of the hands, their first martial ardor cooled, were already deserting the service. A number of them were reported as shipping on merchant vessels in the river. Once more the Naval Committee sent an emissary to the Committee of Safety. Could Commodore Hopkins or any of his captains have permission to search outward-bound vessels for the deserters? Permission "chearfully granted," announced the Committee of Safety, on December 23, with admonitions that the commodore observe "a Discreet Exercise of this Power," and that the officer chosen to do the searching be one "whose prudence may be depended on." [31]

No such backwardness marked enrollments in the first of two marine battalions. Originally Congress had instructed General Washington to raise the battalions out of the army before Boston. The commander in chief had protested the impracticability of the idea at that time; so it was resolved to undertake the recruiting in and around Philadelphia. Rendezvous had been opened early in December with drummers whose drums were gaily and pointedly decorated parading the streets to attract recruits. One of the drums, upon which was painted a rattlesnake, bore the legend, "Don't tread on me." [32]

Lieutenant Craig of the *Andrew Doria* had been particularly successful, probably because he had spent the last ten of his thirty-four years in Philadelphia and was a popular Irishman hailing originally from County Down. Starting his efforts on December 9, he signed nine recruits the first day and four the second, and by December 22 had more than forty men. They came from various professions and trades and included a doctor, breeches maker, weaver, mason, jeweler, butcher, cabinetmaker, hosier, and miller.[33]

Unfortunately, there were few weapons for the marines who now, for the whole fleet, numbered better than two hundred. The Naval Committee had been able to scrape together only about fifty muskets. It had recourse, as usual, to the long-suffering Committee of Safety, which supplied one hundred muskets, one hundred bayonets, and a dozen ramrods.[34] Thereafter the marines were able to relieve details of the First Pennsylvania battalion, which had been on duty day and night since December 2, guarding the ships and stores at the two wharves.[35]

The rules and regulations governing the fleet had been adopted late in November by the Congress, which had at the same time set the pay table and approved the ship's articles.[36] When printed copies of the former became available, Biddle saw at once that they had been modeled upon the rules and regulations of the British navy with which he was of course familiar. The ship's articles, too, showed familiarity with their British prototype. He made sure they were read to every hand signing them, although most of the men probably had not the slightest idea of the meaning of such sonorous phrases as "guilty of any breach contrary to the tenor of this agreement," or "anything herein contained to the contrary notwithstanding." [37]

From his experience on the *Portland* and the *Carcass,* he knew a happy ship depended upon seamen and marines having confidence in their officers. He lost no opportunity to inculcate this idea not only in the lieutenants and warrant officers, but also in all petty officers from boatswain's mate to the quartermasters. For himself, he was solicitous of the welfare of every man jack on board, at the same time maintaining a discipline that won their admiration and, eventually, their affection. He had a wholesome respect for the British navy, and he knew it behooved him to teach everything he had learned while serving in that navy to the crew he now intended to lead against it. This objective he kept constantly before him during the chaotic period while a fleet was being created.[38]

And it *was* a chaotic period. As late as December 22, when the Naval Committee presented to Congress a list of the officers it had appointed, two lieutenants were included who a few days later relinquished their commissions, and three others were omitted who had been in service for several weeks. One of the latter was James Josiah, the first lieutenant of the *Andrew Doria.*[39] Not until that late date was Commodore Hopkins' pay established—$125 a month as against the $32 per month paid the captains. On this same day Congress directed the Naval Committee to give the commodore secretly such orders "as shall appear to the said committee most conducive to the defence of the United Colonies, and the distress of the enemy's naval forces and vessels bringing supplies to their fleets and armies." [40]

There had been high hope that the fleet would be able to sail before the end of December, every effort being bent to achieve that end.[41] The winter was sweeping in. Ice was forming nightly along the shores, bitter winds were whipping across the river, sending shivers down the spines of the marines who stamped their beats along the wharves and of the seamen who blew on icy fingers as they paused in the endless task of loading stores.[42] Aware how pitifully inadequate these stores were, the Naval Committee despaired completing the fleet for sea without much more delay. It did, however, strive mightily to get the vessels ready to sail down the river before they were frozen in at the wharves. If they could reach the head of the bay, where ice could not retard them, the great quantities of still-needed stores could be carted down to them subsequently. With this objective the Naval Committee concentrated on the two ships and two brigs, leaving the sloop *Providence* for later outfitting.[43]

Four tons of powder and four hundred stand of small arms had been requested of the Committee of Safety, the chief source the hard-pressed Naval Committee could find for these essential articles.[44] The Committee had agreed, but had had to request time to collect the small arms from various points in the province.[45] Not until January 5, 1776, had the requisition been completed and delivery made, not only of the powder and small arms, but also eight hundred swivel shot, some saltpeter for the fleet surgeon, and for the marines fifty more muskets and a hundred firelocks.[46]

During this feverish activity the senior officers had been sleeping ashore. Dudley Saltonstall had arrived on December 23 and was quartered with his brother-in-law, Deane.[47] The commodore and his son were living with Stephen Hopkins, and Biddle of course was still at home. Busy as he was, he even found time in December to sit for his portrait—a crayon sketch made by Pierre Eugene Du Simitiere, a celebrated painter of the period.[48] All officers had moved to their ships, however, on January 1, as departure was imminent.

The Naval Committee applied to the Committee of Safety that day for three pilots to conduct the fleet down to Reedy Island and for the loan of sufficient men from the galleys to help the slender crews navigate the vessels during the descent of the river. Both requests were granted, but the Committee was insistent that pilots and hands be returned promptly when Reedy Island was reached.[49]

"The first American fleet that ever swelled their sails on the Western Ocean . . . sailed from Philadelphia amidst the acclamations of many thousands assembled on the joyful occasion."

Thus rhapsodized an editor to whom Christopher Gadsden, of the Naval Committee, subsequently imparted the details of the departure. Somehow or other the account of the massed spectators rings hollow in the light of other comments upon the same event.[50] A British informer, whose story is convincing, makes no mention of a great audience; he would not have been likely to overlook such a demonstration.[51] More acceptable is the simple chronicle as Lieutenant Josiah, of the *Andrew Doria,* penned it in the canvas-bound logbook. His entry is the first in "A Journal of a Cruse In the Brig Andrew Doria Nicholas Biddle Esqr Commander from ye Port of Philadelphia, Begun January 4th 1776." It is brief, pointed: "At 2 P.M. Cast off from ye Warf In Company with ye Comodore Ship Alfred, Columbus & Cabot. Light airs from ye Westward & much Ice in ye River." [52]

A number of officers and many hands were reported absent when the four vessels anchored in the stream. Anticipating this, the Naval Committee had prepared a notice which was posted in coffee house and tavern throughout the city:

"The Naval Committee give possitive Orders," it read, "that every Officer in the Sea and Marine Service, and all the Common Men belonging to each, who have enlisted into the Service of the United Colonies on board the Ships now fitting out, that they immediately repair on board their respective Ships as they would avoid being deemed deserters, and all those who have undertaken to be Security for any of them are hereby

Called upon, to procure and deliver up the Men they have engaged for, or they will be immediately Called upon in a proper and effectual Way.

"Boats will Constantly Attend at Messr^s Welling and Morris's Wharf to Carry all people on board the Ships." [53]

What with one delay or another, the fleet did not drop down the river until late in the afternoon. Darkness had descended when, to quote from the *Andrew Doria*'s journal, "At 6 D^o [P.M.] Came to at ye Pierse at Liberty Iland." [54]

That night turned bitterly cold, and the ice closed in. By dawn an almost unheard of condition had arisen. The Delaware was frozen from shore to shore.[55] The fleet at Liberty Island was hemmed in by ice which thickened with every hour. There was no possibility of breaking through; there was but to wait. To Biddle it was faintly reminiscent of the polar ice pack which had surrounded the *Racehorse* and *Carcass* in the frozen north two years before. In this case, however, there was no danger of ice pressure. At the worst there could be only annoying delay. How serious this might be to the plans of the Naval Committee nobody knew, not even Hopkins; for the committee had yet to supply him with sailing orders.[56]

Instructions for the commodore were drafted by the Naval Committee on January 5, probably reaching him the next day. They were in two sections; the first of a general nature which he could convey in part to his captains; the second, the secret orders for himself alone. Thus Biddle, at that time, was apprized only of certain extracts pertaining to the preservation of "proper discipline good order and peace" on board each ship. Their destination and objectives were matters which remained locked in Hopkins' bosom for the time being.[57]

Specific instructions to Biddle, as captain of the *Andrew Doria,* were penned by the Naval Committee on January 6. He was to put himself and the brig "under the direction of Esek Hopkins, Esquire, Commander-in-chief of the Fleet of the United Colonies, and to follow, observe and obey all such directions, instructions and commands as you may receive from him." He was to observe and answer all signals the commodore might display and to that end to "secure from him an account of the intention and signification of each signal." Finally, he was not to separate from the fleet save on orders from the commodore, and whenever separated should use his "utmost endeavours to join it again immediately at such rendezvous as may be appointed for that purpose." [58]

As long as the ice held—and for more than a week it showed no tendency to break up—there was not much the commodore or his officers could do in the way of executing any phase of the orders save maintaining discipline, guarding against desertions, and exercising the men at the great guns. The enforced delay enabled the officers to become better acquainted, and Biddle found several of the lieutenants on the other vessels well worth knowing. Notable among these was John Paul Jones, of the *Alfred,* the fleet's senior lieutenant. This little Scotsman proved an interesting and talented conversationalist, sharing with Biddle a similar burning zeal for the cause.[59] Another was John Trevett, lieutenant of marines on the *Columbus.*[60] And, as Biddle had more time to observe his own officers, he became convinced his lieutenants were as capable as any in the fleet.

The sloop *Providence* came down through the ice and joined her consorts at the Liberty Island pier in mid-January.[61] She brought some dispatches and letters and a standard for the commodore—a yellow flag with a coiled serpent under which was inscribed, "Don't tread on me!" To command the sloop, the Naval Committee had selected one John Hazard, whose antecedents were unknown to Biddle and are still a mystery.[62]

The sloop's arrival, however, brought activity. There came a spell of warmer weather, a light thaw; the ice thinned out sufficiently for the five vessels to be towed into the stream on Friday morning, January 17. Here a fresh northwest breeze billowed out their canvas and down the river they sailed; through the chevaux-de-frise, past Chester, past the mouth of the Christiana, and on beyond New Castle, where the river grew rougher, the ice floes thicker, the going tougher and more dangerous to the wooden hulls of these converted merchantmen. Behind Reedy Island on the Delaware shore lay the little town of Port Penn; to its piers Hopkins directed his captains. There one after another the vessels nestled for the night.[63]

Winter, after luring them thus far with a few mild days, closed in anew. Further progress southward in the river was again blocked by the ice. Despite this the little sloop *Fly* came up the bay and into the river, bringing forty hands from Rhode Island for the fleet. Half of these newcomers were distributed among the *Alfred, Columbus,* and *Cabot.* The remaining twenty were retained on board the *Fly* by Hopkins,[64] who had just received authority from the Naval Committee to fit out a tender. He appointed another Rhode Islander, Hoysteed Hacker, to command her, and attached her at once to the fleet.[65]

Sensing they were going to be delayed at Reedy Island for a considerable time, Biddle put his crew to work wooding and watering the brig. The other captains followed suit, while Hopkins wrote to Philadelphia for materials still lacking. The plan had been, it will be recalled, to send the remaining supplies to him at the capes. When river pilots refused to take the fleet further until the ice abated, he decided Reedy Island might do as well as the little pilot town of Lewes as a receiving point. Three wagons, containing a little of everything from a cask of cheese to six swivel guns, rumbled out of Philadelphia toward the end of January, and reached Port Penn a few days later. Some of the varied items found their way into the *Andrew Doria.*[66]

Finally, on the morning of Sunday, February 11, Hopkins ordered the captains to drop down another stage on their progress towards the sea. Wrote Lieutenant Josiah: "At 10 A M cast off from yᵉ Pierse in Company with all yᵉ Fleet."

Descent of the bay took two more days.[67] When the fleet dropped anchor close under Cape Henlopen and just off Lewes, a reinforcement of two small vessels awaited them. They were the sloop *Hornet,* of ten 4-pounders, commanded by a Baltimore merchant captain, William Stone, and the schooner *Wasp,* of eight 4-pounders, under William Hallock, another Baltimorean. Both vessels had been outfitted in Maryland by orders of the Continental Congress and dispatched around to join Hopkins' fleet.[68]

Riding in the lee of Cape Henlopen, the commodore awaited more propitious weather before venturing to sea. Desertions became numerous. Patriotic enthusiasm had waned in the breasts of a number of the men who had found the first two months of service largely hard work, frostbite, and constant marrow-penetrating cold. Some of the deserters were rounded up in Lewes and returned to the ships; others were intercepted on the roads and brought in by the militia.[69]

Two men from the *Andrew Doria,* one of them William Green, the former bad man of the Pennsylvania galleys, were caught in this manner and lodged in the Lewes jail. Biddle sent an officer and several marines to bring them off, but the squad returned empty-handed. Green, his companion, and several other deserters had armed themselves, barricaded the door of the jail, and defied anyone to come and get them. The town militia had promptly surrounded the building, but none was brave enough to attempt the door, behind which the prisoners threatened to shoot the first man who entered. Biddle listened to the story, called a midshipman to attend him, and went ashore. The militia were now augmented by curious townsfolk and a number of marines from the fleet. From within the jail Green and his companions were howling defiance and daring anyone to approach. The ring parted to make way for the grim-looking young naval captain.

"Green! Come out of there," he called. "Open the door or we'll break it in."

The deserter swore.

"I'll not come out, and I'll shoot you if you try to come in."

The captain gave brief instructions to a group of militiamen. Within a few minutes they had produced a heavy log and swung it against the oaken door of the jail until hinges gave way and it caved inward. The captain was at the threshold as the militiamen dropped the log and withdrew precipitately out of the line of fire. Pistol in either hand he stepped inside, facing the ringleader whose musket was pointed squarely at him.

"Now Green," said he, with a tone as steely as his set face, "if you do not take good aim, you are a dead man."

The ringleader hesitated and then wilted, awed into submission by the dauntless air of his captain. The musket clattered to the floor; the other deserters relinquished their weapons, and the militia swarmed in.[70]

The story went round the fleet, gaining force if not facts in the retelling; Biddle's reputation for personal intrepidity rose to new heights. As for the captain himself, he returned to the *Andrew Doria* in time to be summoned to a meeting of all commanding officers in the cabin of the *Alfred*.

Since long before leaving Liberty Island, Hopkins had been in possession of instructions which he had imparted to no one. They ordered him to proceed for Chesapeake Bay, to reconnoiter the enemy vessels stationed off Norfolk and, if they were not superior to his own force, to enter the bay, attack, and destroy them. That business executed, he was to search out the enemy vessels off North and South Carolina, make himself master of them, and sail northward to Rhode Island to attack the enemy naval force in Narragansett Bay. Unfortunately, the Naval Committee concluded with a paragraph allowing the commodore, "if bad Winds, or Stormy Weather, or any other unforeseen accident or disaster disable you," to follow his own judgment.[71]

Apparently, between January 5, the date of the instructions, and the middle of February, Hopkins had decided to invoke the clause granting him discretionary privileges. He had heard the British force in Virginia was "considerable" [72]; the Naval Committee had advised him that the enemy vessels in the Carolinas had gone to Georgia, and its further suggestion that if he diligently pursued orders he might have three royal governors "to dine with you on board your own Ship" fell on deaf ears.[73]

So when the captains—Whipple, of the *Columbus;* John Burroughs Hopkins, of the *Cabot;* Hazard of the *Providence;* Stone, of the *Hornet;* Hacker, of the *Fly;* Hallock, of the *Wasp;* and Biddle—boarded the flagship, they found Saltonstall and the commodore awaiting them. Of all these captains save Abraham Whipple and William Hallock, Biddle supplied thumbnail sketches written later that day to his sister Lydia. He catalogued them thus:

"Capt Hazard A Stout man   Very Vain and Ignorant—as much low Cunning as Capacity.

"C Hacker of the Fly an Active Smart Seaman

"C Stone A Very Stout and Very Good kind of Man

"C Saltonstall a Sensible indefatiguable Morose Man

"C Hopkins a Good Natured Man"

And then, because he could never resist joking with his sister, he added a line about himself:

"C B a Mighty good Young Man." [74]

Esek Hopkins had before him long sheets of foolscap upon which his clerks had written with a fair round hand the "Signals for the American Fleet." There were copies for each captain, which they accepted and examined.

Aside from the general signals, there were specific ones for the individual vessels. Biddle noted those for the *Andrew Doria*. If the commodore wanted the brig to chase, a Dutch flag would be flown at the foretop masthead of the *Alfred*. Were the chase to be to windward, Hopkins would hoist his ensign and lower his pennant simultaneously; if to leeward, the pennant would remain flying and the ensign would not be hoisted. A white pennant at the foretop masthead would advise him to give over chase. Should the commodore wish to speak the *Andrew Doria,* he would show a Dutch flag at the mizzen-top masthead.[75]

Once the signals had been read, digested, and tacitly approved, Hopkins asked his secretary to read the orders, copies of which would be given to each captain. The secretary read; the captains listened.

They were to keep company with the commodore, and observe all signals given from the *Alfred*. Should a gale separate them, they should rejoin the fleet as soon as possible, but after four days of failure to meet their consorts they should make their way southward to the island of Great Abaco, in the Bahamas. Off the southern side of this island was the place of rendezvous, where they should await the fleet for fourteen days. No fleet arriving by then, they were at liberty to cruise any place where they felt they could annoy the enemy. All British vessels or any vessels with supplies for the British army in America should be taken and sent into an American port for trial. The final injunction was that in case of their own capture they should make sure orders and signals were destroyed.[76]

The captains returned to their ships. What they thought of the instructions none of them ever recorded, but Biddle, on the eve of departure, penned a letter to his brother James up in Philadelphia. Apparently the experiences of the past two months, the close observation of his fellow officers, and the meeting with the commodore had brought him disturbing thoughts. For what he voiced was this:

"I now muster 109 Men in the Whole, and am in every Respect well equipt. have by great odds the fastest sailing Vessel in the fleet, except a Small Sloop called the Fly and the Schooner [*Wasp*] from Maryland with which I have not had a fair tryal. . . . Tis now twelve Oclock & we are now lying at Anchor in Old keel [*sic,* Whorekiln] Road at C: Henlopen waiting for wind. tis quite calm and like a Summers day. Fare you well my Dear Brother And May the Mercifull God who has upheld Me in all my Dangers and Difficulties Preserve you and Protect you from all Evils. May he who has Mercifully led me through the World keep My dear Brothers Cheek from ever being staind with a Blush for me. I well know the Glorious Cause I am engaged in. And if ever I disgrace it May My Kind father who gave me being instantly Blast me in Mercy to me. I mean not to be desperate beyond measure, But to do my duty to the utmost of My Ability. If in spite of my best endeavoir I should be taken, If Fortune Should frown on me I hope to bear up against it with the Fortitude Patience and Resignation which I usually found Myself Posessed of, Which has hitherto been sufficient for my purpose   And that they ever will be proportionable to my wants Whilst I am conscious of having disc[h]arged my duty I cannot doubt." [77]

Shortly after noon, on Saturday, February 17, with a brisk breeze out of the northeast, Hopkins gave the signal for weighing and coming to sail by loosing the *Alfred*'s topsails and sheeting them home. One after the other, the fleet followed the flagship out around the Henlopen lighthouse; to sea at last! [78]

Chapter VII

New Providence and the Glasgow

ON BOARD THE *ANDREW DORIA*, AS THE FIRST CONTI-
nental fleet began its maiden cruise, Nicholas Biddle had a stout
crew.[1] The black brig had drawn none of the New Englanders
who had arrived in the *Fly*. Most of her complement, including
thirty-seven marines, were Pennsylvanians.[2] By and large they
were well disciplined, could go through a gun drill with a precision to match the British tars on the *Portland* in 1772, and
handed the sails like experienced men-of-war's men. Biddle
could thank Alex McKenzie, the gunner, for a deal of their
proficiency in manning the 4-pounders, and Benjamin Dunn,
the master, for the able way the seamen sprang to their duty in
making or taking in sail.[3] Nor did he hesitate to tell McKenzie
and Dunn so, for he never withheld praise when it was due.
That was one of the reasons he was regarded with affection as
well as respect by all who served with him.[4]

Three leagues beyond the False Cape, which jutted into the
Atlantic below Cape Henlopen, with the course set due southward, the weather clear and the wind strong, the commodore
discharged the pilot. As the little craft bobbed shoreward, the
Andrew Doria's crew gave it a farewell cheer. Thereafter the
land faded slowly away until by nightfall the low Delaware
coast was no longer visible. By dawn the sea was barren of any
sail save the fleet of eight vessels, which, with the *Alfred* ahead,
preserved some semblance of order. All that day they ran southward with a favorable wind over the stern, but Monday,
February 19, brought an end to fair weather.[5]

"Hard gales & thick Weather," recorded Lieutenant Josiah

in the log book, "Lost sight of ye Sloop Hornet & Fly in the Night." [6]

Though masthead watches were maintained constantly thereafter, the two little vessels remained unreported. Barring the one storm, which lasted about twenty-four hours, the weather was propitious and, as they continued southward, turned warm and balmy. Not until they had been at sea for two weeks was a strange sail sighted. Then, with the island of Great Abaco looming ahead, the *Alfred* intercepted and seized two small coastal sloops from New Providence, the principal island of the Bahama group.[7] On the afternoon of March 1 the fleet approached Great Abaco and, as the *Andrew Doria*'s log related it, "came too at ye S west Side in 12 fathoms Water." [8]

There had been no very clear indication to Biddle that Hopkins, until he took the two sloops from New Providence, had any definite idea of what he intended once the rendezvous was reached. Certainly the officers of the fleet were in the dark. From his prisoners, however, the commodore had learned that all military and naval forces had been withdrawn from New Providence island, and that in its two forts were a large quantity of powder and considerable heavy cannon. Whereupon, he conceived a plan to seize the island and called a council of his captains preliminary to putting it into effect.[9]

Included in the officers summoned to the flagship was Lieutenant Thomas Weaver of the *Cabot,* who was well acquainted with the physical features of New Providence, and who drew a rough map for the benefit of the commodore and his captains. Nassau was indicated on the north shore, with Fort Nassau just beyond its western fringe of houses and Fort Montague some two miles to the eastward. The harbor lay open due north of Fort Nassau but was flanked to the eastward by a long narrow island and to the westward by several small keys. Between the keys and the longer island was a sand bar with a channel at the eastern end.[10]

Hopkins' proposal of a frontal surprise attack met with Biddle's approval. The two captured sloops were to be used to carry the marines directly into the harbor for an assault upon Fort Nassau. No one on New Providence, the commodore pointed

out, knew an enemy lay only seventeen leagues away under
Great Abaco. Hence if the marines remained concealed below
deck until the sloops ran close in under the fort, it could be
captured before the inhabitants would be aware of their danger.
After that the fleet could sail into the harbor and, with the
guns of the fort, command the town. All the captains approved
the plan but suggested that the marines be augmented by fifty
seamen drawn from the various vessels and commanded by
Lieutenant Weaver. Hopkins agreed and, as the council did not
adjourn until late in the day, it was decided to postpone the
transhipment of the landing force until the following morning.[11]

On Saturday preparations moved along smoothly. By nightfall the two companies of marines from the *Alfred* and *Columbus* and the half company from the *Cabot,* fully armed and
accoutered, were packed tightly in the two sloops. When the detachment of sailors went on board, there was room for no more.
There were 270 officers and men on the New Providence sloops
when the two vessels stood out from Great Abaco in the dead of
night, the whole force under the command of Captain Samuel
Nicholas. As the heavily laden sloops would make slow going
of it, the commodore had timed their departure so they would
enter the harbor about daybreak. With all but a few hands
hidden below, he was confident they would be mistaken for a
pair of harmless coasters.[12]

That the fleet might be on hand to follow up the initial advantage, he ordered it to weigh and sail several hours after the
sloops had disappeared in the darkness. Because the black brig
was a faster sailer than her consorts, Biddle arrived some three
leagues northwest of the island by dawn and "lay off and on
Waiting for yᵉ rest of yᵉ Fleet." [13] And then Hopkins blun-
dered. Instead of remaining out of sight till after the sloops had
entered the harbor and the marines had secured the fort, the
commodore, coming up in the *Alfred,* ordered the fleet to stand
right on in. They were hard on the heels of the sloops when a
puff of smoke rose from an embrasure in Fort Nassau, followed
by the detonation of a heavy gun. Another puff, and another
gun, and a third puff, and a third gun.[14]

Andrew Doria May the 21st 1776

Sir

The Night after we left New
Port being Chased by a Vessel we took to bee the
Cerberus the Cabot Run a more direct course
for Nantucket Shoals than I thought safe to do
by which Means we have lost company with
her. This Morning we took a Sloop bound
from Saltertudas to Liverpool in Nova Scotia.
Mr Brown my third Mate to whom I have
given Charge of Her will Give You what
further information You may want to know
I am Sir your most Obedient Sert.

N. Biddle

NICHOLAS BIDDLE SENDS IN PRIZE. From the Hopkins Papers,
Rhode Island Historical Society, Providence.

On the *Andrew Doria*'s quarter-deck Biddle groaned.

"That ends it," he said to Lieutenant Josiah. "It would be suicidal to attempt a landing with the guns manned and sweeping the harbor."

Hopkins, too, realized his mistake. The recall signal, a white flag at the ensign staff, was flown from the *Alfred*. After the marine-laden sloops returned, with the squadron standing off and on the harbor mouth, a red pennant succeeded the white flag at the ensign staff—a call for the captains to come on board the commodore.[15]

When the council had assembled in the cabin of the *Alfred*, Hopkins had a new proposal. He would sail around to the west of the island, land the marines, and march upon Nassau from the rear. Biddle led the captains in pointing out its impracticability. There was no fit anchorage to the westward and no road from that part of the island to the town. An alternative was suggested by Lieutenant Jones of the *Alfred*. There was a good anchorage under a key just three leagues to windward of Nassau Harbor where the whole fleet might moor safely. One of the pilots taken on the New Providence sloops had disclosed it to him. Once there, the fleet could effect a landing on the eastern end of the island, where Fort Montague could be outflanked, and a good road would make a rapid approach on Nassau possible. Hopkins, after some quibbling, accepted Jones's offer to pilot the fleet to its new destination.[16]

Headed by the *Alfred*, with Jones and one of the captured pilots in the foretop masthead whence every reef could be seen and avoided, the squadron abandoned its position off the harbor and moved eastward. By ten o'clock, anchors were dropped in Hanover Sound under Rose Island. The sloops, with their cargoes of sweating marines and seamen, were ordered off to the eastward, and the *Wasp* and *Providence* sent along to cover the landing. Into the latter went the half company of marines from the *Andrew Doria* under Lieutenant Craig. They would act as a reserve.[17]

The landing party stormed ashore unopposed that same afternoon at a place called "the Creek," about two miles to the eastward of Fort Montague.[18] Back in the fleet there was suspense, punctuated by the sound of a few heavy guns. In the late afternoon word came that the enemy had spiked the cannon and evacuated the fort. Major Nicholas' men had seized it, but were too fatigued, after twenty hours of close confinement in the sloops with "no convenience either to sleep or cook in," to press on that night.[19]

Meanwhile Hopkins had sent off a manifesto "to the Gentlemen, Freemen and Inhabitants of the Island of New Providence." If they would neither oppose his landing nor his seizure of the powder, cannon, and stores belonging to the crown, he promised safety to the individual and protection to his property.[20] The commodore failed, however, to take the logical precaution of detaching one or two of his squadron to patrol the harbor entrance. This oversight was costly, for a sloop hastily laden with 162 barrels of gunpowder from Fort Nassau, and His Majesty's armed sloop *St. John,* of 8 guns and 30 men, slipped to sea that night.[21]

New Providence's defenses collapsed completely on Monday morning, March 4. Major Nicholas' force advanced without opposition to Government House and Fort Nassau. At Fort Montague the night before they had taken seventeen cannon and considerable shot, but the haul at Fort Nassau was much larger. It included seventy-one cannon, fifteen mortars, thousands of shells and round shot, and many ordnance stores.[22] There were even twenty-four barrels of that precious article, gunpowder, which had not been shipped off, apparently because "sending away the whole of it might enrage a disappointed enemy." [23] The governor himself, His Excellency Montford Browne, Esquire, was peremptorily taken from Government House to Fort Nassau, and word was sent to Hopkins that the conquest was complete.[24]

Aside from attending the several councils on the flagship and dispatching his marines in the sloop *Providence,* Nicholas Biddle had had no active part in the capture of New Providence. None of the captains had, in fact, as the operations were conducted solely by the marines and Lieutenant Weaver's detachment of sailors. The squadron actually did not vacate its anchorage under Rose Island until six o'clock on the morning of March 6. It arrived off the harbor in a few hours, but awaited a bar pilot before it passed through the channel to a safe anchorage off Fort Nassau. The schooner *Wasp* was left without the bar to serve as a lookout.[25]

When Hopkins finally landed, accompanied by his captains, there was plenty for Biddle and all other sea officers to do. Details of seamen were sent ashore to join the marines in the task of dismantling the forts and transferring the cannon and other warlike stores to the various vessels. The first step, however, was to send ashore all ballast and then determine the capacity of each hold. It was at once apparent that the booty bulked too large to be stowed on board the squadron and still maintain the seaworthiness of each vessel. The cannon were therefore stowed in the two ships and in a large sloop engaged for the purpose locally and the shot and other ordnance in the two brigs and the sloop *Providence*.[26]

The arrival of the sloop *Fly,* delayed, they learned, because she had run afoul of the *Hornet* during the February storm, did not add to the fleet's carrying capacity.[27] She was too small to take any cargo. The difficult and laborious job required about ten days and, in the case of the *Andrew Doria*, the hold was finally well filled with "4780 Shott and Sheels of Different Sizes." [28]

Unfortunately, and largely because the officers of the fleet were inexperienced in health and sanitation on crowded shipboard, a general epidemic of fever developed, and cases of smallpox were reported from the *Alfred, Columbus, Cabot,* and *Providence*.[29] Biddle, with his training in the British navy, had maintained a clean ship, and his Pennsylvanians, by inoculations the previous year, were immune from the dread disease. Consequently, before the fleet was ready to sail, the black brig had been called upon to act almost as a hospital ship. Every part of the vessel was utilized, even the longboat being fitted out for the accommodation of the sick. Biddle gave over his own cot to a desperately ill midshipman, sleeping himself upon the lockers in his cabin, an act which led one of his early biographers to remark that "his sterner virtues did not obliterate or subdue the gentler qualities of his spirit." [30] Even if free from the small-pox, the ship's complement did not escape the other epidemic and toward the close of the second week at New Providence Lieutenant Josiah entered in the log: "While we lay here our people takeing very Sickly with the fever, altho as much Care as possible was taking to prevent it." [31]

Into the smallpox-ridden *Alfred,* Hopkins had forced Governor Browne, after the latter had spent about a week under marine guard on shore. Two other gentlemen were also herded on board as prisoners—James Babbadge, a half-pay officer of the British army, who acted as secretary of the colony, and Thomas Irving, a South Carolina Tory who was Inspector General of His Majesty's Customs for North America. [32]

Finally, on March 16, having stowed all loot on board the fleet and the requisitioned sloop, embarked all marines, and watered and wooded all vessels, the commodore signaled to get under way. They weighed and sailed at four o'clock the same afternoon with "fresh Breezes & Clear Weather." By dawn they were abreast of Great Abaco "from which," recorded Josiah, "I take my Departure." [33]

At two o'clock on the afternoon of March 18 the commodore's barge came alongside the *Andrew Doria* to deliver a letter to Captain Biddle. It contained Hopkins' brief sailing instructions:

"You are to keep Company with the Ship I am in if possible —but should you Separate by accident You are then to make the best of your way to Block Island Channel, and there to Cruise in 30 fathoms Water South from Block Island Six days in order to join the Fleet.

"If they do not join you in that time you may Cruise in Such Places as you think will most annoy the Enemy, or go in Port as you think fit and acquaint me by the first Opportunity so that you may Receive further Orders." [34]

Between thirty and forty of the black brig's crew, including both surgeon Thomas Kerr and his mate, had sickened with the fever during the early stages of the northward cruise. [35] Despite this, Biddle had his men "Exercising yͤ Guns and Clearing Ship" for action. He was not going to be caught unprepared should enemy vessels be encountered. What the fleet met with, however, was stormy weather, which set in on March 22 and continued for three days during which they lost sight of the schooner *Wasp*.[36]

The *Andrew Doria* and the *Providence*, on March 25, chased a sail to windward, the latter bringing her to. She was a Carolina schooner bound for France and was permitted to proceed on her voyage. Next day, with the sloop *Fly* in company, Biddle set off after another distant sail and ran her down in an eight-hour chase. No prize she, either, but a French schooner from New London bound for Cap Français. She imparted news which was carried back with jubilation to the fleet: the account of the British evacuation of Boston and its occupation by Washington's army.[37]

The fever epidemic continued not only on the *Andrew Doria*, but throughout the fleet. "Our people still Sickly the Doctor not able to tend them," wrote Lieutenant Josiah, on April 1. A few days before, one of the smallpox victims transferred from the *Alfred* had died and been buried at sea. The following day Sergeant Thomas Vernon Turner of the *Andrew Doria*'s marines passed away. By then they were in cooler weather, about thirty leagues due east of the Delaware capes, and rapidly nearing the Block Island rendezvous.[38]

In the evening of April 3, in thick, foggy weather, the *Andrew Doria* lost sight of the fleet. Early the following morning Biddle encountered the sloop with cannon, escorting her until shortly after noon when, in sight of Montauk Point at the tip of Long Island, they came up with the rest of the squadron and spoke both the *Alfred* and *Columbus*.[39] The latter had earlier taken an armed schooner, the *Hawke*, tender to the British vessels stationed in Narragansett Bay. The *Hawke* carried six carriage guns and eight swivels. She was the first British warship to be captured by a Continental naval vessel.[40]

From Hopkins came orders to Biddle to stand in for Rhode Island, see whether any more British tenders were at sea, and rejoin the fleet in the morning.[41] While he saw nothing in the way of armed vessels on this reconnaissance, the captain did run across a sloop which had left New York three days before, bound for St. Martin's with flour and lumber. He decided to carry her back to the fleet where her papers could be examined rather than release her himself.[42] By the time the *Andrew Doria* returned, on the morning of April 5, the commodore had acquired another prize—His Majesty's bomb brig *Bolton,* of eight carriage guns, two howitzers, and ten swivels, manned by forty-eight men. She had surrendered to the *Alfred* after a few shots.[43]

All that day the squadron cruised within sight of Block Island; nothing of moment transpired. Toward evening a brig and sloop were espied, the whole fleet standing off in pursuit. The *Columbus* overtook the brig; the *Cabot* ran down the sloop. Both were from New York bound to London, and the commodore determined to carry them in and let the courts decide as to their legality as prizes. By then it was well after nightfall, and the squadron was about ten leagues south of Block Island.[44]

At one o'clock in the morning of Saturday, April 6, a lookout in the maintop of the *Andrew Doria* spotted two sail off in the southeast. Biddle was summoned from his cabin, and was able to make out the silhouettes of a ship and small sloop. He surmised them to be a British frigate and her tender and signaled the commodore with a light upon the ensign staff and two false fires. Shortly thereafter, with no signal from the commodore, the various vessels headed for the quarry.[45]

As the fleet bore off toward the distant sails, the *Cabot* was in the van with the *Alfred* less than a hundred yards astern. The *Andrew Doria* was to leeward of the flagship, the *Columbus* on her starboard quarter, and the *Providence* astern. Bringing up the rear was the schooner *Hawke,* now manned by a prize crew from the *Columbus.* The larger stranger was standing directly for them but her consort was lagging astern, a rather clear confirmation of earlier suspicions about them. The order of the fleet's approach was maintained as they neared the presumed enemy; consequently, the *Cabot* was first within hailing distance.[46] So clear was the air and so light the breeze that the words interchanged were audible on the *Andrew Doria,* several hundred yards astern.

"What ship is that?" the stranger called.

"The Cabot, from Plymouth," came the answer after a bit of hesitation. "Who are you?"

"This is his Majesty's ship of war Glasgow, Tyringham Howe commanding," was the reply sent sharply down the wind. "What ships are in your company?" [47]

By now the *Cabot* was close up to the Britisher, and her response was prompt.

"The Columbus and Alfred, a two and thirty gun frigate."

A man in the brig's top punctuated the statement with a hand grenade which exploded harmlessly on the *Glasgow*'s deck.[48] Simultaneously, the *Cabot* fired her full broadside. The enemy was ready. A murderous blast swept the brig. She sheered away as a second broadside was loosed upon her, which killed her sailing master and wounded her captain. In the frantic effort to get clear she almost ran afoul of the *Andrew Doria*. Only through a masterly executed tack to port by the latter was the disaster avoided, but the result was to carry Biddle and his eager crew away from instead of into the engagement.[49] By the time the *Andrew Doria* was clear of the *Cabot,* the *Alfred* had engaged the *Glasgow* on her port quarter, and the *Columbus* had raked her from astern, and then luffed up on the lee beam.[50]

Working back to get into the fight, Biddle's fire had to be withheld because of the *Alfred.* That ship, apparently partially disabled, had broached to and was being raked by the *Glasgow.*[51] The *Providence* seemed content to tack back and forth astern and out of range, while the *Columbus* had worked too far to leeward and had killed her wind. Finally, more than an hour after the engagement had been under way, the *Andrew Doria* got into a position on the larboard bow and opened up with her four-pounders.[52]

By this time Captain Howe, of the *Glasgow,* apparently had decided that a whole fleet was just too much for a twenty-gun British frigate, and that discretion would serve him better than continued valor. The Britisher had received a lot of punishment, but his masts were still standing. So he clapped on all the sail he could carry and bore off to the northward. The maneuver threw the *Andrew Doria* astern, while both the *Alfred* and *Columbus* had dropped away. The *Glasgow* got two stern chasers out of the cabin ports and maintained a running fire on the black brig.[53]

Until dawn the pursuit continued, and the *Andrew Doria* sustained several shots in hull and rigging. One ball only did any damage worth recording. It slashed through the netting, stove in the arms chest on the quarter-deck, and wounded the brig's drummer in the leg. All the while, Biddle was returning the fire warmly and gaining slightly, but at the end of some seven glasses of fighting the recall signal rose to the foretop masthead of the *Alfred*.[54] Hopkins felt they were getting too close for comfort to Captain James Wallace's British ships at Rhode Island.[55] Reluctantly, Biddle obeyed the order and, about dawn, tacked to the southward.

By noon the fleet was reassembled, and the *Hawke,* her prize crew swelling with pride, brought in the *Glasgow*'s little sloop tender—the sole success of the long engagement.[56] The various captains reported their losses to the commodore. On the *Cabot,* in addition to the master, the lieutenant of marines and two of his men had been killed. She had seven wounded, including Captain John Burroughs Hopkins.[57] On the *Alfred* the death toll was five, including the second lieutenant of marines. Seven men had been wounded, three of them seriously.[58] The *Columbus* and *Andrew Doria* each had one man wounded.[59] Most serious damage was to the *Alfred,* which had sustained several shots under water, and whose wheel block and ropes had been carried away by an unlucky shot which had rendered her helpless for a time under the *Glasgow*'s fire. She had, besides, the mainmast shot through and upper works and rigging much damaged.[60]

With visions of Captain Wallace's ships hard upon his heels, Hopkins concluded that safety lay at New London, where the New Providence booty could be landed and where, behind the protection of the forts flanking the river, repairs could be made and the fleet reoutfitted. Orders were issued accordingly and the vessels got under way.[61] By twilight they were northwest of Block Island. That night it began to rain and a fog rolled in from the Sound. At daybreak only the *Andrew Doria* and *Cabot* were in company. Shortly after noon they came to, abreast of

New London lighthouse and, when the fog cleared toward evening, ran in for the harbor and anchored. That night the *Alfred,*
with the rest of the fleet, put in appearance off the lighthouse.
As a grand finale, Lieutenant Josiah inscribed in the black brig's
log on the morning of April 8, 1776: "At 8 A.M hove up   Beat
in a Brest of y town in Company with all the Fleet." [62]

Disgusted with the conduct of the fleet, Nicholas Biddle
wrote a terse analysis of the engagement with the *Glasgow*
for the edification of his brother James.

"As it was well known that the Enemy seldom separated,"
he pointed out, "we had all the Reason in the world to Believe
the Rest of them were not far off.

"If it was thought the Conquest would be easy there was no
Courage shewn in the Attack. If it was judged otherwise there
was no Conduct in Making it before the Prizes had some orders
given them—And as it was I think there was neither. there
was no order in the Matter. Away we all went Helter Skelter
one flying here another there to cut of[f] the Retreat of a
fellow who did not fear us. I kept close to the Admiral that I
might the sooner Receive his Orders. But he had none to give.
And the Cabot Running off Obliged Me in order to Clear her
to go a little out of my way. And before I could Regain My
ground the Alfred had sheered off. Had I behaved as Capt.
[John Burroughs] Hopkins did, had I run on without Orders
and brought on the Action in the Night I think I should have
lost my Commission before now." [63]

And thus the first cruise of the first Continental fleet came to
a safe, if not a brilliant, conclusion.

Chapter VIII
The Scotch Transports

NEW LONDON AROUSED ITSELF TO THE PRESENCE OF the Continental fleet that morning as barge, pinnace, and longboat began to convey the wounded and fever-stricken seamen and marines ashore. The commodore had landed first and sought out the town's authorities. He needed a hospital for better than two hundred sick, and his insistence would not be denied.[1] The little town could not provide such accommodations in its single hospital building, but there were good wives and widows willing to give rooms in their own homes to the overflow.[2] As rapidly thereafter as possible the various vessels rid themselves of the ailing crew members. Hopkins had not exaggerated the number, for there were seventy-two men from the *Alfred,* and thirty-four from the *Columbus*—more than a hundred from just the two ships.[3]

On the *Andrew Doria* the sick list totaled fifty-eight, more than half the black brig's complement. Included among those to be sent ashore was Surgeon Kerr, who had barely survived the ordeal of the cruise. Under Biddle's orders the invalids were gently lowered into boats and as gently laid on litters at the pier to be tended from then on by the sympathetic New Londoners.[4]

The captain was expeditious with it all, as the commodore had ordered him to sea immediately on a reconnaissance cruise. The *Andrew Doria* was the most suitable for the assignment. She was faster than any other vessel in the fleet save the *Cabot,* but the latter had been badly banged up and needed much repair. Also, Biddle had a head on his shoulders, which Hopkins seemed to have recognized from the very start of their associa-tion.[5]

From the shore, after depositing the invalids, the black brig's boats repaired to the *Columbus* and *Providence* for mariners and marines to fill up the crew. About forty hands were added.[6] Hopkins sent on board a Sound pilot. Meanwhile, from the captured brig *Bolton,* Biddle secured an arms chest to replace the one smashed in the fight with the *Glasgow*. From the same vessel he took off a barrel each of oatmeal and salt pork and several hundredweight of ship's bread.[7]

By five o'clock that afternoon he was ready to depart. There was a light breeze from the southward which forced him to bear slowly down stream as far as the lighthouse. There, with a fog rolling in and the tide at flood, he came to for the night. The weather was thick next morning, but about eleven o'clock it lifted sufficiently to heave up and beat out. Three hours later the pilot got them aground a little to the westward of the light-house. But the tide flooding, they soon eased off and towards nightfall rounded Fisher's Island, with no sight of an enemy. More fog closed in and before midnight, having traversed the Sound, the brig ran ashore on Long Island some six leagues from Montauk Point.

"Hove all a back & soon got off," read Lieutenant Josiah's logbook entry, "and came to in 15 fathom Water." [8]

Beginning the morning of April 10, Biddle patrolled back and forth from Long Island to south of Block Island, with one venturesome foray north to near Point Judith, Rhode Island. There was no sign of a British ship although the course em-braced the area where they had fought the *Glasgow*. Then about noon on April 12, while standing in for Long Island on a long tack from the northeast, the lookout discovered a sail under Montauk Point. In an hour they ran her down.[9] She was the schooner *John and Joseph*,[10] which had been taken off the Geor-gia coast some time before by His Majesty's frigate *Scar-borough*. Under a British midshipman and a prize crew of six hands she was headed for Halifax when Biddle intercepted her.[11] Originally the schooner had been the property of Nathan-iel Shaw, Jr., prominent and prosperous merchant of New London. Sent by him to the West Indies, she had taken in a cargo of molasses, coffee, and gunpowder at Cape Nicola Mole, Hispaniola, and had sailed for home. She was a profitable recapture and had been long enough in enemy hands to ensure one sixth of the value of vessel and cargo to the captors.[12]

Biddle removed the midshipman and his prize crew, put a lieutenant and three men on board, and beat up the Sound with the *John and Joseph* in company. For the third time on this short cruise the brig grounded, about midnight, to the westward of Fisher's Island. Once more the captain hove all sails aback and got her off. Then he came to, to await the dawn. Progress next day was slow as there was little wind. Under a fresh breeze from the south on Sunday morning, April 14, they ran close in to the lighthouse and anchored abreast of the *Alfred,* which with the rest of the fleet had dropped down below the town.[13]

Word of the recapture of the *John and Joseph* was conveyed to Nathaniel Shaw, Jr., who came from New London to see the commodore about it. Hopkins agreed to turn the vessel back to her former owner without condemnation in Admiralty court and, upon Shaw's promise "to alow the highest price that Goods were Sold at in this Town" for the cargo, to have the schooner "apprized." It was a fair, if strictly illegal procedure, but the commodore had to endure the censure of a number of his officers, who were fearful they would be deprived of their just shares.[14]

Discord was rife, as Biddle soon discovered, throughout the entire fleet. Partly it was due to a feeling of frustration. No one was happy about the fiasco with the *Glasgow.* Many of the officers resented rumors of cowardice leveled at them, and the majority felt something should be done to retrieve their characters with the public. But the fleet was not in condition to fight.[15]

Deeper than frustration, however, was self-interest, which took the form of politics and wirepulling for preferment. Before the squadron had left the Delaware in February, it was known that Congress had authorized the building of thirteen frigates, and, as Hopkins explained it, there was inattention to present business because many officers had expectations "of getting higher Stations in the new Ships." On the arrival at New London, it was learned a number of these frigates were near launching. Aspirants to commissions on them did not want to be away at sea when Congress started selecting officers.[16]

The general discontent had not permeated the *Andrew Doria,* and Biddle did not intend that it should. For three days after arrival he busied his men putting the brig in repair and was ready, although with a foul bottom, when Hopkins decided to run for Rhode Island and safety behind the defenses of Providence. The commodore had learned that the British fleet had left Newport and that Narragansett Bay promised a safe rendezvous.[17]

To reinforce Biddle's slim crew, for he was forced to return the hands borrowed from the *Columbus* and *Providence,* the commodore had sent him another lieutenant of marines, in the person of John Trevett, a Rhode Islander who had been serving on the *Columbus,* and seventeen soldiers to act as marines.[18] The soldiers were part of 150 men from one of his regiments which Washington had loaned to the fleet.[19]

They weighed at ten o'clock in the morning of April 19, and two hours later the *Alfred* went aground on a ledge of rocks southeast of the lighthouse.[20] While in his official report Hopkins pooh-poohed the matter as unimportant, getting the flagship off proved a long task.[21] It was necessary to take out her guns and start her water. She was floated by the following afternoon, and the fleet thereupon ran back into New London Harbor.[22]

By this time Hopkins had decided that Biddle should unload the shot and shells brought from New Providence and place them in the care of Nathaniel Shaw, Jr. The commodore's varied and contradictory orders on the guns and ordnance from the Bahamas had been puzzling everybody. At any rate, the *Andrew Doria* ran up abreast of the town and for two days disgorged the ammunition. Thereafter she returned to the fleet, where the captain asked permission to heave down and clean the brig's bottom. There was grudging consent and on April 25, Biddle "gott in to Mr. Shaw's warf & got out our guns." [23] That day, just before the *Alfred* and her consorts made the second and this time successful departure, the commodore sent further orders to him.

"You are to make what dispatch you can to clean your Brig," Hopkins wrote, "and you may take the Ballast out of the Bomb Brig and what more you want you must make up with Stones. You must apply to Mr. Shaw for whatever you may find necessary. When you get ready I desire you may take Care of the Merchant Vessels & Convoy them clear of the Land if the Coast is so clear that you can do it with Safety to them—and make what dispatch you can to Providence for further directions as I intend [to go] there as soon as possible." [24]

Careening and cleaning the black brig consumed a week's time and was not accomplished without mishaps. First Biddle put all hands to getting out guns, provisions and water, and every bit of movable gear. Then they attached cables and hove her to larboard, but were too strong with the last haul. The gunwale dipped beneath the surface; the water rushed in, and the *Andrew Doria* overset. They righted her only after striking topmasts and topgallant masts, and two days later got her safely on her side. It took the balance of that day and part of the next to burn and scrape off the accretions and pay the exposed half hull with pitch. A similar mishap occurred in putting the brig on her starboard side. Again they hove too heartily and she filled, but the cables kept her from turning over. They righted her, and next day performed the job successfully so the other half of the hull could be graved.

Meanwhile New London had been particularly hospitable to Biddle, and the fair sex had made much of him. To his sister Lydia he penned one of his typical jocular letters, his subject being the Connecticut misses. He remarked that he might be in love, but was not quite certain of it.

"To be sure I was a few days ago," he continued. "But there never was a more free sociable set of dear Creatures got together in any one place as in this. And so I went into another Company. And so I attended my Mind   And so I am at a Loss. Yes at a Loss to know which I love most. I am sure I begin to grow Old for My Love fits dont hold half their Usual time.

I have known the day when I have been held in Chains during a while tide of Ebb."

From this humorous analysis of his emotions, he turned serious momentarily: "I am now (I do not mean at this instant I am writing) Cleaning my Brig for a Cruise and hope in three or four days to sail. Should I feel in a writing humour before I go out you may probably hear from me again. If you should not, swear that I had not time, or any thing else you Please except that I want Inclination."

Lydia must have given credence to some of his remarks, for a rumor circulated among Nicholas' friends in Philadelphia that he was to wed a young lady of New London. "What is the dear Girls name that is to be favord with your Heart & hand?" inquired his cousin Nancy Biddle. "Heart I say, as I have so good an Opinion of My Cozen Nicholas as to think he never will give his hand unless Accompanied with his heart." [25]

By May 2 the *Andrew Doria* was cleaned and they were ready to reship the guns, restow the gear, and take in ballast. The few remaining provisions were brought aboard.[26] Shaw had advised Biddle of orders received from Hopkins to supply the *Andrew Doria* with provisions for a three months' cruise. These were itemized by the merchant and delivered next day —ten barrels of pork, twenty barrels of beef, ten barrels of flour, and ten bushels of potatoes, together with linseed oil and candles for ship's lanterns.[27]

Before parting, Biddle repaired to Shaw's office to go over and approve the charges for the overhaul and also the merchant's preliminary accounting for the prize schooner *John and Joseph*. The overhaul account was most detailed and exact, and the captain's eye ran down the items and their costs. There was a charge of £1 10s. 0d. for eight days' wharfage of the brig and her stores and 15s. 0d. for the use of stage and kettles. The other items were for labor and materials, including tallow, plank, putty, blocks, ropes, pitch, and ironwork.[28]

With the prize account Shaw was just as meticulous. As he pointed out, he had had to have the molasses and two tierces of rum gauged and stored, and the powder, coffee, and cocoa weighed and also stored. There had been 10,202 gallons of molasses, 13,545 pounds of coffee, 5 bags of cocoa, 105 gallons of rum, and 103 casks containing 1,578 pounds of gunpowder. Total value, including the hull appraised at £150, was £2,126 7s. 7d. Expenses had been £9 12 s. od., and his commission, at 2½ per cent, was £53 3s. 4d.

That left, he explained, £2,064 12s. 3d., which, by the resolves of Congress, was divided; one half to the former owners; two sixths to the United States, and the remaining one sixth to the captors. The gross amount due the captors was £344 2s. 2 ½ d. But, explained Shaw, out of that would have to be paid the commodore's share of one twentieth before there could be distribution of the balance to the crew of the *Andrew Doria*. Biddle sighed, agreed that all seemed in order, and initialed both accounts.[29]

On Friday, May 3, the captain rounded up from the crews of the *Alfred* and *Columbus* a number of invalids who had sufficiently recovered from the fever to be shipped off to the fleet. At six o'clock Saturday morning, with a moderate breeze, the *Andrew Doria* bade farewell to New London. Two outbound merchantmen had accepted convoy and sailed at the same time. Several hours later, nearing Long Island, Biddle spied a sail far to the southward and signaled the convoy to stand in while he investigated. He spoke her near Montauk Point—a schooner from the West Indies bound to New London. Then about noon, off to the southward of Block Island, he saw a large ship, undoubtedly a British cruiser. Apparently the distant enemy failed to make out the three vessels under Long Island, for when Biddle bade the merchantmen farewell as they stood off to the southward the ship below Block Island had not changed position.[30]

The *Andrew Doria* then bore away for Rhode Island. She entered Narragansett Bay by the western passage on Sunday morning, May 5, and with a spanking southwest breeze to help her along stood northward under full sail. Shortly before noon she came to off Conimicut Point and that afternoon ran up the river and anchored below Providence and near the *Alfred*. Biddle reported his presence to the commodore and dispatched to their respective ships the men he had brought from the New London hospital.[31]

The commodore's barge brought him a communication that evening—a brief summons to attend a court-martial the following morning at ten o'clock to inquire into the conduct of Abraham Whipple. The captain of the *Columbus,* as Biddle learned later, had demanded the trial, being much upset by various and sundry rumors that his conduct had been cowardly when the fleet attacked the *Glasgow.*[32]

The court-martial, which sat in the cabin of the *Alfred,* was presided over by Captain Dudley Saltonstall and comprised twelve members: three captains and five lieutenants of the line, and two captains and two lieutenants of marines. After hearing Whipple's own account of his actions, and "sundry evidences, who were present in different vessels during the engagement," the court concluded that the captain's mode of attack on the *Glasgow* "proceeded from error of judgment, and not from cowardice." [33] Biddle duly signed the verdict, and two days later was recalled to the *Alfred* for another court-martial, this time of Captain John Hazard of the *Providence.*[34]

The officers of the *Providence* had signed a series of complaints against their captain, which they proceeded to prove at the proceedings which consumed most of Wednesday, May 8. As a result the court convicted him of breach of orders at Reedy Island in January, of neglect of duty in not preparing for action promptly the night of the fight with the *Glasgow,* of embezzling part of the sloop's stores, and of breach of orders in Providence River in late April. He had, said the court, and Biddle subscribed to the findings along with the other eleven members, "rendered himself unworthy of holding his commission in the Navy of the United Colonies of North America." On May 9 Hopkins confirmed the sentence and demanded Hazard's commission.[35] Next day John Paul Jones, senior lieutenant of the *Alfred,* was given a captain's commission by the commodore and assigned to the command of the *Providence.*[36] By the sloop, under her new commander, Hopkins returned the soldiers borrowed from Washington to the camp in New York, and Biddle received directions to send his seventeen men on board her. He complied on May 12 [37] and the same day Hopkins issued orders for a cruise for the *Andrew Doria* and the *Cabot.*

"You are to take as many men out of the Alfred as will make your Complement eighty-five," Hopkins directed Biddle, "and proceed on a Cruise against the Enemies of the United Colonies for three or four Weeks in such places as you think will most annoy the Enemy if you do not take as many Prizes as you can well mann sooner.

"You are also to endeavour to keep Company with the Cabot, and give such directions to Lieutenant Hinman her Commander as may be necessary for the Public Good."

Word of the action of Congress in broadening the field of naval activity had reached Hopkins as was evident in his defini- tion to Biddle of the prizes he could take.

"You are to send in for Tryal," he pointed out, "all British Property and all Vessels bound to Great Britain or to any of the British Plantations which are now under the British Minis- try." [38]

Somewhat similar instructions were sent to Elisha Hinman, who was commanding the *Cabot* in the continued absence of her wounded captain, John Burroughs Hopkins. Hinman was to get additional men from the *Alfred* and *Fly.* Also his orders stated, "you are likewise to take such directions from time to time as you may receive from Captⁿ Biddle."

The prospect pleased Biddle not at all, and, while he still lay off Providence, he voiced his discontent to his brother James.

"I have been here this week Ready for Sea and waiting Only for orders," he wrote. "The Cabot is to go with me And I ex- pect to sail in a day or two on a Cruise. I wish with all my Soul I was not Obliged to be taging after these Dam'd Ships   I ask Nothing more of the Congress than the Vessel I have   Good God of Heaven I am out of all patience with being in such a port. Do get Me a Cruizing Commission if it is possible to obtain it. And then you may expect to hear from me. Before, you Cannot." [39]

With drafts of additional hands on board, the *Andrew Doria* and *Cabot* dropped down the river as far as Pawtuxet and came to for the night. The wind was out of the southwest when they weighed the following morning and they had to beat down. Toward dusk the black brig ran aground on the Gull rocks off Prudence Island. They pulled her off near dawn; with the air calm, Biddle and Hinman got out their boats, towed both brigs southward through the eastern channel, and finally brought to in Newport Harbor.[40]

They were windbound for several days, using the opportunity to fill up water casks. Biddle sent a boarding party to investigate a sloop tied up at a Newport wharf and reported as bound to Halifax. She was brought alongside, overhauled, and discharged, as suspicions proved groundless. On Sunday morning, May 19, the two brigs weighed and had proceeded to about abreast of the lighthouse when the wind died. Not until noon could they get under way again, when with a moderate breeze they stood off into the southeast. By six o'clock the following evening the island of No Mans Land bore five leagues north by west. An hour later a large ship was observed astern. She was standing towards them, so Biddle spoke the *Cabot*.

"I believe she is the Cerberus," he called across. "If she comes up too fast we had best separate." [41]

Hinman was in agreement. Both knew the *Cerberus*, a twenty-eight-gun frigate, had been reported watering at Block Island within the week.[42] They knew also that their two brigs were no match for her. By nightfall the *Cerberus*, if she it was, was gaining rapidly and the captains decided it was time to strike out each for himself. The *Cabot* bore away to the eastward toward Nantucket Shoals while Biddle, fearing those treacherous waters, turned the *Andrew Doria*'s head into the southward. An hour later he had lost sight of both brig and pursuing ship.[43]

In the early morning, many leagues south of Nantucket, a lookout reported a sail to leeward, and orders were given to chase. By eight o'clock they were near enough to see she was a large but unarmed sloop. When two swivel guns were fired in warning, the sloop's sails came down on the run. As they drew abreast, the *Andrew Doria*'s pinnace was lowered, and Biddle hailed: "Send your captain on board us."

The captain boarded the pinnace and was brought to the

brig where Biddle questioned him.[44] The sloop was the *Two Friends,* Abraham Copland, master.[45] She was bound from the Virgin Islands to Liverpool, Nova Scotia, with a cargo consisting of 22 hogsheads of rum, 20 barrels of sugar, 26 tierces of molasses, and 950 bushels of salt.[46] Bound in the journal of the *Andrew Doria* is a page apparently torn from the *Two Friends*'s logbook. It was kept by the mate and the first entry in it describes her capture as follows:

". . . at ½ past 4 A M we Saw a Sail in Chase of us and She soon Came up with us and hild and ordered the Capt. on Bord and Sent the penance for him & afterwards for me with N Bowen George Barber and N Russell and Sent the Capt on Bord with a Prize Master and 4 Sailors and took out one of our Sailors and left the other on Bord the Sloop and sent her for Newport and the Brig stood to the W S W the Brig N[ame]d Andrew duriah of 14 Guns belonging to Philadelphia Commanded by Capt. Biddle—and so end the day." [47]

Before the day had ended, however, Biddle had written a letter to Hopkins, entrusted it to a master's mate, Philip Brown, as prize master, and dispatched him for Rhode Island. The letter was brief and to the point, thus:

"The Night after we left Newport being Chased by a Vessel we took to be the Cerberus the Cabot Run a more direct course for Nantucket Shoals than I thought safe to do by which Means we have lost company with her. This Morning we took a Sloop bound from Saltertudes to Liverpool in Nova Scotia. Mr. Brown my third Mate to whom I have given Charge of Her will Give You what further information you may want to know." [48]

The prize sloop reached Rhode Island on Saturday, May 25. Prize master Brown sailed her up to Providence, where she was libeled against and condemned less than a month later as lawful prize.[49]

Under the latitude given in his orders, Nicholas Biddle could cruise where he chose; in the places where he would "most annoy the Enemy." Hence, after dispatching the prize sloop on the evening of May 21, he summoned his officers to a council

to outline his intentions. They would proceed generally eastward until south of Cape Sable, where transports with troops
or supplies bound for Halifax would most likely be encountered.
As he pointed out, this was the logical time of year for reinforcements to be at sea, if the British government intended a
determined effort during the summer and fall to regain foot-
holds in the rebellious colonies.[50]

As the *Andrew Doria* nosed along the air was light, the
weather hazy, the sea smooth, and the horizon empty. Thus for
three days, and then small breezes and a large swell from the
eastward. Biddle ordered the guns housed, and they sailed
under single-reefed topsails. Fresh gales out of the northeast
followed and by Sunday, May 26, they were bowling along
close-reefed at a ten-knot pace. That night the barge pulled out
of its chocks and "had like to kill one of the Seamen that was
Sleeping under it." Fortunately, it was secured without further
casualties.[51]

All next day, amid rain and frequent squalls, the black brig
continued eastward, tacking to north and then to south, as
Biddle sought to cover as much area as possible. Lookouts
strained their eyes through the murky atmosphere but saw
nothing to report. At noon on Monday, May 27, with a brief
break in the weather, Sailing Master Dunn took their bearings
—39°35′ north latitude and 60°27′ west longitude. He estimated Cape Sable as bearing north, thirteen degrees east, a
distance of 292 miles. Thereafter rain and thick weather set in
again.

By Tuesday Biddle had about concluded to venture no further eastward. He determined upon one last long tack to the
northeast, and then a return toward the Continent. They were
on the first tack, when at four o'clock in the morning of Wednesday, May 29, a lookout hailed the deck.

"Two ships to the northward," he called, "but too dark, sir,
to make 'em out." [52]

Biddle was summoned from his cabin; in a trice the black brig
hauled her wind, her nose swinging due northward in pursuit.
In the widening dawn it could be seen that both vessels were
turning away in flight, and within another hour they were close

enough to be identified as merchantmen or transports. By then the brig's crew was at quarters, matches lighted, tompions knocked out of the guns, and the *Andrew Doria* ready for a fight if needs be. That danger seemed imminent for the nearest stranger showed numerous cannon bristling from her gunports. They came abreast of her just at six o'clock, and Biddle hailed:

"Heave to, or we'll sink you. What ship is that?"

"The Oxford transport, Stewart, master," came the reply, "from Glasgow with troops. Don't fire! We are unarmed."

"Hoist out your boat and come aboard, Captain," were Biddle's directions. Her sails were taken in, the ship's boat was lowered and Stewart was rowed across to the *Andrew Doria*. The master and his boat crew were ushered over the rail, and the brig set off for the second vessel. While they pursued, Biddle extracted details of both ships from the captured master.[53]

The *Oxford*'s formidable array of cannon consisted of sixteen wooden guns. She carried a company of the Forty-Second Royal Highland regiment, commanded by Captain John Smith and numbering about one hundred men. The other ship was a transport also, the *Crawford,* John McAlister master, with Captain Norman McLeod's company of the Seventy-First regiment, likewise about a hundred strong, but largely recruits coming out as replacements. They had sailed from Greenock in April in a convoy of thirty-three transports but had become separated in stormy weather.[54]

As they came up with the *Crawford* her sails were being taken in. There was no more fight in her than there had been in the *Oxford*. She did not even have wooden guns to bluff with. Lieutenant Josiah went over to her in the *Andrew Doria*'s pinnace to take command. Sending back her master and four men, he proceeded to inventory his captives. On board were Captain McLeod and his lady, Lieutenant Roderick McLeod, Ensign Colin Campbell and his lady, a lady's maid, five servants, and about 110 soldiers of the Seventy-First, some of them with wives and children along.[55]

Meanwhile Biddle was securing similar information about the *Oxford*. Of the Forty-Second regiment in addition to Captain Smith, there were Lieutenants Robert Franklin and Harry

Monroe, Ensign John Campbell and about 110 noncoms and privates, with a few women and children. Here was a problem. The *Andrew Doria*'s crew numbered about eighty. Adding the British seamen manning the two transports to the soldiers made a total of more than 260. The captives outnumbered the captors by more than three to one. The solution, of course, was to separate sea officers from their crews, land officers from their companies, and make sure that all navigators were brought on board the brig.[56]

Instructions went to Lieutenant Josiah, and Midshipman Evan Bevan, who was appointed prize-master's mate, was sent to the *Crawford* with four seamen.[57] All arms and accouterments and the officers' field equipment were to be transferred to the *Andrew Doria* along with the English seamen. The troops were to be taken on board the *Oxford,* and the officers, together with Mrs. McLeod and her maid and Mrs. Campbell, were to remain on the transport and be courteously treated as prisoners of war.[58]

For the *Oxford,* Biddle picked as prize master his third lieutenant, John McDougall, with Lieutenant John Trevett as mate and a crew of nine. McDougall was instructed to send all arms and British seamen to the *Andrew Doria,* as well as the officers of the Forty-Second.[59] At the last moment, because of the crowded condition on the *Andrew Doria,* the captain had sent two invalid officers of the Forty-Second, a passenger, and several servants to the *Crawford.*

"I lost one of the Ship[']s and one of my own Boats in carrying the People and things from one Vessel to the other," Biddle said, "but happily no lives were lost." He had, he remarked, taken both prizes "with the Speaking trumpet." [60]

When they got under way, heading westward and homeward at last, the *Andrew Doria* in addition to her own crew carried forty prisoners and the muskets, bayonets, broadswords, and small arms of the two companies.[61] The *Oxford* had 300 on board, of whom 220 were soldiers. How many were women and children even John Trevett admitted later he "never knew." [62] Fewest of all were the number on board the *Crawford,* which, including the prize crew, totaled but twenty.[63]

The brig and her two prizes kept close company as they made for home. The weather, barring a haze and rain on the night of May 31, continued pleasant but the winds were contrary and progress was slow. Without anything of moment occurring, they logged an average of seventy-five miles every twenty-four hours for a period of ten days. This brought them by Tuesday, June 11, to a position some thirty leagues south of Martha's Vineyard. Early that morning Biddle spied five sail in the northwest, one of them seemingly a good-sized man-of-war. They were heading his way; so he signaled the two prize ships to come within speaking distance, and gave the prize masters orders to separate—Josiah in the *Crawford* to stand to the southwest, and McDougall in the *Oxford,* due west. The *Andrew Doria* then made off eastward.[64]

Whether or not the five distant sail really chased is a matter of conjecture. Had Biddle been aware of their identity, however, he would not have taken the precautions he did to evade them nor have been so precipitate with his orders to separate. The five comprised His Majesty's frigate *Mercury,* of twenty guns, convoying four merchantmen from New York to Halifax, and carrying dispatches for Vice Admiral Molyneux Shuldham at that latter port.[65] Unfortunately, in eluding the *Mercury,* the *Andrew Doria* also lost sight of the transports. By the time Biddle got back on his course they were over the horizon, and he did not see them again.

"About 9 o'clock we heard several Guns to the N.E.," he stated, "But I was in no condition to know the Occasion. I had forty Prisoners who did duty on Board and when I cleared Ship for Action they were put below under guard and I had but fifty three men and boys sick and well to fight." [66]

Three days later, on Friday, June 14, the black brig hauled into Newport Harbor. Hopkins was on shore—had come down from Providence to get some of his fleet to sea—so the captain reported in person upon his successes. But the *Crawford* and *Oxford* had not arrived and the commodore remarked glumly, but nonetheless prophetically, that he supposed they had been retaken.[67] That night Biddle landed his prisoners, turning them over to a militia guard.[68] Next day, the *Andrew Doria* dis-

charged into the commodore's custody the arms and accouterments, and a clerk checked them off, securing Hopkins'
signature on the invoice. Quite a haul it was: 191 firearms with
cartouche boxes, 2,600 musket cartridges with balls, 3 fuses, 2
hangers, or short swords, 162 bayonets, 80 broadswords, 8
halberds, 2 drums, 273 pounds of gunpowder, and as unique
trophies, but of little value to the captors, 2 pair of Scotch bag-
pipes.[69]

To return to the captured transports. Before the *Oxford* was
out of sight of the *Andrew Doria,* on June 11, the Highlanders
and a few British seamen led by the ship's former carpenter
rose on the prize crew. How they overpowered the eleven men
has never been disclosed.[70] Lieutenant Trevett, whose comments are usually pertinent, merely remarked in his journal,
"I could not blame them, for I would have done the same." [71]

Without a competent navigator, the new captors decided to
make for Hampton Roads, which they concluded to be about
due west of their position. There they expected to find safety
with Lord Dunmore, who they believed held Norfolk. Nine
days later by good fortune they made the Virginia capes and
got inside about sunset. The air was calm, and the roadstead
barren of any sails save two small craft, which they assumed to
be pilot boats. A sergeant of the Highlanders and a private,
with one of the prize-crew seamen to do the rowing, put off
from the *Oxford* to query the supposed pilot boats as to Lord
Dunmore's whereabouts. They were told he, with his fleet, was
some miles up James River; a beautiful misstatement of fact,
as the deposed Virginia governor had assembled his force on
Gwynn's Island some forty miles to the northward in Chesapeake Bay.[72]

The unsuspecting British, according to Trevett, "after giving
three cheers," weighed and stood up the river with "a light air
of wind." Alas for expectations! The American seaman in the
small boat had managed to convey the true situation to the
skipper of one of the "pilot boats," and both closed in toward
midnight. Pilot boats? Not they, but two small armed boats
with commissions from the colony of Virginia, and commanded

by Captain James Barron and his brother Richard. Wary of so large a ship and not knowing that Biddle had removed all the arms, nor that the frowning cannon were wooden guns, Captain Barron seemed puzzled as to his next step. Trevett, who had somehow gotten undetected on deck, resolved his dilemma.

"I'm an officer of the Andrew Doria," he called, "and a prisoner on board, but there isn't a weapon in the ship."

The Virginia boats swept alongside then and a dozen well-armed seamen sprang to the *Oxford*'s deck. There was no fight in the Highlanders, as they had nothing with which to fight.[73]

Transport ship and her small captors continued up the James through the night and moored off Jamestown next morning. A company of frocked riflemen—"the finest I ever saw," commented Trevett—marched the Highlanders off via Williamsburg to a prison camp at Richmond. The British seamen were jailed, and Lieutenant McDougall and his American prize crew, having established their identity, drew orders on Congress for expense money.

"We were supplied with what cash we wanted with pleasure," Trevett said, "and were treated very politely by one and all in Williamsburg." [74]

They set off for Philadelphia, while the *Oxford* was libeled against by the brothers Barron. Having been in the enemy's hands after recapture for a period of greater than ninety-six hours, she was, according to resolve of Congress, one half the property of the new recaptors.[75]

And now the *Crawford!* Misfortune overtook Lieutenant Josiah the day following the separation from the *Andrew Doria* and the *Oxford*. On the early morning of June 12 he spotted a sail off to the northeast and promptly turned away from her. There was an immediate pursuit, and at seven o'clock the *Crawford* was being so rapidly overhauled that the pursuer, easily identifiable now as a frigate, fired a warning shot. Not to be frightened so easily, Josiah crowded on all the sail he could carry and fled westward. All that day the chase continued, and at frequent intervals the enemy yawed to fire a gun. They sounded like 9-pounders to Josiah, and toward evening the shot were falling uncomfortably close. At sunset, when the frigate was almost abreast, and a single broadside could have sunk the defenseless transport, the plucky lieutenant gave up. The *Crawford*'s sails were lowered as a midshipman, heading a British prize crew, took possession of her for His Majesty's frigate *Cerberus*.[76]

Josiah, Bevan, and the four members of the crew were unceremoniously removed to the frigate.[77] Rummaging through the former's sea chest, the captors found his private journal of the *Andrew Doria,* beginning January 4, 1776. It was confiscated, eventually finding its way to the British Admiralty in London, being forwarded because it contained an account of the engagement of the rebel fleet with the *Glasgow*.[78]

The British army officers and wives remained temporarily on board the *Crawford,* while Captain John Symonds of the *Cerberus* decided what disposition to make of her. When they learned he intended to put a few hands on board and send her to Sandy Hook, under convoy of an armed sloop tender, their decision was to stay where they were. The tender and *Crawford* parted with the frigate on June 16. Three days later, off Fire Island and within a few hours of their goal, they were intercepted by Captain Charles Pond, in the Continental sloop *Schuyler,* one of a fleet of small vessels Washington had commissioned for patrol duty off New York.[79]

That afternoon Pond ushered his prizes into Fire Island Inlet and sent the chagrined prisoners off to army headquarters on Long Island, where the arrival of three women, "two of quality," threw General Nathanael Greene into consternation. He found camp accommodations for them, next day forwarding them all to New York.[80] From the transport, Pond removed thirteen tierces of beef, eleven tierces of pork, three hundredweight of bread, four puncheons of rum, two firkins of butter, and a cask of cheese.[81] These were carted across the island to add to the army's commissary stores.[82] Then Pond filed a libel against the *Crawford,* which, like the *Oxford,* had been long enough in repossession of the enemy to entitle the recaptors to one half her value.[83]

Thus Biddle's prizes, after divers unusual experiences, and with their complete cargoes—human, arms, and provision—fell eventually into the hands of the Continent. But the *Andrew Doria*'s share of the spoils dwindled much in the accomplishment.

Chapter IX

Final Exploits in the Black Brig

ANCHORED IN NEWPORT HARBOR IN MID-JUNE WERE four vessels of Hopkins' fleet. Besides Nicholas Biddle's black-sided *Andrew Doria,* they were the ship *Columbus,* the sloop *Providence,* and the little sloop *Fly.* Having left the *Alfred* at Providence only half manned, the commodore had journeyed to Newport to order the quartet to sea—the *Columbus* and *Andrew Doria* on cruises, the *Providence* on escort duty to Boston, and the *Fly,* with a cargo of twenty of the New Providence cannon, to New York.[1] Almost identical sailing orders, providing the broadest latitude to the captains, were issued for the *Andrew Doria* and *Columbus* on June 16; Hopkins then returned to Providence.

"You are to go to Sea with your Brig, as soon as possible," his directions to Biddle read, "and Cruise till your Provisions are out or you have weaken'd your Brig by Manning Prizes so as to make it unsafe to Cruise, in such Places on our Coast as you will be most likely to intercept the Enemies of the United Colonies."

There followed the usual definition of the enemy and directions as to prizes. Then, for the first time in orders to his captains, Hopkins conceded the authority of the Marine Committee, which had succeeded the original Naval Committee. Biddle should, he advised, "transmit to the Marine Committee or their Agents, or to me, an Account of your Circumstances." [2]

As certain necessary stores could not be procured in Newport, Lieutenant Elisha Warner had gone to Providence for them. Meanwhile the captain proceeded with watering and wooding and managed to recruit a few additional hands. Master's Mate Philip Brown and his prize crew, which had brought in the *Two Friends*, came down to augment the crew further, and Lieutenant Warner returned on the morning of June 16 with Hopkins' instructions as to officers. Sailing Master Dunn should act as a lieutenant, and Brown as master, but the commodore thought it not prudent to issue a commission or a warrant "till we hear further from Mr Josiah—for if he returns he must have his old Birth." [3]

In the cabin of the *Andrew Doria* that Sunday afternoon, June 16, Biddle completed a letter to his brother James, with a postscript that epitomized his life. The captain had written at length of the capture of the Scotch transports and the subsequent separation from his prizes. He must have settled back in his chair lost in thought, and then, leaning forward, added these inspiring words:

"I fear Nothing but what I ought to fear. I am much more afraid of doing a foolish Action than of loosing My Life   I aim for a Character of Conduct as well as courage And hope never to throw away the Vessel and Crew merely to Convince the world I have Courage   No one has dared to impeach it yet. If any should I will not leave them a moment of doubt."

From Providence, Hopkins fired another order on June 18. He had just learned that the British blockading fleet had been driven from Boston Bay and that two more Scotch transports had been taken. Therefore, if Biddle took "any Prizes Eastward of the Shoals its Safest to send them to Boston." Also, if the *Andrew Doria* happened to put into that same port, the Captain should call on the Continental agent and, provided the sloop *Providence* had not arrived there, "take a Vessel Loaded with Coal & Convoy to the Capes of Philadelphia or into the River." [4]

That same day Abraham Whipple in the *Columbus* stood out of Newport Harbor on his projected cruise. The wind was from the southwest, so the ship made slow way as she tacked out the East Passage. She was well south by west of Brenton Reef when lookouts on Castle Hill observed a distant sail— probably the *Cerberus*—standing in from Block Island. The alarm raced across Newport Neck to Biddle, who ordered the *Andrew Doria* and the *Providence* out to the support of the endangered *Columbus*. Two Rhode Island galleys were hastily manned and dispatched on the same mission.[5]

While the rescue vessels were still beating down the passage, the *Columbus* and her opponent delivered broadsides, the reverberations of which the wind carried to an excited Newport. Then the enemy vessel was seen suddenly to haul by the wind and bear away to the eastward. A little later the *Andrew Doria* spoke the *Columbus,* which was standing in on a strong flood tide. Their opponent had been the *Cerberus,* all right, Captain Whipple related to Biddle, and she had fired three broadsides into the *Columbus,* killing one man.[6]

"I got in one broadside," he added, "but probably did her no damage. I think she hauled off to clear Brenton Reef, as the tide and wind were carrying her that way fast." [7]

The *Columbus, Andrew Doria, Providence,* and galleys returned by nightfall to Newport Harbor. The encounter made necessary a postponement of the *Columbus'* cruise. Sails and rigging had been badly enough shot up to require a week or more of overhaul. And the appearance of the *Cerberus,* with her superior armament of twenty-eight 9-pounders on her main deck and six 4-pounders on forecastle and quarter-decks, indicated there might be a delay in the departure of Biddle's black brig also.[8]

Discontent in Congress over Hopkins' lack of initiative with the fleet had begun in May. It took the usual form—a committee to consider how far he had complied with orders and, "if he has departed therefrom, to examine in to the occasion thereof." [9] When on June 13 the Marine Committee reported it too had complaints of breach of orders and "other mal-practices" against the commodore as well as against Captains Saltonstall and Whipple, Congress ordered all three to Philadelphia "to answer for their conduct." [10] Next day John Hancock wrote to Hopkins, transmitting the resolution of Congress, and adding: "The command of the ships, will, of course, devolve in your absence, upon the eldest officer, to whom you will give the command, with this direction, however, that he take no steps with respect to the ships until further orders."

The injunction restraining the "eldest officer" from showing any initiative must have been an afterthought of the Marine Committee, of which Hancock was chairman. The Congressional resolve did not encompass anything which would render further inactive a fleet whose inactivity was the chief cause of the investigation.[11] However so, the letter went forth by express for Providence, where its contents would represent the first problem for Nicholas Biddle, who, with Hopkins, Saltonstall, and Whipple ordered to Philadelphia, became the senior officer of the fleet.[12]

Certainly the Hancock letter, when he received it at Providence on June 20, could not have been a complete surprise to Hopkins. His elder brother Stephen, a member of the Naval and later the Marine Committee, had apprized him of the discontent as early as the end of May. In fact, replying to Stephen Hopkins, he had written on June 8, suggesting that he welcomed a successor if it was desired to replace him with somebody "more able to serve the common Cause than I am at these Years." [13]

The account of the abortive engagement between the *Columbus* and *Cerberus* had reached Providence just before the letter from Philadelphia, so he knew Whipple was still at Newport and surmised Biddle was there also. Two letters were sent off that same day. To Whipple he enclosed a letter from Hancock alike in tenor to the one he had received and commented that, as he and Saltonstall were similarly directed to appear before Congress, they would "take pleasure in your Company" to Philadelphia.[14] To Biddle he was more explicit. After pointing out that "the Command of the Fleet devolves upon you as oldest officer," he cautioned care in taking "no Steps with the Ships 'till further Orders from Congress."

The letter concluded with an injunction to forward immediately "an Account of the State of your Brigs Stores, of every kinds of Provisions, a list of the effective and non-effected [*sic*] Men, and in short every thing relative to the Vessel under your

Sir   New London June the 28th 1776

I arrived here the 26th of June in company with Capt Hacker in the Fly. Who sailed for New York with a fair wind yesterday morning There are several Vessels here outward bound Capt Kennedy who commands one of them shew me a paper signed by one of the Committee of Congress Directed to the Commanders of Continental or Provincial Vessels of War Desiring they would Assist them in getting Clear of the Land And Another to the same purpose signed by General Putnam. As soon as a favourable opportunity offers I purpose going out a Head of them and to give them a Signal to Return in case I see danger.

Capt Jones has according to Your Orders gone to Boston. I shall send you with this the Account of Stores &c on board the Doria And have Ordered Capt Jones and Capt Hacker to transmit You theirs as soon as possible.

I am Sir your Humble Sert

Nicholas Biddle

NICHOLAS BIDDLE REPORTS TO THE COMMODORE.
From the Hopkins Papers, Rhode Island Historical Society, Providence.

Command." Jones, of the *Providence,* and Hacker, of the *Fly,* were to furnish similar lists.[15]

These instructions arrived in Nicholas Biddle's hands on June 21; had he been without initiative, he would have accepted them as superseding all previous ones. To abide by the letter of the latest Hopkins order, all he had to do was forgo a cruise, void the *Providence*'s departure for Boston, and the *Fly*'s for New York, and simply sit down in Newport Harbor and await developments. But that was foreign to Biddle's nature. He was satisfied that, regardless of the tenor of the letter from Hancock, which Hopkins had cited but not produced, the Congress did not want its war vessels rotting in port. The *Columbus,* because of needed repairs, would have to remain idle for a time, but not so the *Andrew Doria, Providence,* and *Fly.*

To John Paul Jones and Hoysteed Hacker he gave instructions to carry out their respective orders. As the *Providence* was ready, and the *Cerberus* nowhere in sight, Jones got to sea on June 22, stretching away for Vineyard Sound and the eastward. Because the *Fly* would have to run the gauntlet of the British cruiser or cruisers based on Block Island, Biddle decided to give her convoy as far as New London just as soon as he felt that section of the coast fairly clear.[16]

The same express which had brought such disquieting orders to Hopkins, Saltonstall, and Whipple was the conveyer of very good news to Biddle. It was purely unofficial, coming by private letter with an injunction to secrecy until Congress saw fit to make it public. On June 6, according to this advice, captains had been appointed for the four frigates building at Philadelphia, and, in the order named, they were Nicholas Biddle, John Barry, Thomas Read, and Charles Alexander. Names had been bestowed upon all thirteen frigates at the same time, and the Marine Committee empowered "to affix the names to each particular ship, and determine the vessel which each captain is to take command of." [17] The most advanced on the stocks, the letter advised, was the frigate building by Joshua Humphreys in Southwark, and it was at least a month from launching. As to armament, there was none in sight, so Biddle need not grow impatient. It would be a long time before any Philadelphia-built frigate would be ready for sea.[18]

Whereupon the captain turned his attention to the more immediate problem, and on June 24 the *Andrew Doria* and *Fly* went out past the Dumplings, stretching away past Beaver Tail for Point Judith. The *Cerberus* was not visible around Block Island, and the weather was hazy. Hugging the shore, and with pilots who knew the entire stretch of the coast, the brig and sloop slipped through the treacherous channel between Fisher's Island and the main, entering the Thames on June 26, to anchor off New London that afternoon. Near by was the brig *Cabot,* just in from the cruise begun in company with the *Andrew Doria* more than a month before.[19] Captain Hinman reported some success; in fact, had sent a prize into Rhode Island, which Biddle could assure him had arrived safely.[20]

Since the captain's previous visit to New London, Nathaniel Shaw, Jr., had been appointed Continental agent. Consequently all naval vessels reported to him, and all supplies and repairs fell under his jurisdiction. Biddle consulted Shaw, and with his concurrence dispatched the *Fly* unescorted for New York on June 27.[21] Then he took the opportunity to requisition some five dozen shirts and as many pairs of shoes for his seamen, and twenty-two pairs of trousers, probably for his marines.[22]

When he wrote Hopkins, on June 28, he addressed him as "Commander in Chief of the Continental Navy in Philadelphia." First announcing his arrival with the *Fly,* and her departure through the Sound, he proceeded to indicate clearly that, orders or no orders, he was not standing by in idleness.

"There are several Vessels here outward bound," he explained. "Capt Kennedy who commands one of them Shew me a paper signd by one of the Committe of Congress Directed to the Commander of Continental or Provincial Vessels of War Desiring they would Assist them in getting Clear of the Land And Another to the same purpose signd by General Putnam. As soon as a favourable opportunity Offers I purpose going out a Head of them and to give them a Signal in case I see danger." [23]

But, in case he saw danger, what about the *Andrew Doria?*

No mention was made of his own return. He had no intention of doing so. When he cleared New London, danger or no danger, it would be to execute the cruise authorized by Hopkins on June 16, all subsequent orders to the contrary notwithstanding.

In foggy weather, which concealed the *Andrew Doria* from the British vessels off Block Island, Biddle made his departure on the last day of June. He carried provisions for one month only. Several merchantmen accompanied him to sea, but parted company after a safe offing. The captain headed into the southeast, past No Mans Land and out into the Atlantic. His course was the same as the one he had followed a month before, but this time there were no Scotch transports to fall into his clutches.

For almost two weeks the black brig met nothing. Then on July 11 they spied a large vessel off in the northeast. There was a short chase, with the fleet *Andrew Doria* overhauling her quarry, a lumbering merchantman, in less than an hour. She was the ship *Nathaniel and Elizabeth,* William Hoar master, from Jamaica for London with a cargo of West India produce. Sailing Master Brown and four seamen went on board as a prize crew, and the British master and his hands were sent to the brig. The *Nathaniel and Elizabeth*'s manifest was produced —three hundred hogsheads of sugar and one hundred hogsheads of rum—and Biddle realized he had a rich haul. He ordered Brown to make for the first port he could reach and saw the ship off on a plodding gait to the northwestward before resuming his own course.[24]

Two or three more days of profitless cruising, and Biddle concluded he had ventured far enough for the present and had best turn homeward. Provisions were getting low and would suffice for not more than ten days without short rationing. So he bore away for Rhode Island with favorable winds. Passing Block Island in the dawn of July 21, he spotted two British frigates close in and under easy sail. As he had the wind and was already approaching Point Judith, they attempted no pursuit. That afternoon the *Andrew Doria* anchored off Gravelly Point in Newport Harbor, hard by the *Columbus,* which Biddle could see was groomed for sea.[25]

Hopkins, Saltonstall, and Whipple were still absent. Lieutenant Joseph Olney, in temporary command of the *Columbus,* had heard nothing from them. Letters from Philadelphia awaited the captain, however, and contained a little information. The trio had arrived in that city on July 2, and the Marine Committee had been ordered to "enquire into the complaints exhibited" against the two captains. Hopkins, it appeared, would have his hearing in the halls of Congress, where the Declaration of Independence had just been adopted.

So to Hopkins, at Philadelphia, Biddle directed the official report of his cruise:

"I sailed from this place in the Continental Armed Brig Andrew Doria on the 25th of June, and accompanied the Armed Sloop Fly as far as New London on her way to New York. On the 30th I saild from New London on a Cruise And on the 11th of July took the Nathaniel and Elizabeth a Ship bound from Jamaica to London commanded by William Hoare who is the Principal Owner. Just as I had taken the Captain and Crew out of the Ship and Mann'd her another Vessel came in sight to which I gave chase ordering the Prize Master to make the best of his way to the first Port of safety he could get to. The Vessel I Chased Proved to be a French Ship. Cap Hoare sailed in Company with a fleet of fifty Sail under Convoy of a Fifty Gun Ship.

"I Cruised till the 15th without seeing any of the Rest of the fleet and as the wind blew hard from the S W had no doubt of their having passed me. I then Steerd for Newport and Arrived here Yesterday. I had the Misfortune to strike on a Rock coming out of New London which makes it Necessary for to Careen the Vessel. I shall make what dispach I can in getting Ready for Sea And wait for Orders." [26]

Biddle's letters from Philadelphia had some advice for him also about the frigates. One of the four, named the *Randolph,* in honor of the late president of Congress, Peyton Randolph, of South Carolina, was to have been launched on July 10, and another shortly thereafter. Rumor had it the *Randolph* would be assigned to him by the Marine Committee, but there was yet nothing definite on that point. [27]

One correspondent asked a favor. There was a Captain

Golly, who had been taken in a vessel from Philadelphia and carried to Halifax. Golly had escaped and in making his way homeward had been stopped and jailed in Providence on suspicion of being an enemy to the liberties of America. This was a grave injustice, the letter writer pointed out, to the aforesaid Captain Golly, whose wife and friends were most uneasy about him. Would Biddle intercede with the executive authority of Rhode Island in behalf of this unfortunate mariner? The captain would indeed and penned a note to Governor Nicholas Cooke—a note which was a model of tact and diplomacy, concluding:

"The subject I write on, will, I hope apologize for my troubling you, and the mentioning the matter induce an enquiry into the cause of his confinement, which, if it is (as is apprehended) only on suspicion of being inimical to the cause, may be the means of procuring him his liberty." [28]

He learned, too, did the captain that first day back in port, of the misadventures of his Scotch transports. Two seamen who had been members of the prize crew placed on the *Oxford* had returned to Newport, via Philadelphia and New York, and could tell him all about the events which ultimately saw her arrived in Virginia.[29] The Newport *Mercury*'s news columns supplied the details of the *Crawford*'s advent in Fire Island Inlet. And just when Biddle had reconciled himself to the diminished prize shares which would come to the *Andrew Doria*'s crew for the two transports, an express from New London arrived with word of another misfortune.

The *Nathaniel and Elizabeth* had been chased on the rocks behind Fisher's Island and probably would be a complete loss! [30]

When the *Nathaniel and Elizabeth* parted with the *Andrew Doria,* on July 11, Prize Master Brown knew she was cranky and slow. Within twenty-four hours he learned she was likewise very old and very fragile, with much rotten timber below decks and frayed and worn rigging above.[31] So he nursed her along, not daring to carry much sail, and praying for continued fair weather. His good luck held day after day until, on the morning of July 26, he passed to the eastward of Block Island, standing before a breeze out of the southeast which should waft him into New London by the following day.[32]

Then his luck ran out. Lying southwest of Block Island that morning was His Majesty's frigate *Cerberus*. At six o'clock one of her lookouts "saw a Sail over the Island." She "weighed & Gave Chase." [33]

Upon the complaining masts of the *Nathaniel and Elizabeth* Brown crowded every inch of sail and headed for Fisher's Island, hoping he could get behind it before the frigate could come up. As pursued and pursuer came into sight of the Connecticut shore, glasses were trained upon them and word went to the militia to assemble at Stonington. It was apparent the fleeing ship was trying to round the eastern end of Fisher's Island, where shallow and unfamiliar water might deter the enemy from following.[34]

At noonday the *Cerberus* had narrowed the distance. At no time did she yaw to fire, for her captain knew he could not afford to lose ground by such a maneuver. Hour after hour through the afternoon, with the frigate hauling closer and closer, the long stern chase continued. Then at six o'clock, as the *Nathaniel and Elizabeth* rounded the island tip, the enemy gave over the pursuit and tacked to the westward. The reefs and sands of an area uncharted on the British maps were too dangerous to risk His Majesty's frigate.[35]

Brown's triumph was short-lived. Scarcely had the *Cerberus* veered away when the old merchantman's bottom was gouged by the teeth of a rock ledge stretching between the island and the shore near Watch Hill. She grounded with a stop so sudden that her masts snapped and she bilged. From Stonington the militia came off in boats to her defense should the frigate send in a landing party. The enemy, however, tacked again, toward the southward, and stood off for Block Island.[36]

Next day the *Cabot* came out from New London to the assistance of the stricken ship. By herculean efforts, they got eighty-six hogsheads of rum and ten hogsheads of sugar into the brig before the *Nathaniel and Elizabeth* went to pieces.[37] Nathaniel Shaw, Jr., as custodian of the salvaged goods, reported "the

Remainder of her Cargoe is lost." And that was the story Brown and his men brought to Newport when they rejoined the *Andrew Doria* a few days later.[38]

Another long-absent crew member turned up on the afternoon of July 28, with an account of British brutality which mightily incensed Biddle. He was Frank Gould, a mestee lad who had been a member of the prize crew placed on the transport *Crawford*. The previous night, while the *Cerberus* had been lying about three miles from Block Island and the day after she had chased the *Nathaniel and Elizabeth* ashore, Gould had slipped unseen into the water and swum to the island. There he had found a small cedar boat with two sails. In this flimsy craft he embarked alone and naked and set off for Rhode Island. He landed at the fort on Brenton Point the next afternoon, told his experiences, and was rushed off to relate them in greater detail to Captain Biddle.[39]

In the captain's cabin he produced a water-soaked, but still readable, missive from Lieutenant James Josiah, who had been held on board the *Cerberus* as a prisoner ever since the *Crawford* had been retaken on June 12. In few words Josiah painted a picture of brutal treatment.

"I am used worse than I ever thought one Englishman could use another," he wrote. "I was sent before the mast with the rest of the prize crew, but upon refusing to do duty, I was given under the charge of a boatswain and his mates, and am daily threatened with the gangway." [40]

Young Frank Gould supplied more details. Not only Josiah, but many others were treated ill "for refusing to act against their country." Of the six members of the *Crawford*'s prize crew, Gould, and one Edward Kirk had entered on board the *Cerberus,* but the former had done so only to facilitate his escape.[41] There were, all told, about 40 Americans on board the frigate, her whole force totaling 160. On the Block Island station she had taken 18 vessels, mostly small sloops and schooners, 16 of which she had burned.[42]

That same day Biddle wrote to the Marine Committee, protesting against the harsh treatment being accorded Josiah, and asking that steps be taken to alleviate the condition of all the prisoners on the *Cerberus*. He quoted the captive lieutenant's letter, but cautioned against any disclosure that such a letter had been received, as "it might prove injurious in case he is not exchanged." [43] He also, according to his brother Charles Biddle, wrote to Admiral Richard Howe off New York, threatening that "however disagreeable it was to him, he would treat a young gentleman of family, who was then his prisoner, in the same manner they treated lieutenant Josiah." [44]

Of this second letter there is no further record. Of the one to the Marine Committee, however, there is. It was presented in Congress, on August 7, and produced an immediate result, thus:

"Resolved, That the General [Washington] be directed to propose an exchange of Lieutenant Josiah, by giving in exchange for him a lieutenant of the navy of Great Britain, and that the General remonstrate to Lord Howe on the cruel treatment Lieutenant Josiah has met with, of which the Congress have received undoubted information." [45]

Washington protested to Howe on August 17, commenting "From your Lordship's character for humanity, I am led to presume, that the hardships imposed on Lieutenant Josiah are without either your knowledge or concurrence." [46] In reply, two days later, the British admiral agreed that "insults and indignities, to persons of whatever rank, who are become parties in this unhappy dispute, cannot be justified." The *Cerberus* being absent, however, he had no information on the treatment accorded Lieutenant Josiah, but would inquire into the matter when possible. [47] Meanwhile the unfortunate lieutenant continued his unhappy existence on the frigate, "insulted with the name of rebel" and "damned for a rascal." [48]

In Philadelphia the Marine Committee had completed the hearings of the charges against Saltonstall and Whipple and had concluded them unfounded. Congress in turn, on July 11 had approved the return of the captains to their commands. [49] That same day the Marine Committee drew up instructions for Biddle. In so doing it removed him entirely from under the direction of Hopkins and placed him "under the Orders and

Commands of this Committee." [50] He was informed of his appointment to the frigate *Randolph* and directed to proceed upon one more cruise in the *Andrew Doria* to terminate in Philadelphia before the end of September.

Transmission was delayed while the Marine Committee prepared instructions for Saltonstall and Whipple. When the captains finally started for Rhode Island they were accompanied by Lieutenants McDougall and Trevett, of the *Oxford*'s prize crew. This pair had arrived in Philadelphia from Williamsburg and settled their accounts with the navy paymaster. To McDougall the Marine Committee had given the letter of instructions to Biddle. Lydia McFunn had also entrusted him with a letter to her brother: "Dear Nicky Your Vessel is to be launch'd on Monday Next," she wrote. "we long to see you." The actual date the officers departed northward is not specified, but they traveled via New York and were delayed in crossing the Hudson by the British frigates and tenders in the North River. They arrived on August 6 in Newport, where McDougall and Trevett at once rejoined the *Andrew Doria,* and the former delivered the letter to his captain. [51]

Whipple too had been ordered to cruise; with the *Columbus* ready, he proposed going out with Biddle. Both ship and brig were shorthanded; even a draft upon the *Alfred* for men did not fill their complements. The *Columbus* put to sea with 176 men on board, the *Andrew Doria* with about 90. [52] Their departure, on August 10, would have passed unnoticed save for an unusual incident which the Newport *Mercury* mentioned two days later:

"Last evening a drowned man was found at gravelly point in this town; 'tis said he belonged to the Andrew Doria, Cap. Biddle, who sailed the day before with the Columbus." [53]

The joint cruise of the two Continental vessels terminated about ten days later when, in latitude 36°, they ran afoul a British twodecker of sixty-four guns. They took to their heels and, as the enemy gained, separated. The ship of the line kept after the *Columbus* as the larger quarry; by nightfall the *Andrew Doria* was alone on the ocean. Whipple did not reappear, so Biddle proceeded on his own course and centered his activities off the island of Bermuda, cruising between it and the main.[54]

Within a few days he had his first prize. A lookout picked her up in the early morning, a large ship standing eastward and apparently heavily laden. The captain hailed as they drew abreast, receiving an evasive and unsatisfactory answer.

"This is the Continental brig Andrew Doria," he called across the water, his voice threatening. "Heave to and send your master on board."

The master came, one Bridger Goodrich, member of a Tory family that had become anathema in Virginia. From him Biddle learned that the ship was the *Molly,* formerly the property of a Maryland merchant, but seized long since by Lord Dunmore. She had 15,000 bushels of wheat on board, which the royal governor had pilfered from Virginia plantations and was dispatching to Halifax.[55]

There was other news, too. Dunmore and his force had been driven from Gwynn's Island and had sought safety on shipboard, and the motley fleet had retreated down the bay to Hampton Roads. His Tory supporters, their property loaded in anything that would float, were departing daily, making chiefly for Bermuda. According to Goodrich, the governor himself intended to join Lord Howe off New York.[56]

A prize crew manned the *Molly,* Biddle having removed to the *Andrew Doria* two negro slaves, as well as Goodrich and his hands.[57] She parted from the brig shortly afterwards, and the records are silent as to what happened to her.

Another of the Dunmore fleet was picked up within twenty-four hours—the brig *Maria,* John Marshall master, in ballast and loaded with Tories and their household furniture. The *Maria* was short of water and provisions; so the captain took out four negroes and let her continue her voyage to Bermuda. He had no compunctions in separating the slaves from their erstwhile owners. Notoriously Dunmore had seized them from the plantations bordering the Chesapeake, or induced them to run away from their masters by promises of freedom. He had been roundly cursed as a "negro-snatcher," and his army derisively called a "black legion." To deprive the Tories of their ill-gotten gains, therefore, was a satisfaction to the captain.[58]

In the next two days the *Andrew Doria* intercepted two more prizes, neither however from Dunmore. The first was a 100-ton brigantine, the *Lawrence,* George Leyburn master, from Barbados for Newfoundland, with a valuable cargo of rum, sugar, limes, sea coal, wrought copper, and tinware. John Trevett was placed on board as prize master with a crew of seven.[59]

The second was also a 100-ton brigantine, the *Elizabeth,* William Ryson Johnson master, from Cape Fear for the British army and fleet off New York. She had a cargo of salt, flour, rice, tobacco, turpentine, and two carriages—a phaeton and a chaise. To her went John McDougall as prize master with seven men. Biddle ordered both brigantines for Providence and directed them to keep company if possible. To McDougall he added instructions to repair to Philadelphia once he had turned his prize over to the proper authorities in Rhode Island. There was a lieutenancy on the frigate *Randolph* awaiting the young New Yorker, to whom Biddle had become quite attached, and who had demonstrated all the attributes of a fine sea officer.[60]

Next day the *Andrew Doria* intercepted the brig *Betsey,* John Rynoe master, another of the Dunmore fleet. Like the *Maria* she was in ballast, with a number of Tories and their possessions on board. Like the *Maria* also, she was short of water and provisions. Biddle's procedure was the same as that he had applied to the previous cargo of Tories. All the negro slaves were removed—there were five of them—and the *Betsey* was permitted to depart.[61]

The final prize, which likewise came from Dunmore's scattering forces, was the brig *Peggy,* William Cook master. She, however, was bound to St. Augustine instead of Bermuda. As her cargo contained rum, molasses, and linen as well as the usual number of Tories, their belongings, and three negroes, the captain decided to send her in. The slaves were removed—fifteen of them had been taken on the *Andrew Doria* by now—and Philip Brown was put on board with a seven-man prize crew. She, too, was ordered for Providence, and Biddle decided to run in toward Bermuda before turning his helm homeward.[62]

Meanwhile, on September 7, the brigantines *Lawrence* and *Elizabeth,* safely escaping the observation of the blockading frigates, got into Rhode Island where Esek Hopkins libeled against them in the Admiralty Court at Providence.[63] Later he was advised by the Marine Committee that he had no one twentieth as commander in chief coming to him from either of the two prizes, as he had been definitely legislated out of the picture as a participant in any of Biddle's prizes taken after July 11.[64]

Not so fortunate as the two brigantines was the prize brig *Peggy*. That nemesis of Biddle's prizes, the *Cerberus,* sighted her when between No Mans Land and Block Island on September 11 and set off in pursuit. Prize Master Brown headed for the latter island and crowded on all the sail she could carry. But the *Peggy* could not outrun the *Cerberus*. As the frigate was coming up fast, Brown finally ordered out the boat. He and his crew piled into her and rowed off.[65] They reached Block Island while the enemy took possession of the *Peggy*. After nightfall, the *Andrew Doria*'s eight men began a long row which took them to Newport the next day.[66]

From the time the *Andrew Doria* had parted with her last prize until she entered Delaware Bay, Nicholas Biddle had never left the deck. Of his original crew, the 104 who had sailed with him out of that same bay just seven months before, but 5 remained. Some had been left at New London or Newport sick, one or two were dead, a few were prisoners, and many were off in the prize crews. There had been replacements from the *Alfred,* and during this last cruise he had enlisted seamen from his prizes. But this was risky business, as he very well knew. Consequently, with many prisoners below decks, and numerous hands of dubious loyalty in the crew, the captain maintained eternal vigilance day and night. Only Benjamin Dunn and Isaac Craig could spell him. All other officers were off commanding prizes. When he slept, therefore, it was rolled in a blanket on the quarter-deck, a pistol within reach of his hand.[67]

With no untoward incident the *Andrew Doria* passed between the Delaware capes on the morning of September 17, and ran up the bay and river to anchor off Chester by nightfall. The newspapers hailed her advent, thus:

"Arrived the Continental brig Andrew Doria, Captain Biddle, from a cruise, in which he took six vessels." [68]

The captain, however, by the time that article appeared, had turned the brig over to the Continental shipyard for overhaul, reported to the Marine Committee, relinquished the command, and secured a short leave of absence. Then he had departed for Reading, where his mother had taken up her abode with his elder brother, the ailing Edward, and where the exploits of the black brig were recounted to the family.[69]

Down in the West Indies another brother, Charles Biddle, was also learning about the accomplishments of the black brig, and in a manner which indicated that Nicholas Biddle's successes at sea were sitting illy with the enemy. Charles, having been taken in a brig while carrying a cargo of flour from Philadelphia for Port-au-Prince, was hauled before Clark Gayton, British admiral commanding at Jamaica.

"Biddle, eh?" leered Gayton, when the prisoner's name was announced. "Any relation to this rebel?" He pointed to a Philadelphia newspaper he had been reading, which told of the return of the *Andrew Doria* from her latest cruise.

"That rebel is my brother," Charles answered with a grin.

And Gayton, having damned the Biddles, the Congress, the rebellious colonies and everything in them, ordered Charles into irons.[70]

III

The Randolph

Chapter X
Continental Captain Number Five

TEN OF THE THIRTEEN FRIGATES HAD BEEN LAUNCHED before Nicholas Biddle returned to the Delaware in the *Andrew Doria*.[1] Twelve frigate captains had been named, although by resolve of April 17 rank had not been established but was to be settled by Congress "before commissions are granted."[2] A total of twenty-four captains had been appointed so far; so rank involved more than the seniority of those named to frigates. It affected every one of the two dozen commanders. Successors also had to be selected for naval vessels whose captains had been honored with frigate assignments. As some of the new ships were nearly outfitted, it behooved prompt Congressional action. To solve these problems the Marine Committee was meeting nightly, with influence on behalf of various captains being exerted through members of Congress.[3]

Biddle's reputation and achievements would assure him preferment and high standing on the list regardless of politics. So, as he still had warm champions in the halls of Congress, he saw no reason for dallying in Philadelphia to put in personal appearance, either before the Marine Committee or before the Pennsylvania delegates. He would let the accomplishments of the *Andrew Doria* bear testimony to his worth, and the fair-mindedness of Congress determine a rank proper to his merits.[4] Nor was his confidence in the justice of the Continental fathers misplaced, for on October 10, when the seniority list was promulgated, Nicholas Biddle stood fifth.[5]

There might be questions as to some of those who preceded him on this famous list. Certainly James Nicholson, who had not entered the Continental service until June 6, 1776, had no warrant to be appointed as "first captain," nor had Hector McNeill, whose services began June 15, to be chosen third. As to John Manley, who stood in second place, there could be justification based upon his previous Continental naval employment in 1775 under General Washington. Dudley Saltonstall, whose original commission in 1775 had predated Biddle's, deserved even better than fourth on the list.[6]

As James Nicholson's frigate was outfitting in Maryland, Saltonstall's in Connecticut, and Manley's and McNeill's in Massachusetts, the fact that they outranked Biddle was of little importance. In Philadelphia, where a number of Continental captains were forgathered at the time the list was announced, he was the senior. Next in line were the other three frigate commanders—John Barry, Thomas Read, and Charles Alexander. Others included Isaiah Robinson, who had succeeded him as captain of the *Andrew Doria,* and his former lieutenant, Elisha Warner, who had been assigned to the sloop *Fly*. Still another of the lieutenants who had served in the *Andrew Doria* had been given a captaincy—James Josiah. But, as Josiah was still a prisoner of the British, no definite command was assigned him.[7]

The seniority list had been settled and Congress, to avoid more headaches, had wished the ranking of the naval lieutenants upon the Marine Committee before Biddle's visit in Reading had ended. He bade farewell on October 11 to his mother—his last farewell had he known it—and departed for Philadelphia and his new command, that frigate *Randolph* of which he had heard much and seen but a glimpse.[8]

If Biddle had not yet examined the frigate, nearly all of Philadelphia had. The good citizens had strolled down the riverside all through the spring and summer to watch her building, her launching, her rigging. The joiners, the shipwrights, the carpenters, and the riggers had finished her now.[9] Fully rigged, from jib boom to spanker gaff, she lay moored beside the wharf at Humphreys' shipyard, with a guard of marines on twenty-four-hour duty to protect the precious gear which the commissioners of naval stores had been delivering daily since the launch.[10]

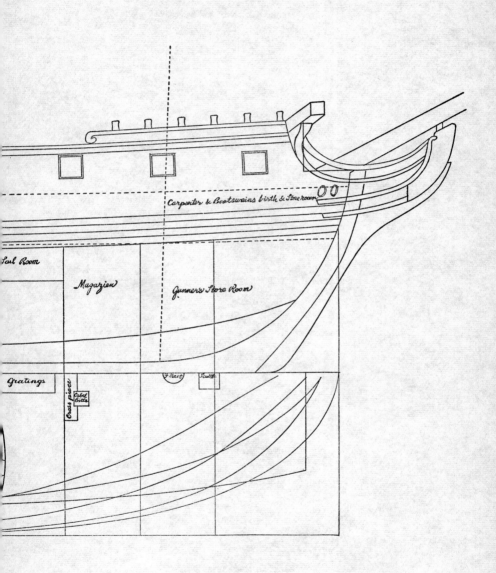

Carpenter & Boatswains birth & Store room

Sail Room

Magazien

Gunner's Store Room

Gratings

Cross piece

Cabel Bitts

Mast

Scuttle

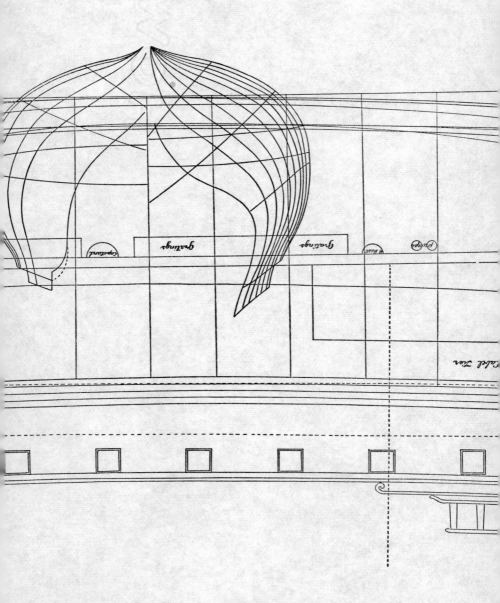

Capstan Gratings Gratings Bitts Pumps

Cable Tier

Wharton & Humphreys's Draft

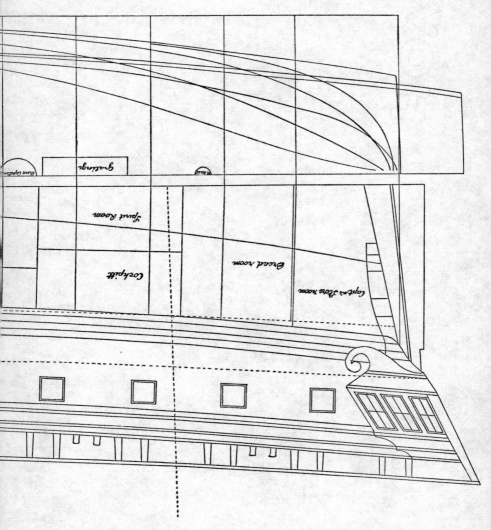

Grating

Spirit Room

Cockpit

Bread Room

Captain's Store Room

Continental Frigate Randolph
drawn from the original by
T. R. Hawley Jr

The *Randolph* was "a beautiful frigate" [11] in the eyes of all who saw her, and Biddle, as he boarded her in mid-October, could but echo the same sentiment. She rode lightly in the water, for as yet she was unarmed and but partially ballasted. Along her 137 feet of gun deck were the gunports where eventually 12-pounders—thirteen to a side—would thrust forth their ugly iron nozzles. [12]

Forward the forecastle deck stretched for twenty-seven feet, with better than a six-foot clearance between its planks and those of the gun deck below. In the forecastle were the quarters for the warrant officers and midshipmen. Aft rose the quarter-deck, beginning just abaft the mainmast and extending a full third of the ship's length to the stern post. In the closed-in space beneath the quarter-deck, where lay the spacious quarters of the commanding officer, the clearance was just shy of seven feet. Headroom on the long main deck below was but five feet two inches; so officers and men would have plenty of chances to bump their polls on the heavy beams of the gun deck above. The main deck, from fore to aft, housed in turn the gunner's storeroom, magazine, sail room, crew's quarters, galley, officers' quarters, cable tier, cockpit, bread room, and captain's storeroom. With a breadth of thirty-four feet six inches, the *Randolph* afforded ample space for a crew of better than 250 officers and men. [13]

The frigate's masts reared skyward amid a network of rigging—the foremast piercing the forecastle deck, the main-mast rising through the gun deck just seven feet forward of the quarter-deck, and the mizzenmast springing aloft about midway along the quarter-deck. They were tall masts, too, with the tallest of the trio—the mainmast—rising to a height, including topmast and topgallant mast, of nearly 150 feet above the gun deck. [14]

Ready in the sail loft ashore was a complete suit of canvas to be spread upon the tall masts and broad spars whenever there would be a crew to do the spreading. In October there was none. Other than the captain, but two officers had been appointed. One was the first lieutenant, William Barnes, a capable Pennsylvanian who had sailed several ships from the port of

Philadelphia before the war.[15] The other was the second lieutenant, John McDougall, who was on his way by land from
Providence with the prize crew which had brought in the brig
Elizabeth. Before the end of the month the Marine Committee
had named as third lieutenant, Joshua Fanning, who had been
sailing master of the *Columbus,* and who could boast of a father
and two brothers in the Continental naval service.[16]

A well-trained company of marines, quartered in the barracks in the Northern Liberties, just above the city's limits on
Second Street, was ready to go on board the *Randolph* whenever needed. In fact, the frigate guard was maintained out of
this same company.[17] Back in June, when the first frigates were
near the launching state, Congress had determined to raise a
battalion of marines in Philadelphia, had appointed four each
of captains, first and second lieutenants, and had sent them out
recruiting.[18] One of the most successful of these recruiters was
tall, thin Samuel Shaw, who was captain of one of the companies. Under him, as first lieutenant, was Franklin Reid, a Philadelphian.[19] In September a down-at-the-heel Frenchman from
the West Indies—one Panatiere de la Falconniere—had memorialized Congress and wheedled the Marine Committee into
appointing him a second lieutenant in Captain Shaw's company.
It was this company, fifty strong, which had been selected for
the *Randolph.*[20]

Original plans had specified the frigate as of thirty-two guns
—twenty-six 12-pounders on the gun deck, and six 6-pounders
on quarter-deck and forecastle. Having examined this armament as proposed, Biddle believed it inadequate. He felt she
could easily mount four more 6-pounders, and thus be rated
as thirty-six guns instead of thirty-two. In October he carried
his proposal to the Marine Committee, and found ready approval when he explained that he would mount four 6-pounders
on the forecastle and the other six on the quarter-deck.[21]

The long-awaited guns were received in early November,
having been cast in furnaces in Berks and Lancaster counties.
Accounts of the commissioners of naval stores record their
arrival with entries such as "Hawling 2 Twelve pound Cannon
—7 . . 6," "Martin Wert for hawl⁵ Cannon—5–," and

"Martin Brooke for hawl^g 2d^o—10—" [22] By the middle of the month a member of the Marine Committee could report, "Biddle has all his Guns on board." While this was technically correct it did not, however, mean they were mounted and ready for use. The carriages which had been provided all had to be altered to fit the cannon, and this proved a long and tedious operation. [23]

The captain left outfitting largely in the hands of his three lieutenants. Details were innumerable, as a glance again at the accounts of the commissioners discloses. Water casks painted; the magazine whitewashed; hickory and oak wood to be hauled, sawed and corded; porterage to be provided for almost every item received; a canvas awning to be sewn as covering for part of the quarter-deck; a wire screen to be woven around the magazine lantern—to mention but a few.

The *Randolph* had her complete suit of colors, and the sempstress who produced them, a Mrs. Mason, had been paid £6 for her handiwork. The record is silent as to when the Grand Union was first raised aboard, but it probably occurred shortly after Biddle took command. The colors had been ready by July; at least, Mrs. Mason's account was settled by then. [24]

Affairs of the *Andrew Doria* took a bit of the captain's time, too. The first item was the matter of securing prize money for his men. Officers and crew had petitioned Congress in October for an accounting, and the Continental agents in Philadelphia had been directed "to make an estimate of all the prizes taken by the Andrew Doria," which, if approved by the Marine Committee, would result in a payment of "one half of what may be estimated to be due to them." As the Continental agents had not the haziest idea of the black brig's captures, they could only base an estimate upon the information that Biddle could supply. [25]

Another problem was the status of the numerous negro slaves brought into port not only by the *Andrew Doria,* but by several other of the small Continental cruisers. Congress had appointed a committee of three, on October 14, to consider what was to be done with them. [26] Whether this committee ever reported or, if it did, whether Congress took any action, is not recorded in the journal of that body. At any rate, because the value of the prizes could not be determined without knowing the value of the slaves, Biddle on November 11 filed a libel in the Pennsylvania Admiralty Court against the fifteen he had brought in, "to Wit, Luke, Baile, Jack, Phil and Ben . . . Jacob . . . Henry and Jacob . . . Sol, Moses, Charles and Jacob . . . and Romeo, Joe and Frank." The "owners or masters of the said Negroes," stated the libel, could show cause, if they had any, "why the same should not be condemned as prize," when the court convened on November 28.[27] But, as events will disclose, the court was not held then, nor at any other time during the remainder of the captain's stay in Philadelphia.

Sometime in late October or early November Biddle, attired in his new uniform, presented himself by appointment at the home of Charles Willson Peale for a first sitting for his portrait. The artist, who would later become famous for his canvases of Washington and other Revolutionary celebrities, had come to Philadelphia from Maryland the previous summer. When not drilling his militia company, he was busily engaged with palette and brush. Already he was looked upon as an artist of promise. Peale's painting could not have been begun before October 14, when Biddle returned from Reading, and must have been finished before November 30, when the artist led his militia company off to join the Continental army.[28]

In that portrait, which exists today, the captain appears in the uniform which the Marine Committee authorized in September for its naval captains—blue coat with red lapels and flat yellow buttons each bearing an upright anchor. The waistcoat is red, the same shade as the lapels, and a high white stock fits tightly beneath a rather pointed and resolute chin. The captain's hair is trimmed fairly short and seems a bit unruly, particularly over the ears. Alert brown eyes are shaded by dark eyebrows, and the nose is long and straight. Add a pair of firm lips, and you have the picture of a man of action, not words. That is Nicholas Biddle as you see him today by means of the brush of Charles Willson Peale, and as he was in the fall of 1776 in the beginning of his twenty-seventh year.[29]

Philadelphia had not considered the British invasion of New York in September a serious peril to the young republic's capital. True, a report of a large enemy fleet standing southward from Sandy Hook had rather upset the city in mid-November, but this ship movement had later been diagnosed correctly as a convoy of empty transports headed for England. Before this diagnosis had been completed, however, Congress had directed the Marine Committee to make such disposition of its naval force in the Delaware "as will best conduce to defeat the designs of the enemy." [30]

One of the measures taken by the Marine Committee was to instruct Biddle to open a rendezvous in the city and start recruiting a crew. A committee member was sanguine, on November 16, that the *Randolph* would be ready for sea "by the latter end of this Week." [31] Samuel Shaw's company was ordered to the frigate from the barracks. There is probably no significance in the fact that shortly afterwards the commissioners of naval stores paid out £10 15s. for a barrel of country rum and a keg of West India rum delivered about the same time the marines came aboard.[32]

There is significance, however, in an indent of slops needed, which Biddle issued on November 19 to Alexander Todd, a Philadelphia merchant. He wanted on the frigate, said he, among other things, 200 each of outside jackets and shirts, 240 "Woollen Trowsers," 300 pairs of stockings, 260 pairs of shoes, 250 caps, and 280 pairs of mittens.[33] The captain seemed to have the same optimism as to his recruiting efforts. But from a statement by a member of the Marine Committee made five days later, it appeared that the men to fill this indent of clothing were still wanting; for he reported, "Captain Biddle's frigate Randolph. . . is now completely ready, except that she wants men which we hope to remedy." [34]

The movements of General William Howe, since August, had served to lull Philadelphia into a fatuous feeling of false security. The enemy, from Flatbush to White Plains, had definitely inclined northward. As long as the British and their Hessian minions were seemingly pinned down in Westchester

County there was no need for alarm. But that had changed when the enemy struck and in a single day engulfed Fort Washington on upper Manhattan Island, whose commander had boasted an ability to withstand all assaults. Fear gave way to consternation when it was learned the enemy had crossed the Hudson into New Jersey and had almost cut off the garrison of Fort Lee. Panic mounted as Washington retreated to Newark, dispatching General Thomas Mifflin with an urgent request for militia support and a confidential message to Congress that he intended to continue falling back until he had placed the Delaware between himself and his opponent.[35] Inspired by Mifflin's eloquence at a mass meeting in the State House yard, the Philadelphia militia battalions started northward for the Delaware at Bristol.[36]

Faced with inactivity because of the inability to man their ships and get to sea, five of the naval captains—the only ones in port at that time, and headed by Biddle—addressed Congress with an offer to join the army with such force as they could muster. The offer was referred to the Marine Committee with directions "to pursue such measures as they think proper in consequence thereof." [37] The decision was to hold Biddle and his men on the *Randolph*, and John Nicholson, youngest brother of the senior James Nicholson, on the sloop *Hornet*, both vessels being completely outfitted.[38] The other three captains—Barry, Read, and Alexander—headed two nondescript companies of seamen and landsmen who were enrolled as volunteer artillerymen and who set off in the wake of the militia.[39]

As with the militia had gone all artisans from the various shipyards, journeymen and apprentices in every trade, and even the registrar and marshal of the Admiralty, industry in Philadelphia came to an abrupt halt, and the Admiralty Court to a lengthy adjournment.[40] Townsfolk began loading their belongings into carts and drays and forsaking the city for protracted visits with relatives in the back counties.[41]

"This City alarmed with the News of Howe's army's being at Brunswick, proceeding for this place," recorded a diarist on December 2, "Drums beat; a martial appearance: the shops shut, and all business, except preparing to disappoint our enemies, laid aside." [42]

Included in the plan to "disappoint our enemies," the Marine Committee urged Biddle to get his frigate ready for immediate departure. The captain was quite agreeable, provided someone would conjure up a means of procuring enough hands to sail her. That problem was promptly passed along to Congress, who empowered the committee "to advance 20 dollars to each seaman who will enter to serve on board the Randolph . . . the same to be deducted out of their share of the prize money." [43] Of course, nothing happened, as the seamen who might have been attracted had already marched off to join the army. Five days elapsed, and on December 7, in desperation, Congress resolved:

"That Captain Biddle be empowered to inlist into the continental service such of the sailors in prison as he shall think proper." [44]

Meanwhile, from General Washington came word that he had retreated across the Delaware into Pennsylvania, that the British had entered Trenton, and that the enemy objective was certainly Philadelphia. He had ordered General Israel Putnam down to fortify the city, and "Old Put," arriving the night of December 9, brought further intelligence of danger. There was every reason to fear, wrote one member of a jittery Congress, that soon we will "perhaps hear the thunder of their cannon and mortars and feel the effects of shots and bombs." [45]

Before Biddle could take the drastic step of enrolling seamen who had been sent to jail as felons, or disaffected persons or prisoners of war, an express rode in from one of the watchdogs at the Delaware capes. The *Roebuck*, of forty-four guns, and a sloop of war, had anchored at the mouth of the bay, blocking exit to the sea.[46] Congress began panicky legislation when this news reached the State House. The Marine Committee was directed to send one or more fast sailing vessels off the capes to warn inward-bound merchantmen. General Putnam was to have complete charge of the defenses, and was to have combustibles prepared to burn the frigates and other Continental vessels should they be in "imminent danger of falling into the enemies' possession." The general also should employ all private armed vessels in the harbor for "the security of the city." Next Congress turned its attention to the two naval vessels which were in the most forward condition—the *Randolph* and the sloop *Hornet*. Both, it directed, should act as Putnam might order "in preventing the enemy from passing the Delaware." Then, thinking of their pride in that beautiful frigate, which by now had dropped down the river and lay anchored at Fort Island, they passed one further bit of legislation:

"But when it shall happen that the General has no further occasion for the use of the frigate Randolph, for the defence of this city, if the same should fall into the enemies hands, should Captain Biddle in that case carry the frigate safely to sea, and thereby save her from falling into the enemies' hands, this Congress will reward him and his people with a present of 10,000 dollars."

That afternoon, despite previous protestations that it would stick to the last, Congress adjourned to Baltimore and gave to General Washington dictatorial powers "in all things relative to the department, and to the operations of war." [47] Behind it were left three delegates who refused to be panicked into flight; one of this trio was Robert Morris, the most aggressive and determined member of the Marine Committee.

Morris did not intend that the Continental vessels in the harbor should be put to the torch until he had exhausted every possible measure to get them to safety. Nor did he subscribe to the idea that they were of importance to the defense of the city from attacks by land. So, scarcely had the last delegate departed for Baltimore before he was on his way to the commanding general.

"I waited on General Putnam," Morris explained later, "and proposed that the frigate Randolph and sloop Hornet should be sent to sea immediately, as it was plain to me they would be of no use here, and I had received certain advice that there was not any British men of war in our bay. The General very readily consented." [48]

Just where Morris got his "certain advice" that the Delaware was free of enemy frigates, he did not say. Regardless of source, though, it was erroneous. Both the *Roebuck* and the sloop *Falcon* were in Whorekiln Road at the time, and on December 11 a warning had gone northward from Lewes, Delaware, that "the two Capes and to the Southward are Lin'd w'h Men of War." [49] Admiral Howe actually had ordered four ships, which sailed from Sandy Hook on December 8, "to remain off the entrance of the Delaware until there is reason to believe the Communications by that River to the Town of Philadelphia, has been by the State of the Weather entirely prevented." [50]

Unaware of this formidable force waiting to pounce on anything that might come down the bay, Morris proceeded to supply the *Randolph* with her powder and ammunition. From the prison Biddle had secured a few men of dubious loyalty but well qualified as seamen. He had added some landsmen; so Morris believed the frigate had "Seamen & Marines sufficient to work the Ship," and that it was better to risk sending her out shorthanded than "to let her remain & be destroyed." [51]

On December 13, the day after Congress forsook the city, the captain received his sailing orders.

"You are to repair on b[oar]d the Randolph Frigate of w[hi]ch you are Commander," Morris directed, "and proceed with all possible dilligence to Sea. We shall not at this time prescribe to you where you are to Cruize nor form any plan whereby to distress our Enemies—the first Object is to get the Ship well manned and for this purpose you may Cruize where you think is the best Chance of meeting Merchantmen or Transports without Encountering Frigates &c we find by [expe]rience that Seamen taken in prizes are in General very [wi]lling to enter into our Service we think you will be able [in] this Manner to compleat your Number admitting such as enter freely & [to] induce them thereto shew [them the va]rious Encouragements given by Congress."

After Biddle felt himself sufficiently manned or in good condition for fighting, the orders specified he should "return on this Coast, cruize for some of the Provi[sion] Vessels or Store Ships that will be coming from Europe [to New Y]ork & particularly keep a look out for the Galatea [Captain] Jourdan as we should be well pleased to see that [vessel] among the Number of your Prizes. . . . We are willing to suppose the business now recommended may employ you for two or at most three Months after which you will put into some safe Port & let us hear from you." Morris had heard that the *Galatea,* a new twenty-gun ship, was cruising off the coast of Virginia.

There were, of course, the usual admonitions for a display of humanity to prisoners and an adherence to discipline and good command. Also the orders contained the routine directions as to prizes.[52]

Instructions to John Nicholson of the *Hornet* directed him to keep company with the *Randolph* until outside the capes, and then proceed for South Carolina and subsequently Martinique.

"I have this afternoon given Captain Biddle and Captain Nicholson their instructions," Morris reported on December 13 to Congress, "signed by me on behalf of the Marine Committee. They will depart early in the morning, and I entertain the most sanguine hopes of their escape." [53]

At Fort Island, Biddle was indeed about ready to sail. He had a pilot, Henry Tudor, discharged from the Pennsylvania ship *Montgomery* to "go on board the Randolph." [54] He had a crew which, while nothing to boast about, could, as Morris had said, work the ship until he could pick up more hands. Lieutenant Fanning came in that morning of December 14, with a request. Would the captain witness his will? The captain would and did so. John McDougall and Samuel Shaw were the other two witnesses.[55] Thereafter, the *Randolph* cast off and dropped down with the tide to the chevaux-de-frise below Hog Island, the *Hornet* in company.

An express overtook them in the river above Chester, on December 15, with letters for Martinique to go by the *Hornet*,[56] and a request to Biddle to await at Chester until a ship for France, laden with tobacco, could come down and join him. While at Chester, in behalf of a master's mate, John Rogers, Biddle sent a certificate to the navy paymaster, James Read, attesting that Rogers was entitled to a share of the prize money for the guns captured at New Providence.[57]

Just as they were getting under way—the *Hornet* was already out of sight below Wilmington—a pilot boat from Philadelphia came alongside with a letter from Morris. To Biddle's disappointment it was an order recalling both the *Randolph* and *Hornet* because of the heavy enemy force off the Delaware capes—the *Roebuck, Falcon*, and two bomb ketches, according to the latest information.

"My labours appear to be lost," Morris wrote to Congress in explaining the reason for the recall, "and sorry I am for the disappointment." He was hopeful, however, that "the first smart northwester" would drive away the blockaders and open the way for the frigate to push out.[58]

There was nothing for Biddle to do but comply with the order, and by December 20 he was back again at Fort Island. The *Hornet,* too, came back to moor across the pier from the frigate.[59]

On Christmas Day Morris and Biddle decided to make another try. The weather was favorable but cold.[60] The captain had secured "more seamen than we expected," and two little Continental vessels—the sloop *Independence* and Biddle's former command, the *Andrew Doria*—had eluded the British frigates and got into and up the bay.[61] Before the effort could be made, came the electrifying news of Washington's Christmas-night victory at Trenton, followed by the appearance of the Hessian prisoners parading down Front Street in double file on December 30. Even so, Morris was disappointed, because, as he announced regretfully to Congress as the year ended, "Six of the enemy's ships are still in Delaware Bay, so stationed that Captain Biddle cannot pass them." [62]

Then winter closed in, with ice forming in the river, the winds howling through bare poles and whistling along decks deserted save for half-frozen sentinels.[63] And while the frigate, snow-swept and wind-blown, rode at the pier, the war had begun to move away from Philadelphia.[64] Trenton had removed the immediate threat, and the victory at Princeton a few days later had rolled the embroiled armies back into northern New Jersey.[65]

No longer was it necessary to save the *Randolph* by venturing her to sea.[66] Prospects of the $10,000 present from Congress, which Biddle probably had taken none too seriously from the start, had vanished along with the old year.

Chapter XI
The First Cruise

From Baltimore, Congress had appointed its three stalwarts who had dared to remain behind when it fled, a committee with power to execute all Continental business in Philadelphia. Joined with Robert Morris, therefore, were George Clymer, another Pennsylvanian, and George Walton of Georgia.[1] These two, however, deferred to Morris in all matters pertaining to the marine department; so the direction of the *Randolph* and all other naval vessels continued in his hands.[2]

Toward the close of the first week in January, 1777, the Continental schooner *Georgia Packet,* coming from Georgia, slipped in through the capes without encountering any enemy vessels. She made her way up the river despite the ice, and her skipper, Lieutenant Isaac Buck, reported to Morris that the mouth of the bay seemed clear of blockaders.

"We hope they may be gone for N. York again," Morris wrote to Congress, "but we must send down to see before any Movements can be made with our Shipping and We fear being interrupted by Ice." [3]

The intelligence brought by Lieutenant Buck was communicated to Biddle, who was more interested in the fact that the little schooner had been able to push its way through the ice than in the belief that the enemy ships had given over winter vigilance at the capes. He was more concerned by possibilities of damage by the heavy cakes churning the surface of the river than by the guns of British frigates. Given an adequate crew, he could combat the latter. The ice, as he knew from experience, was a relentless and dangerous foe.[4]

Actually the situation in which he found himself during early January was reminiscent of a year before, when in the *Andrew Doria* he had lain moored to the very same pier waiting for the river to open. The comforts in the warm cabin of the *Randolph* far exceeded, however, those of the black brig. He appreciated those comforts even more when, a day or two later, James Josiah, just back from captivity, came down to Fort Island to see him.

The former first lieutenant of the *Andrew Doria* had had bitter experiences at the hands of a brutal British captain, and these he related over a substantial dinner which Biddle's steward had prepared. He told of Captain John Symons' vituperations and abuse, of the daily threats of flogging, of being forced to do the meanest duties in the waist of the ship, and of other captives kicked about the deck.[5] For the whole period of the *Cerberus'* cruise off Rhode Island he had been kept aboard, not being transferred to the prison ship *Whitby* in New York Harbor until November 16, more than five months after he had been captured in the *Crawford*.[6]

Even his discharge from the prison ship had been conducted with malice. The British lieutenant for whom he was to be exchanged had been sent in ten days before Josiah had been released. He had petitioned to be landed in New Jersey, as it was nearer Philadelphia. Instead he was put on shore in Connecticut without a pass; this forced him to encircle the entire British front in the dead of winter to get home. For all this suffering there had been some recompense.[7] Upon reaching Philadelphia he found that Congress had made him a captain and that Morris was outfitting his new command, a recently purchased prize ship now named the *Champion*.[8]

Biddle told Josiah of the receipt of his letter through the mustee lad who had swum to Block Island and of the steps taken thereafter to secure an exchange. He asked also about Midshipman Bevan and the others of the *Crawford*'s prize crew. Three of them had been transferred with him to the *Whitby,* Josiah said, and were still in the prison ship. The remaining hand had signed up as an able-bodied seaman on the *Cerberus* the day the transport had been retaken and was now serving His Majesty's navy.[9]

"He'll not serve long," Biddle remarked. "He's probably like the British seamen I have on board. Give them half a chance and they'll desert."

To prevent such desertions the captain had ordered Captain Shaw to maintain a double marine guard on the frigate night and day. It had been successful, but on the night of January 15, to the mortification of the earnest young captain of marines, four of his men ran off, leaving the ship momentarily unguarded. Three days later another marine slipped away from his post at the main gangway, and two of the recruits signed on from prison went with him. These latter two were landsmen, however, and had been jailed for felonies. Biddle advertised for them in the *Pennsylvania Evening Post,* offering a reward of £5 for each man, or £35 for the whole seven "on their appearance on board the Randolph frigate, or if secured in any of the jails of Philadelphia." [10] Whether any of them were ever apprehended is not apparent.

Meanwhile advice had come from the capes confirming Lieutenant Buck's report that the bay was unguarded. In fact another Continental vessel, the sloop *Sachem* from Martinique, had slipped past Cape May and gotten into Morris River, on the Jersey side of the bay. The *Sachem*'s captain had sent word to Philadelphia that he had been chased about the coast for some ten days outside the bay. He also advised that he had attempted to come on up the river but, meeting with solid ice, had turned back.[11]

By January 26 the Philadelphia committee was writing despondently to Congress that "the Delaware continues too full of ice for Ships to sail which is a pity as Capt Biddle has now 200 men onb^d the Randolph & is ready to push out the first opening." [12]

Then there happened an unusual two-day thaw, a shift of the wind, and the receipt of a letter from Silas Deane, American agent in France, announcing shipment for Martinique in October last of great quantities of warlike stores. The Philadelphia committee took heart and Morris advised Congress:

"Our River is now nearly clear of Ice and I propose pushing out Capt Biddle   I do think we cannot employ him & the small Vessells better than to send them to Martinico for the Stores mentioned in M^r D's letter, and I will send out the Indico [*sic*] now here as a remittance towards paying our debts in that Island." [13]

Between January 28, the date of the foregoing letter to Congress, and January 30, when new sailing orders were drafted for Biddle, Morris changed his mind. The smaller Continental vessels ready for sea would be sent to Martinique. The *Randolph* would not. Undoubtedly Nicholas Biddle had much to do with the revised decision. The captain had gone up to Philadelphia on January 29 to see Morris. Learning what was in contemplation, he had remonstrated against using the *Randolph* as a merchantman. He had pointed out the frigate had been designed for fighting, not freighting. True, he wished for more seamen, but even shorthanded he felt himself a match for anything in the British navy under a twodecker. [14]

A letter to Esek Hopkins at Providence from the Marine Committee in Baltimore, which was sent to Morris for forwarding, also helped to alter the original idea. In this letter the Marine Committee asked the commodore to expedite the outfitting of the frigates *Warren* and *Providence* and dispatch them on a cruise from Newport south to the Virginia capes against the enemy ships of war "that are now interrupting the Commerce of the United States." [15] Such duty for the Rhode Island frigates would indicate the desirability of similar instructions for Biddle.

The previous sailing orders, which would have sent the *Randolph* forth after British merchantmen until the captain had proselyted a sufficient crew, clearly needed revision. The frigate had better than two hundred men on board now and Morris, having reread his draft of the December orders, superseded it with a new set of instructions. He was positive the capes were clear—a large merchantman had just come in unmolested—and the ice in the river, while still dangerous, was not a barrier to a determined effort to get out. Certain returns were essential—boatswain's, gunner's, carpenter's, and other stores. A list of officers and men on board was also required, but waiting for these could cause needless delay. Therefore, said Morris, "as I would wish you not to loose one Moments time in getting out to Sea these returns can be made out as you go down and may be sent up from the Capes."

The sloops *Hornet* and *Fly* were in readiness to proceed with the *Randolph* and should be kept ahead of the frigate to look out for enemy ships at the mouth of the bay. Also Biddle was to give convoy to several merchantmen and see them "fairly off to sea," keeping with them a few days on their voyage. "Soon as you find yourself fairly out at sea," continued Morris, "you will no doubt try the ships sailing and I expect she will perform wonderfully in that way."

For specific cruising instructions, he repeated to Biddle the orders sent by the Marine Committee for the frigates *Warren* and *Providence,* and added, "I think they must be proper for you." Then Morris dropped the role of director and became inspirational.

"I must observe that there are no Cruizing Ships an over match for you except the two Deckers," he declared, "for altho you think you have not seamen enough yet this is just their case; except the Roebuck there is none of them halfmanned, therefore you have only to avoid two Deckers or engaging when there is more than one in sight.

"Any of their other single Ships you need not fear, especially if you can persuade your men to board. remember what a glorious exploit it will be, to add one of their frigates or 20 Gun Ships to our Navy in a few days after you get out."

Nor was Morris dubious about that possibility, for "if the Randolph has but Heels I think you can and will do it, you will then get seamen plenty. If your ship sails remarkably fast you may take libertys with them, If she does not be more cautious and try to find out her trim."

At the time he forwarded the returns from the capes, Biddle should also supply signals for identifying himself in case it was necessary to send a small cruiser after him with further orders from Congress. Also in view of this possibility of additional orders, he should look into the bay occasionally, and if there was anything to communicate a large white sheet would be flown from the lighthouse at Lewes under Cape Henlopen.

"You will be careful of the Randolph her Stores and Materials," Morris concluded, "kind to your officers and men, but observing Strict discipline, humane to your Prisoners, and send your prizes into safe ports. With the best wishes for your success I am Sir Your obed^t ser^t" [16]

The *Randolph* was indeed ready for sea. Her magazine was stored with powder, her lockers with an adequate supply of round and double-headed shot for both 12- and 6-pounders, together with small shot for swivels and cohorns and two hundred hand grenades.[17] Only the ice in the river held her to the Fort Island pier, and each day saw the drifting pack diminishing.

With departure imminent, there began the usual flow to the quarter-deck of seamen, who wished to make their last wills and testaments. The captain was authorized by a Marine Committee resolution "to take Acknowledgments of the publication of the Wills of Sailors & Marines"; so Biddle along with several of his officers witnessed a number. There is a bit of pathos in a little group of eight such testaments drawn up at that time and signed by Bernard Garland, Joseph Barry, Thomas Tivy, Dennis McCarthy, William Connolly, Alexander Leyburn, Jeremiah Twig, and Thomas Saunders Pascho. They tell a story of impecunious sea dogs and a Philadelphia boarding-house mistress, who fed and slept them and was content with their promise to pay on death. In the old will books of Philadelphia is the evidence that she was reimbursed— the probate, two years later, of the eight wills, each naming Jane How as "Friend & Executrix." [18]

Just before she cast off, on the afternoon of February 3, the *Randolph* received her last consignment from the Philadelphia jail—nineteen former British seamen who had been taken in various ships. The authorities called them volunteers, but one of their number, Joseph Frost, formerly of His Majesty's sloop *Swan* and taken in a prize, told a different story. After

his capture he was sent to Amboy and then removed to Philadelphia.

"Continued there until the 3rd February, 1777," said he,
"with 18 more was hand Cufft and sent on board the Randolph." [19]

Frost's statement, made later before a British examining officer, may have been a bit exaggerated as to the handcuffs. Another of the nineteen sent to the frigate at the same time makes
no mention of irons, but is emphatic that "they took me out [of
jail] and put me on board the Randolph." Upon one point both
agreed; that was that Biddle's crew then numbered 240 officers
and men. [20]

"The Randolph Frigate is on her way down the River with
several Merchantmen under Convoy, the Hornet & fly attending them and we hope they will get safe out," the Philadephia
committee advised Congress on February 4; "that being accomplished we shall be impatient to give you good accounts from
Capt Biddle." [21]

Neither ice nor the enemy interfered as the *Randolph* negotiated the chevaux-de-frise guarding the river pass and
dropped downward through the broad river into the widening
waters of the bay. Biddle brought her to in Whorekiln Road on
the morning of February 6, and sent a boat ashore to Lewes
with a letter to go off express to Robert Morris. Only a fragment of this letter has come to light—an excerpt as to the dis-
tinguishing signal the frigate would fly ". . . to be known to
small Cruizers by a White Jack at the fore top mast head and
a pendant over it." For the rest, he probably enclosed his muster
roll and return of any supplies, and discussed the merchantmen
he was to convoy—three large ships laden with tobacco and
bound for France and dozens of smaller vessels destined for
the West Indies. [22] The tobacco ships, guarded by the sloop *Fly*,
were still lying off Reedy Island at the head of the bay. He
hoped to pick them all up and give them safe escort when, in
line with his orders, he had returned from a shakedown cruise
off the capes for a few days. He spoke of himself as "not badly
manned," and said of the frigate that she "sails well." [23]

That afternoon of February 6, the *Randolph* nosed out around Cape Henlopen—the first of the thirteen American frigates to put to sea!

In Baltimore the Marine Committee had given enthusiastic approval to Morris' suggestion that the frigate as well as the smaller vessels be sent to the West Indies for the warlike stores promised by Deane.

"We have determined to send all the Armed Vessels mentioned in your Letter to be now at Philadelphia and the frigate *Randolph* likewise on this business," it advised him on February 5. "The Island each Vessel is to go to and the port she is to aim at returning is left to your discretion. You will please Sir to give the necessary orders for the quickest possible execution of this important service." [24]

Whether there was delay in sending the letter or detention along the road, the instructions failed to get into Morris' hands for ten days. When they reached him he promptly drafted new orders for Biddle advising him to go directly to Martinique, load "a quantity of Arms Ammunition Cloathing and other Stores," and return immediately to a safe American port as the supplies "are exceedingly necessary for the service of the ensuing Campaigne."

Were there no warlike stores at Martinique, Biddle was to seek them out at St. Eustatius, or Curaçao, or finally Cap Français. There was much detail in the letter, Morris trying to cover every contingency. It also contained a patriotic urge, to wit: "As you command the first American frigate that has got out to sea, it is expected that you contend warmly on All necessary occasions for the honor of the American flag." [25]

How to get these new orders to the captain presented a problem. Morris knew from Biddle's letter from Cape Henlopen that the sloop *Fly* was at Reedy Island. To reach her he rushed the outfit of the tiny four-gun sloop *Mosquito* and managed to send her off down the river, on February 18, with the new orders to Biddle and a letter to Elisha Warner, commanding the *Fly*.[26] To the latter he wrote:

"I send down to you by the Muskeito sundry Packetts for

Captain Biddle of the Randolph frigate which is now a Cruiz-ing on the Coast. . . . These dispatches are of great conse-quence and must be delivered Captain Biddle soon as possible."

There were instructions as to identifying the frigate; how to advise the lighthouse to signal her, and how to avoid being cut off from shore by the enemy while out seeking her.[27] Morris quietly congratulated himself upon his forethought in prear-ranging a system of signals and advised Congress:

"I have sent the Fly in search of the Randolph Capt Biddle with orders for him to proceed to Martinico. . . . The Fly being too small to carry Remittances I have ordered her after Speaking the Randolph & delivering the dispatches to proceed off the Capes of Virginia to turn from thence the inward bound vessels & I sent the fly two M^s, provisions for that Cruize." [28]

The *Mosquito* delivered the dispatches to the *Fly* at Reedy Island, and Warner went out in search of the *Randolph*. For four weeks he cruised between Capes May and Henry, but not once did his lookouts espy her. Finally he came into and up Del-aware Bay, and the packets for Biddle were returned to the sender in late March. By then Morris knew why they could not have been delivered.[29]

After sticking her nose into the Atlantic on February 6, Bid-dle watched the *Randolph*'s sailing qualities with a critical eye. He tried her before the wind, athwart the wind, against the wind. He tested her under full canvas, with light canvas alow and aloft, with sails aback and in stays. For three or four days he cruised within sight of Cape Henlopen until satisfied the frigate was "the very best vessel for sailing that ever I knew." [30]

Three Tory officers, hiding with friends in Lewes after an escape from jail in Baltimore, saw the *Randolph* on this shake-down trial and mistook her for a British frigate. One of them, Captain John Ferdinand Dalziel Smyth of the Queen's Rang-ers, told about it later.

"During this time [of concealment in Lewes] the rebel frigate Randolph of 36 guns, came down from Philadelphia," said Smyth, "proudly cruised off and on the Cape for three days, then stood out to sea. Taking her for a king's ship, we had almost gone on board, but were soon undeceived by our friends." [31]

Once satisfied with the manner in which the frigate handled, Biddle stood in for Henlopen, sending notice to the tobacco vessels at Reedy Island and to the fleet that was under Cape May and bound for the West Indies, that he was ready to give them convoy. It was probably at this point when Smyth of the Queen's Rangers almost boarded the *Randolph*. There were some delays in getting all the vessels out, but the last of the tobacco ships finally cleared the bay. Like a mother hen watching her brood, the frigate stood eastward amid some forty or fifty bottoms of all sizes and descriptions.[32] For three days she escorted them on their way. They parted on February 15, the vessels bound for the West Indies veering southward, the tobacco ships continuing eastward for France, and the frigate swinging her bow into the northward, bound for the coast of New England.

"She stood farther Northward," related the master of one of the tobacco ships, who had spoken the *Randolph* before they parted, "to pay her first compliments to the Milford." [33]

The *Milford,* a British frigate of twenty-six guns, had been a thorn in the flesh of New England shipping for many months. Congress had tried to send the two Massachusetts-built frigates out after her the previous fall, but could not get them armed or manned.[34] Biddle apparently had considered it within the latitude of his orders to make a try himself for this much hated enemy. How far along on his northward swing he proceeded on this quest is not in the record. Probably he had attained the general area where in the previous May, in the *Andrew Doria,* he had taken the two Scotch transports.

A strange sail was sighted about this time, and the *Randolph* displayed her sailing qualities by running the quarry down in an hour's chase. She proved to be a French vessel. A boarding party found her papers in order and let her go, but not before Lieutenant Panatiere de la Falconniere, a member of the party, had "Begged a large Jug of Wine of the Capt" This rather deplorable act on the part of the marine officer came to light later.[35]

Thereafter, unkind fortune put an abrupt end to Biddle's intentions to seek out the *Milford*. The *Randolph* sprung her foremast. How it happened is not disclosed, but, when it was discovered, the captain immediately ordered the mast stripped of yards and topmast. It was the one measure which might prevent it from going over the side. Then he set about the job of stepping it back into place, but found that the base was rotten. The only alternative was to get it out and rig a spare spar as a jury mast.

Before this could be completed, and with a high sea running and a stiff wind blowing, a second and more serious accident befell the frigate. From amidships came an ominous cracking, and on the quarter-deck an officer shouted a startled warning: "Stand clear the mainmast! She's going by the board!"

There was just enough time for those in the proximity to leap to safety, when, with a final splintering crack, the mast gave way even with the deck. Held upright by rigging only, the tall stick gyrated menacingly about. Biddle reached the deck and paused aghast.

"To see it stagger from side to side with the roll of the vessel," he commented later, "was as unpleasant a sight as ever I wish to behold."

He acted with his characteristic promptness and ordered the mast cut away before more damage might befall the ship. Seamen leaped with axes to the attack on taut ropes until, freed at last, it toppled over the side. The carpenter examined the slivered stub protruding from the gun deck and reported it rotten to the core. Some member of the crew, whom Biddle identified only as "a person of credit," told the captain then that "he knew those spars our masts were made of to have lain these 18 years in the water at the mast yard." [36]

Literally helpless, and at the mercy of any enemy who might happen upon them, the *Randolph* wallowed in the sea. Working under capable instructors, for the frigate's officers were experienced men, the crew proceeded to get out the sprung foremast and rig a second jury mast. Meanwhile, lookouts at the mizzen masthead strained their eyes for the sight of any vessel, friend or foe, and saw nothing.

Biddle had no desire to meet the *Milford* now nor, further south, the new frigate, the *Galatea,* of which Morris' first orders had spoken. What the captain wanted most was to get into some friendly, convenient port on the American continent, anywhere from Philadelphia southward. But with the grave possibility that the British might have re-established the blockade off the Delaware capes and the knowledge that a considerable enemy squadron had been based in Chesapeake Bay, he selected Charlestown, South Carolina, as the most promising, attainable haven. So he turned the *Randolph*'s bow to take advantage of a northeast breeze then blowing, and the frigate responded sluggishly as the meager sails on the jury masts filled.[37]

Probably Biddle hoped to encounter the *Warren* or the *Providence,* which, according to the advice in his orders, were cruising between Newport and Georgia. Either frigate could have given the crippled *Randolph* safe escort. But, if the lookouts had orders to watch for those particular ships, their vigil would have gone unrewarded for both still lay in Providence River, barred from the sea by the British fleet in Narragansett Bay.[38]

No, Biddle could hope for nothing but his own good seamanship and a bit of luck which might take him undetected through the areas presumed to be patrolled by Lord Howe's cruisers. He maintained ironclad discipline, sensing that the large number of British hands enrolled from the Philadelphia jail might consider the vulnerable state of the frigate as an ideal reason to rise. It was well he took the precautions he did, for just such an effort to seize the *Randolph* was brewing below. We do not know very much about it. All we have is the account by Charles Biddle as his brother related it to him.

"While they were bearing away for Charlestown," the story goes, "the English sailors with some others of the crew formed a design to take the ship. When all was ready they gave three cheers on the quarter-deck. By the decided and resolute conduct of Captain Biddle and his officers, the ringleaders were seized and punished, and the rest submitted without further resistance." [39]

The foregoing leaves unexplained how the mutineers got on

the quarter-deck, and what "decided and resolute" steps were taken by the officers. Just as a surmise, it would seem more likely that the British seamen tried their "three cheers" on the gun deck, and that Captain Shaw's marines had been assembled quietly and armed on the quarter-deck ready to put a quietus to the attempt. However it was, the mutiny was nipped promptly, and the ringleaders most likely had a taste of the cat-o'-nine-tails while triced, barebacked, to a grating near the quarter-deck ladder.[40]

Thereafter, as the *Randolph,* buffeted by high seas, made her way laboriously south by west, sickness put in appearance on board. Half the crew was stricken shortly with a malignant fever, from which one man or more died daily through the ensuing week. Fifteen had been sewn into canvas coffins and buried at sea by the time the frigate came within sight of the low, palmetto-lined shore of Sullivan's Island.

Bad weather was threatening ahead as Biddle brought to on the morning of March 11, 1777, and awaited a pilot boat. Then, proceeding under the skilled hand of a man accustomed to negotiate the dread Charlestown bar, the *Randolph* went in, Fort Moultrie to starboard, and in the afternoon dropped anchor in the harbor. The captain breathed a sigh of relief. The cruise just concluded had been, said he, "one of the most disagreeable passages that I ever experienced." In a letter to his brother that night, he added that he "very fortunately had got in just before a gale of wind came on that would undoubtedly have put us ashore." But he concluded with high praise of his ship. "The Randolph," said he, "is the very Best Vessel for Sailing that ever I knew   I hope soon to be out in Her again." [41]

That letter, and others written by members of the crew, reached Philadelphia before the end of the month. In the newspapers of the capital appeared, as early as March 29, an announcement that "The Randolph frigate, Capt. Biddle, having sprung a mast at sea, is put into South Carolina to refit." [42] So, it had been indeed no surprise to Robert Morris when Elisha Warner of the sloop *Fly* reported a few days later that he had been unable to deliver the orders directing Biddle to go to Martinique.[43]

Chapter XII

Romance

JOHN DORSIUS, ONE OF THE JOINT CONTINENTAL
agents for South Carolina, came out to the *Randolph* on the
morning of March 12. As he climbed aboard and crossed the
gun deck to the quarter-deck ladder his practiced and apprais-
ing eye took in the jury rig. He met Biddle with a wry smile.

"Welcome to Charlestown, Captain," was his greeting. "I'm
John Dorsius, one of the joint agents for this port. Looks as
if you've had some bad weather."

"The foulest cruise I've ever been on," Biddle admitted,
"and, as you can see, we stand in need of a lot of repairs."

"Just where we're going to find the sticks for new fore and
main masts for you is a puzzler," the agent mused. "Plenty of
good plank timber in these parts, but we're shy on booms and
spars."

"My first problem," the captain pointed out, "is not masting.
The frigate is ridden with fever. We need a shipyard where
we can heave down and clean her, inside and out and from stem
to stern. And I've a number of men who ought to be in the
hospital." [1]

"That's easier to take care of," Dorsius said. "We have an
agreement with Begby & Manson's shipyard at the mouth of
Hobcaw creek, to handle all Continental vessels. With the wind
blowing out of the southeast like she is, you can run up Cooper
river to the yard in jog-time. I'll arrange with the health officer
to have your sick men taken off, and we'll talk about any indents
you may want later."

Being a most expeditious man, the Continental agent departed for shore leaving in Biddle's mind a feeling that the

Randolph would be in good hands.[2] Other visitors who arrived
on board that morning confirmed this. Dorsius was well esteemed in Charlestown.

Among those who came off to the frigate was Brigadier
General William Moultrie, the heroic defender of the Sullivan
Island fort the previous June. Moultrie was delighted to see
one of the Continental frigates riding in the harbor and particularly pleased to meet the captain whose reputation had preceded him into the southern states. As Moultrie later expressed
it: "The North Carolina troops being ordered away, and most
of our regular troops in Georgia, gave great uneasiness to the
inhabitants for the safety of Charlestown; but upon the arrival
of the Randolph frigate, their fears were a little subsided, looking upon her to be a great additional strength to our batteries,
and protection to the harbor." [3]

To provide that additional strength and protection, the
Randolph certainly needed a thorough overhaul, and Biddle
proceeded without delay to follow Dorsius' advice. By nightfall
the frigate was moored beside the shipyard pier at the mouth
of Hobcaw Creek. With a caution to Captain Shaw to maintain extra sentinels throughout the ship to prevent desertions,
the captain went in his longboat to Charlestown for a formal
call upon John Rutledge, president of the Privy Council of
South Carolina. Probably the arrangements had been made
through Moultrie. There is no record of this official visit, save
in its result—an immediate order from the president to the commissioners of the navy of South Carolina "to Assist the Continental Frigate Randolph." [4]

Apparently the help of the commissioners was not required.
Dorsius seems to have solved all problems, secured all supplies,
provided every needed bit of equipment without once resorting
to them for aid. Not that all of this could be accomplished over-
night. The masts had to be brought from North Carolina; this
alone would take weeks. Meanwhile there was much to do. The
powder had to be removed for drying. Sails must be hauled off
to the sail loft for mending. Bowsprit, jury masts, and mizzenmast had to be unrigged; the ship had to be thoroughly cleaned,
scrubbed, and fumigated.

For all these duties there were daily fewer hands. Despite the vigilance of the marine guard, the British seamen who had been herded on board from the Philadelphia jail slipped quietly away, singly or in pairs. Some sought merchant ships in the harbor, and others made their way into neighboring states. Those who were caught protested they had deserted only because they feared the fever; then they took the earliest opportunity to vanish for a second time. A large number turned up in France months afterwards, where to an inquisitive captain they protested they had left the *Randolph* "on Acct of the Sickness on board." [5] Two men, who managed to get clear to Gothenburg in Sweden, told how they had "run away to Georgia," there shipping on a brig bound to Europe. [6]

What with desertions, deaths from fever, and removal of invalids to a hospital on shore, Biddle's complement dwindled to less than a hundred, including marines. With this totally inadequate crew, he inaugurated a program of ship cleaning which he felt sure would bring an end to illness. The holds and between-decks were ventilated daily and washed with vinegar. Powder was burned as an additional fumigant. Hammocks and bedding were hauled on deck for daily airings. Fresh paint was applied throughout. [7]

A Charlestonian, who went over to Hobcaw about a month after the frigate had arrived, and who ignored the absence of masts, commented that he had "lately seen one of our 36 Gun Frigates which is [as] noble and compleat a one as ever sailed from Britain in every respect; the Randolph she is called, built in Philadelphia." [8]

Apparently Biddle's efforts to restore the frigate to her former splendor were beginning to show results. Dorsius, with an optimism he would later regret, reported to the Marine Committee by letter, on April 14, that he believed the *Randolph* would be fitted and ready for sea by the time the said committee's orders for her future operations could be received from Philadelphia. [9] Biddle, the same day, also asked the committee for orders. He explained that his crew was greatly weakened by sickness and desertions, but that he hoped to recruit sufficient additional hands in Charlestown. [10]

Early in May the masts had arrived and had been stepped. Riggers went to work thereafter, and by May 14 the *Randolph* was ready save for one rather important item. Her crew numbered a scant one hundred officers and men. Recruiting efforts had produced nothing. A rendezvous opened in Charlestown attracted no seamen. Privateers, with their higher wages and larger shares in prizes, were enrolling everybody who was inclined for the sea service; in fact, they were even enticing men from Biddle's slender crew.[11]

Then by express from Philadelphia came two packets; one sealed and marked "not to be opened until July 10," [12] the other containing comprehensive instructions from the Marine Committee. The instructions revoked those previously issued by Robert Morris and presumed that "the Randolph will be fitted and ready for Sea by the time that this reaches you." The captain thought ruefully of the overoptimism which had prompted his last letter, and perused the directions he knew he could not possibly carry out.

The Marine Committee was much agitated about the financial status of Stephen Ceronio, its agent at Cap Français, and was positive that because of no remittances "his Credit is nearly ruined there." British cruisers had bottled up in Delaware Bay three vessels laden for his relief. So, to save his credit as well as the credit of the United States, it was proposed that Biddle receive from Dorsius as many casks of indigo as he could carry "without injuring the fighting or Sailing of the Ship." Whether the quantity should be "50, 60 or 70 Casks of Indico" the committee was not certain. Dorsius was to load several vessels in Charlestown with more indigo for Ceronio, and the *Randolph* should give them convoy.

The British cruisers out of Jamaica had nearly destroyed the American trade with Hispaniola. Hence the committee wanted Biddle to delay at Cap Français no longer than necessary to land his "indico," take in fresh provisions and stores, and proceed on a cruise against them. It was currently believed the enemy force consisted of two frigates, two brigantines, two sloops of fourteen guns each, and four or five small schooners.

"The Randolph by all accounts comes to our ears has the

Heels of most ships that swim," the committee wrote; "therefore if the Frigates Cruize together you can avoid them, if you meet either single we hope you can & will take them but particularly exert your utmost diligence and endeavours, to take sink or destroy all the small Cruizers of our enemies that infest that Coast."

He was empowered to arm a tender, if he captured a vessel suitable for that purpose; he was to give safe convoy out of Cap Français or Môle St. Nicholas to merchant vessels laden for the American continent and to continue such cruising until July 10, when he was to open "the Sealed Instructions," which would "require from you an other service." [13]

Dorsius came aboard that day with a letter he had received from the Marine Committee, and they compared notes. Said the committee to the Continental agent: "The Service Captain Biddle is now Ordered upon being urgent and the objects in veiw important, we request your utmost exertions to get him out to sea as soon after the receipt of this Letter as it possibly can be done." [14]

The captain and Dorsius probably replied by return of the express, each telling the Marine Committee that the only thing preventing execution of the orders was lack of men.[15] Then Biddle stowed the sealed packet in his sea chest, hoping that by July 10 his crew problem would have been solved, and he would be well on his way for Cap Français.

Not all of Nicholas Biddle's interests were centered in the *Randolph*. His visits to Charlestown were frequent, and of such duration that he had provided himself with suitable town lodgings. The city had not materially changed since his one previous visit, when, as a youth of sixteen, he had spent a month there shortly after his shipwreck on the Northern Triangles. Then, because of his age, he had met no one who had left sufficient impression upon him to be remembered. Hence in the Charlestown of 1777 he was seeing new faces, meeting new people and, because he was an agreeable and most attractive young man, being sought after for social functions.

There may have been some friends of his late brother

Thomas in Charlestown at that time, who could have introduced him into some of the exclusive homes. Thomas, the youngest of Mary Biddle's children, had studied medicine and taken up practice in Georgetown, South Carolina, in 1774, but had died there in the following year.[16] However, Biddle's merits were sufficient in themselves to open the doors of the most select mansions, particularly as he was in the councils and confidences of government. John Rutledge welcomed him as a friend. So too did Lieutenant Governor William Henry Drayton, and General Moultrie, and Colonel Charles Cotesworth Pinckney, of the First South Carolina regiment, and Edward Blake, first commissioner of the South Carolina navy, and numerous others whose names were locally or sectionally famous in the Revolutionary period. Joshua Ward, one of the city's most patriotic men and a celebrated attorney at law, and Thomas Farr, a wealthy merchant and later speaker of the South Carolina Assembly, were numbered among his closest companions.[17]

At somebody's home, shortly after his arrival, he was introduced to a lieutenant in the Second South Carolina regiment, a handsome and ardent young patriot whose name was Richard Bohun Baker. The chance acquaintanceship developed into a warm friendship, and one day Baker proposed a visit to his family home out on the Ashley River, the stream which formed the southern boundary of the city and then merged with the Cooper River to create the harbor. He had an invalid father, he explained, who had expressed a great desire to meet the celebrated captain of the *Randolph*. While deprecating any claims to fame, Biddle agreed willingly to the proposal, and they used the frigate's barge for the first visit.[18]

As they proceeded up the picturesque river young Baker prepared his guest for what lay in store ahead. He told of his family and its ancestral home, Archdale Hall, on the right bank of the Ashley. The original house had been built by his great-great-grandfather around 1680. The present structure, however, dated back to 1710, when his great-grandfather had erected the spacious and livable mansion in which the family had dwelt ever since. Just when it had acquired the title Archdale Hall he did not know, but thought maybe it was about the same time the name Bohun got into the family, some fifty years ago. That was when his grandfather, Richard Baker, married Mary Bohun. That grandfather had been killed in a duel, according to family tradition—pistols at forty paces, no doubt! He had left six children, of whom the narrator's father, Richard Bohun Baker, Sr., had been the youngest, and as the only surviving son had inherited Archdale Hall.

Young Baker spoke feelingly of his father, who had been for more than a year suffering from an incurable disease. The senior Baker had been twice married; first to Elizabeth Elliott, who had borne him five children; and after her death, to a widow, Elizabeth Miles, for whom the five had deep affection and who had but recently added an infant brother to the Baker family.

That brought the story down to the present generation; Biddle, who had never been too much of a ladies' man, learned to his great surprise, that at the end of the long river excursion he would meet not only an ailing father and stepmother, but four sisters of his young host. They were Elizabeth, who was eighteen years old; Mary, two years younger; Harriett, not quite fourteen; and Charlotte, aged twelve.[19]

Not that the entire trip was devoted by young Baker to a genealogical discourse about his family. He took pains to point out the great plantations along the river as the barge swept past them. Outstanding of course were Ashley Hall, the ancestral home of the Bull family; Drayton Hall, where the lieutenant governor dwelt; and Arthur Middleton's magnificent home and gardens some miles beyond. Then the oarsmen ceased the long pull, and the barge slid into the landing place at the journey's end.

Biddle was struck instantly by the beauty of the place. Where the landing pier met the shore lay an open brick porch, flanked on either side by stone benches. Beyond that a double avenue of live oaks lined a broad pathway leading gently upwards to a tree-bordered fish pond. Beyond that Archdale Hall itself came into view, but between its massive brick walls and the fish pond stretched a majestic Old World garden, with bed after

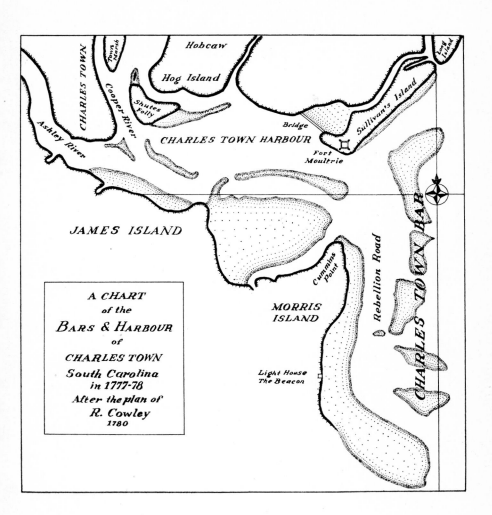

A CHART
of the
BARS & HARBOUR
of
CHARLES TOWN
South Carolina
in 1777-78
After the plan of
R. Cowley
1780

bed of plants sent from England. The long walk, passing through the garden to the house, split midway in the ascent to circle a bronze and artistically engraved sundial. Up a flight of brick steps the captain made his way to an open piazza, flagged with old tiles, and thence into the cool of a hall which ran through the center of the house to the main entrance way in the front. His host explained that Archdale Hall faced north, that the channel of the Ashley at the landing ran due east and west; so they had entered the estate from the south and through the rear.[20]

Of the meeting with Richard Bohun Baker, Sr., and his family there is no record. Nor is there even family tradition as to the romance which blossomed that day, of undetermined date in early 1777, when Nicholas Biddle first visited Archdale Hall. Only this we know; that the charming eldest daughter, Elizabeth Elliott Baker, who bore the maiden name of her dead mother, proved an attraction which brought the captain back again and again to the Baker home on the Ashley. Sometimes it was by the river; sometimes by the old Dorchester road, which passed by the front of Archdale Hall. Sometimes it was a visit of a few hours, sometimes for a weekend; and sometimes he escorted Elizabeth to a ball, or rout, or soiree, which featured the gay social season in Charlestown.

Whether it was love at first sight; whether there were other suitors to be reckoned with; whether the course of true love ran smoothly through the courtship; whether the wooing proved a long or short siege of the heart; these are matters of which nothing is known. It can only be deduced from subsequent events that they were engaged before the summer was done.[21]

No painter has consigned Elizabeth Elliott Baker to canvas. No family record has remained to tell whether she was tall or short; whether brunette or blonde; whether her eyes were blue, or brown, or gray, or even green; or of the tone of her voice, or the shape of her mouth, or aught of any of her physical attractions. One bit of testimony there is to her cultural attainments—an old receipt from a private tutor who, in 1773 and 1774, was paid liberally to teach her and her sister Mary.

French and Italian were included in their curriculum, along with
a quarter's course in writing legible and womanly hands. With
these fragments we must rest content, save for the definite fact
that Elizabeth was born on April 25, 1759; so she was at the
threshhold of her nineteenth year when Nicholas Biddle came
into her life.[22]

On June 8 the *Randolph,* with new foremast and mainmast
in place, fully rigged and completely overhauled, was brought
down from the shipyard into the harbor. Several days later,
in a typical Charlestown late-spring storm, a bolt of lightning
splintered the mainmast from cap to deck. The mast had to
be replaced, but fortunately Dorsius had had extra spars
shipped in at the time he ordered the first replacements. All
this took time, however, which Biddle tried to utilize in renewed
efforts to augment his crew.

Recruiting posters were printed offering a bounty of thirty
dollars—an advance upon prize money—to each able-bodied
seaman who would enlist. The bait failed. Privateering continued to lure the sailor, and the frigate's hands were constantly
enticed away.

"Several Capts. of Privateers have been detected in carrying
off my People," Biddle reported to the Marine Committee, "but
I can get no redress of them. From one I had taken four Men
in lieu of as many he had enticed & taken from me but the Civil
Power obliged me to give them up   I applied to the President
and he ordered the Capt to replace my Men or he would not
let him pass the Forts. The Capt. Sailed without giving me a
Man." [23]

Nor did the forts take any steps to stop that privateer. On
the other hand, the authorities did make every effort to keep
the state navy vessels from proselyting among the *Randolph*'s
hands. Witness the instructions issued to the captain of the brig
Notre Dame, which concluded, "Pray be . . . particularly
Carefull that you do not Enlist any men belonging to the Continental Frigate." [24]

Added to Biddle's troubles was the conduct of one of his

officers, the second lieutenant of marines, Panatiere de la Falconniere. That gentleman, you will recall, first conducted himself in a manner unbecoming an officer when he begged a jug of wine from a neutral French ship. Proceeding from that point, he had bottled the wine and peddled it to the people on board the frigate at a dollar a bottle. That he was no fit companion in the wardroom every officer could attest. He was blasphemous, obscene, and vindictive. On shore he was a constant problem to the captain, who heard continuous complaints against him of association with vagabonds and prostitutes, of drunken brawls in one of which he stabbed a soldier, but fortunately inflicted no serious wound, and of bullying and threatening any who questioned his authority.[25]

Amid these discouragements, Biddle's brother Charles arrived in Charlestown on a visit and afforded a welcome respite to worries. Charles Biddle we last encountered being cast into prison by Admiral Gayton in Jamaica. Eventually transferred, still a prisoner, to His Majesty's frigate *Antelope,* Charles's release from captivity could be traced directly to his younger brother. On board the *Antelope* was a lieutenant who had been a midshipman on the *Portland* in 1772 with Nicholas Biddle and "who had a great affection for him." Learning of the relationship, the lieutenant advised Charles to apply to the captain of the frigate for permission to go ashore at Port Royal, but to wait until said captain was in his cups. Then the lieutenant made sure the proper degree of intoxication had been attained before notifying Charles to make the application. The drunken captain gave consent and Charles, once ashore, soon contrived to ship in a vessel for the Continent. Undoubtedly, in relating this experience to his brother, the British lieutenant was identified. Unfortunately, however, in retelling it later the name was omitted, so his benefactor remains unknown.[26]

Through Charles came recent news from home. He had been in Reading visiting their mother, sister Lydia McFunn, and brother Edward. When he had left them on June 1 all were well save Edward, whose long illness had reached a critical stage. Accompanying Charles Biddle to Charlestown were two gentlemen who wanted to purchase goods for the northern markets. Charles, however, had but one motive, namely to see his brother, "who was very dear to me."

"I let nothing delay me," he explained. "Yesterday at Georgetown I was requested, as I speak a little French, to go talk to a Frenchman who had just arrived. But I've a mighty poor impression of the French officers who come over to enter the American service."

"So have I," remarked Nicholas feelingly, "if my second lieutenant of marines is any criterion."

"Well, anyhow," continued Charles, "I told those who asked me that the officer probably was only a barber or tailor, and I wasn't going to waste time on him." [27]

The French officer arrived in Charlestown a few days later. His name was Marie Jean Paul Joseph Roch Yves Gilbert du Motier, the Marquis de Lafayette! [28]

Charles Biddle's stay in Charlestown was about ten days, and one of these days included a visit to Archdale Hall, where he met Elizabeth Baker and quite approved of Nicholas' good taste. Toward the end of June the elder brother departed for Beaufort and, eventually, on to Philadelphia.[29]

By then the third mainmast had been stepped in place, and the rerigging of the *Randolph* had proceeded to a point where a few more days would see her ready for sea. When Charlestown, on July 4, put on a gala celebration on "the first anniversary of the glorious formation of the American empire," the frigate, no better manned than before but trim in appearance, rode at anchor in the harbor ready to contribute her part to the day's events.

"Ringing of bells ushered in the day," runs the old chronicle. "At sunrise American colors were displayed from all the forts and batteries, and vessels in the harbor."

Perhaps during that morning Elizabeth Baker came on board the *Randolph* to see the frigate decked with gay banners and with the Grand Union flag at the mizzen peak. And no doubt the captain escorted her to the parade where Colonel Pinckney's First South Carolina regiment passed splendidly in review before the president, the vice-president, and the members of the Privy Council. No doubt, too, Elizabeth covered her ears as the forts began firing discharge after discharge until seventy-six had been counted, "alluding to the glorious year 1776." Then the infantry and Captain Thomas Grimball's battery fired "three general volleys" and quite deafened all the ladies present.[30]

Not for the ladies, however, was the subsequent dinner in the council chamber, which his excellency, President Rutledge, tendered "all the members of the Legislature then in town, all the public officers, civil and military, the clergy and many strangers of note, to the amount of double the number that ever observed the birthday of the present misguided and unfortunate King of Great Britain." As one of the "public officers, military" Biddle attended the dinner and, being an abstemious man, drank in water the thirteen toasts which thundered across the banquet boards. Outside, "with admirable regularity," the two field pieces of Captain Grimball's battery punctuated each toast with thirteen guns. One of these toasts, mayhap, the Captain drank in wine. It was the fourth on the list: "The American Army and Navy—may they be victorious and invincible."

In honor of the ladies, the president had reserved the evening for illuminations, which "far exceeded any that had ever been exhibited before." Thus concluded a day "of the most conspicuous joy and harmony." [31] That day, also, the captain confided to Elizabeth, no doubt, that despairing of getting more hands he intended to sail within a week with those he had on board.

From his sea chest, on July 10, Biddle extracted the sealed packet he had received two months before. He smiled grimly at the opening sentence which remarked, "We expect you will be cruizing near the Island of Hispaniola, and that agreeable to our former orders you will have the Randolph Frigate in good order and every way fit for Action." As he read on, however, he realized that perhaps he was in a better position to act upon these new orders than if he had been at sea off Hispaniola as the Marine Committee had anticipated.

What was in contemplation was a bold stroke against the Jamaica sugar ships, which generally sailed from that island about July 26 of each year, under convoy for England. The course of this fleet was always through the Windward Passage between Cuba and Hispaniola and then northward through the Gulf of Florida.

"Our design is to intercept this Fleet, and take, sink, burn and destroy as many of them as possible," the instructions continued. "You are therefore to repair to the Island of Abacoa [sic] near New Providence which is the place we have appointed for the Rendezvous of such Ships & Cruizers as we may find it in our power to order on this service and you must make it a point to be there on or before the 25ᵗʰ July that being the day we shall fix for every Ship or Vessel being at Abacoa." [32]

Biddle sent for Dorsius and gave him the letter to read, as well as several pages of Marine Committee resolutions which contained detailed directions for the senior officer, who would command the fleet when once it had assembled off Abaco. Most elaborate these were, and seemingly anticipated assemblage of a number of the new Continental frigates.[33]

"Can we induce President Rutledge to offer a bounty to help us fill up the Randolph?" Biddle asked the agent.

Dorsius shrugged: "We can try, but I doubt it."

They called on the president that afternoon, and Rutledge regretfully declined. His grounds were, as Biddle pointed out to the Marine Committee, that "some of the State Armed Vessels being in Port nothing could be done by the State until they were manned." [34]

The captain's barge conveyed him out toward the *Randolph*. He had concluded it would be a better risk to try and get men from prizes at sea "than Lie here on an uncertainty at this Season so bad for the Worms." One of Charlestown's frequent summer squalls was sweeping in from the east, where beyond the bar thunder rolled and lightning flashed. Biddle boarded the frigate and summoned his officers.

"Bend sail," he told them. "Half manned though we are, we're going out."

Sheets of rain swept across the deck as he spoke. The storm broke sharply overhead. Darkness almost as of night closed in, punctuated by vivid streaks of lightning that split the clouds to bury themselves jaggedly in the water of the harbor or the marsh of the island of Shute's Folly. All save one, that is, of the brillant bolts; it, by some perverse chance, struck the mainmast of the *Randolph*. A blinding flash, a crash, and the mast was splintered as had been its two predecessors.[35]

Sick at heart, Biddle surveyed the wreck of his third mainmast, while the storm passed on and the sun shone brightly. There would be no rendezvous at Abaco for the frigate. If Dorsius could conjure one more mainmast it would still take another month to get the ship ready for sea. Had the captain but known the truth about the projected attack upon the Jamaica sugar fleet he might have felt a little better. Not a single Continental vessel was bound for Abaco. Absence of the *Randolph* meant absolutely nothing to the Marine Committee plan which while looking good on paper had proved entirely impracticable.[36]

Chapter XIII

The Second Cruise

WHILE JOHN DORSIUS BEGAN THE REPAIRS ON THE *Randolph,* and a new mainmast was floated down the Cooper River from Hobcaw, Nicholas Biddle approached President Rutledge upon a new tack. The captain had abandoned all idea of a rendezvous at Abaco. The frigate could not be in readiness to fulfill the Marine Committee order for a July 25 meeting with other Continental ships. Also, the Continental agent had "procured Shipping to make Remittances to Mr S. Ceronio at Cape Francois," so the necessity of a voyage to the West Indies no longer existed.[1] There remained, therefore, the obvious possibility of a cruise out of Charlestown. Such a cruise would recommend itself to the president if he could be shown how advantageous it would be to the trade of South Carolina. In turn, Rutledge might be induced to reconsider his refusal to offer a bounty for seamen.

The arguments in behalf of such a cruise were sound. His Majesty's twenty-gun ship *Perseus* had cruised within sight of Charlestown in the spring and "had taken so many Prizes off the Carolinas, that for want of Hands, she was obliged to carry them to the West Indies." [2] By now she, and possibly other frigates, were likely on the way to renew profitable picking among merchantmen entering or departing the harbor. The enemy could be driven off or destroyed by the *Randolph* if enough seamen could be signed on to give her a complement of about 250. But experience had shown that without help from the state, Biddle could not recruit an adequate crew.

"Your trade is very extensive when there are no interruptions from British cruisers," the captain pointed out. "Other states benefit as well. Therefore I propose to stay on this coast, between here and St. Augustine.[3] The Randolph will have her new mainmast in place any day now. If you will offer an additional bounty of twenty dollars, to add to the thirty I have already advertised, I believe we can man the frigate."

So favorably inclined was the president with the protection promised for the South Carolina trade, that he agreed to urge the bounty upon his Privy Council. While the state vessels were not fully manned, he could justify favoring the *Randolph* because she alone was powerful enough to cope with an enemy frigate. His recommendation, after some questioning, was accepted by the Council.[4]

Just the day before the *Randolph*'s fourth mainmast had been stepped into place, seamen on shipping in the harbor and loiterers on the parade stared agog. Tapering above the maintopgallant masthead was a slender iron rod. Men rubbed their eyes and looked again. Yes, there it was—a lightning conductor on the frigate! The good folk of Charlestown had long accepted the lightning rod as a needful contrivance to protect home and public building from electrical storms. But who had ever heard of its use at sea?[5]

Well, Biddle had, for one. There were probably others, too, who had tried it before, for more than twenty years had passed since Ben Franklin had advocated it in his *Poor Richard's Almanac* and had written: "Vessels, also, having a sharp pointed rod fixed on the top of their masts, with a wire from the foot of the rod reaching down, round one of the shrouds to the water, will not be hurt by lightning."[6] But to Charlestown it was new, and the novelty "excited much attention."[7]

Probably the captain escorted Elizabeth on board to explain it to her and point out the wire that ran from the conductor down one of the topgallant backstays to the bulwark and then dangled into the water of the harbor. Maybe he told her that the old adage of lightning never striking twice in the same place had been so thoroughly disproved that he had had to do something unusual to protect his fourth mainmast. Also, if he were romantically inclined that afternoon, he may have referred to the shattering of his masts as combining good with bad fortune.

He had been delayed in port in idleness, but how else could he have been able to spend so much time with such a charming companion?

If the captain had inclined to the poetic over the lightning rod on the *Randolph,* not so John Dorsius, who was of a practical turn of mind. He saw nothing but annoying delays in the frigate being "twice Struck" and was hopeful his troubles were over as "a Conductor is since fixed to the Mainmast." But Dorsius was happy to find that the *Randolph* weathered several local storms virtually without harm. He could report the frigate ready for sea in every department save one—that, as usual, was the crew.[8]

Fortunately, something was being done about that. Biddle had ordered him to have handbills printed and posted throughout the city telling of the bounty now being offered by the state. He had obliged promptly and, as seamen began to respond, he wrote to the Marine Committee that "they engaged for Thirty Dollars P Man Bounty   Ten Dollars P dº I agreed to Advance in part of Prize Money that may become due on the Cruize and Twenty Dollars Bounty offered by this State."

With a fifty-dollar bonus—one fifth payable in advance—the rendezvous began to do a better business than during previous efforts to drum up a crew. Several privateers returned from cruises in early August, and "a Number of Men entered out of them." This was an achievement indeed, for generally the shoe was on the other foot. The additional bounty, said Biddle, proved a help by which "I have got many Men." [9] Not enough to fill all requirements, but far better than hitherto. Also, there were reinforcements from an unexpected source. Among Biddle's many new friends were a number of gentlemen with seafaring experience, who were willing to volunteer and bring with them their sea-trained negro hands. Among them, and the only one identified by name, was John MacQueen, a prominent South Carolinian, who came aboard with several of his slaves.[10]

On August 16, after a farewell to Elizabeth and a final conference with Rutledge, the captain went down to the wharf, took boat out to the frigate, and "dropped down into Rebellion Road in order to embrace the first fair Wind & proceed on a

Cruize." While he waited, a number of vessels came in across the bar, favored by the very winds which held him in the roadstead. Three sloops and two brigs arrived on August 18 from St. Eustatius. Biddle recognized one of the brigs. She was the privateer *Fair American*, Charles Morgan master, who, some months before, had enticed a number of men from the *Randolph*.

"I had certain intelligence of his having four of my Men on Board," the captain said; "so I ordered Lieutenant Barnes in our barge to board him. He would not bring to."

Biddle would brook no such affront. He ordered a gun crew to one of the 6-pounders and sent a warning shot across the brig's bow. Morgan's disdain for the frigate ended precipitately. Sails came down on the run, and the vessel hove to while Barnes' boarding party climbed over the rail.

"It was a good thing he stopped," the captain remarked, "for if he had not I was determined to Sink him."

Presently the barge returned with two men who had been recognized as former seamen on the *Randolph*. Lieutenant Barnes made his report. He was able to apprehend the pair he had brought back, but the other two known to have shipped with Morgan had been sent off some days before in a prize.

After the *Fair American* had gotten into the harbor and her crew had been given liberty in Charlestown, one of Biddle's recruiting officers identified five of them as seamen who had deserted the frigate. He even induced them to accompany him to Rutledge and swear that Morgan had shipped them in full knowledge that they belonged to the *Randolph*.

"It is easy for those Fellows [such as Morgan] to act so as to make it difficult to prove they know of their being on Board until they Sailed," Biddle pointed out in a most involved sentence, "but this was not the case in this instance."

To have secured the five men, however, would have entailed a tedious law suit, and the captain was determined to permit no further delays.[11] Unfortunately, the wind continued contrary, pinning the *Randolph* in Rebellion Road through the balance of August. Biddle made the most of the opportunity to train his crew, exercising them at the great guns and drilling them for boarding. Each day in the Road made them more proficient and gave him greater confidence in them.[12] The same could not be said as to the *Randolph*. She was most unseaworthy, and it troubled him as he tested her. He knew the difficulty. There was nothing wrong with her construction, nor her masting. The truth was, "The Ship does not Sail well owing to Her being foul." About that he could do nothing without returning to Hobcaw; this was a step he could not have been induced to take.[13]

Before Biddle could get to sea the problem of the obstreperous lieutenant of marines, Panatiere de la Falconniere, arose to vex him. The other officers of the frigate had had their fill of the Frenchman. They wanted no more of him, so they filed a formal complaint with the captain setting forth that "he has in many instances behaved very unbecoming an officer and is a disgrace to the Randolph."

"As there is not Officers Sufficient to form a Court of inquiry," began the complaint, "we are sorry to be under the disagreeable necessity of addressing you." Then they arrayed the evidence in a series of damning charges. Here are the principal ones as Biddle read them there in the cabin that last day of August, 1777:

"He has suffered himself to be beat on shore without resenting it—

"He gave an Order for Eighty Pounds on Mr. [Edward] Blake, with intent to defraud the Person to whom he gave it—

"He allways when on shore Associates with the worst of Vagabonds, and those houses no Gentlemen ever go to—

"He was one Night put under the Town Guard for stabbing a Soldier; but shewing his Commission and the wound not like to prove Mortal, was let go—

"He is the most Obscene talker, and greatest Reprobate and blasphemer we ever heard—

"He has been heard to Damn the Trinity in the most shocking expression—

"He has frequently declared that if any Man affront him, he would Assasinate him for it if it was 20 Years afterwards."

There were a couple more charges listed, and the address concluded:

"For these and a Thousand more instances we could mention (if necessary) of the same Nature we think him not only unworthy of holding a Commission in the Randolph, but a Nuissance to the Ship, and therefore beg you to Rid us of him."

Captain Samuel Shaw was the amanuensis as well as a signator. First Lieutenant William Barnes likewise signed, as did John McDougall and Joshua Fanning, the second and third officers; Sailing Master Robert Johnson; and Surgeon Thomas Hore.[14]

The captain laid the address aside for the moment to sniff the changing air through the stern windows. The wind was shifting—the tide was in. He hastened to the quarter-deck where the pilot greeted him with a cheery promise to take the frigate over the bar that afternoon. The breeze increased, and with all sail set the *Randolph* stood eastward. Leadsmen at the bow cast their line, as the pilot with practiced eye directed the helmsman through the tricky channel. The water shallowed, deepened, shallowed again, and toward nightfall they were clear of the last shoal water.

Next morning, ere the pilot departed, Biddle composed a letter to the Marine Committee.

"I have the pleasure to acquaint you," he began, "that I have at last gone once more without the barr of Charles Town." He recited his troubles: the mainmast twice split by lightning, the raids on his crew by privateers, his various futile efforts to recruit seamen until the state came to his aid with an extra bonus, and his doubts as to the sailing qualities of the frigate. Then he picked up and reread the officers' complaints against the French lieutenant of marines, after which he again dipped his quill and penned a final paragraph.

"Lieut Falconier of Marines," he wrote, "is so exceeding Troublesome and had behaved in so many instances unworthy the Character of an Officer that I can not hesitate a moment to comply with the Request of the Officers which I inclose under cover to you and which contains the principle Charges against him. I have ordered him to proceed to Congress." [15]

The pilot boat waited alongside. Across the rail and down into it went Panatiere de la Falconniere, followed by the pilot.

With a stiff breeze blowing out of the west, the *Randolph* stood
to sea, and, as the small craft dropped astern, the officers of the
frigate caught their last glimpse of the detested lieutenant of
marines. Whether the Frenchman ever reported to either the
Marine Committee or Congress is a matter of doubt.[16]

Nicholas Biddle ordered the *Randolph*'s bow turned into the
southward in the afternoon of that first day of September, 1777.
Under a good press of sail the frigate moved through the water
at a rate which was none too pleasing to her commander. He
compared it with the speed she had demonstrated in the previous February under similar conditions as to wind and canvas
spread, and the comparison reflected adversely upon her present
performance. There was no doubt that her sailing qualities
were much impaired by the condition of her bottom. However,
most important, he was at sea and, given an opportunity, he
would demonstrate that foul though her condition might be
she could still render a good account of herself.

There had been expectations of encountering British cruisers
as she moved along off the coast, keeping within soundings until in the latitude of St. Augustine. No enemy appeared. In fact
no sail of any sort was sighted. Biddle concluded there would be
better picking further seaward in the path of the Jamaica trade
to New York. The weather during the two days spent running
southward had been balmy, but when the *Randolph* nosed eastward she quickly ran into squalls. If anything she made better
going in the rough seas than she had before, and toward nightfall on September 3 was a good twenty leagues east of St. Augustine.

Over the port bow at twilight, the masthead lookout sighted
a distant sail and promptly hailed the quarter-deck. A midshipman scurried aloft with a glass and soon reported five sails visible, all standing northward. Biddle ordered all lights doused,
and the frigate kept on a course toward the distant vessels,
which with darkness showed an occasional lanthorn.

Through the night the *Randolph* drew closer; so at dawn
the captain would be able to identify the quarry. The sails when
first sighted had been almost over the horizon and later, when

they had been brought closer, it had been too dark to determine their rig. He surmised they were a small group of merchantmen bound for New York or Newport, possibly under convoy of a sloop of war, or even of a frigate. He could be wrong, he remarked to Lieutenant Barnes, as they stood together peering through the false dawn, and he might be running into some two-deckers. In that event the frigate, despite her barnacles, would have to show a good pair of heels.[17]

All doubts were resolved on the morning of September 4. They were near enough to make out each vessel—two ships, two brigs, and a sloop. Biddle sent the crew to quarters, ordered the Grand Union hoisted, and bore down upon them. That they were British was apparent the moment they spied the frigate's ensign. Although the distance was great, one of the ships and the sloop opened fire, while the other ship and the two brigs mounted more sail in an effort to escape northward.

The *Randolph* closed in rapidly, the captain withholding his fire, although by now the enemy, within range, were plying their guns as fast as they could be loaded, run out, aimed, and discharged. The ship carried 6-pounders and the shot, which at first had peppered the sea between them, now began to whistle overhead. From the sloop also came a galling fire, although with lighter weapons.[18]

Captain Shaw was a tall and remarkably thin young man, and had always insisted that he was too skinny a target for an enemy cannon ball. On the quarter-deck that morning, while the gunfire increased, he turned to Biddle to joke anew about his immunity from danger, when a shot carried away a mizzen shroud at his back. He blinked, took one look at the dangling lines that had been so neatly severed, and concluded that perhaps his joke was not as funny as it had previously seemed.[19]

A few minutes later another shot crashed into the forecastle rail. Hurling splinters felled Midshipman John McPherson, severely wounding him in the groin and right leg. He was carried to the cockpit where Surgeon Hore applied tourniquets and with great skill saved the youngster's life as well as his limb.[20]

But still Biddle would not give the order to fire. He had sized

up the situation and had concluded he wanted all the vessels as
prizes, not just one. He knew that a single broadside from the
frigate would disable the ship. To fire that broadside, however,
he would have to yaw, and so lose precious time which might
mean the escape of the rest of the fleet. With the frigate rushing down upon the ship, he counted upon the enemy crew becoming panicky and failing to serve the guns effectively. Thus he
could chance some slight damage, but maintain his headway.
His surmise proved itself. When within pistol range he ordered
a single gun to be fired—one of the 6-pounders on the forecastle. That was sufficient. Scarcely had its reverberations ceased
when the enemy's colors came jerking down from the mast.[21]
As the *Randolph* drew abreast, Biddle hailed—

"Who are you?" he demanded.

"The True Briton, from Jamaica," came the answer.
"Thomas Venture, master."

A prize crew under Lieutenant Barnes was sent on board,
and the *Randolph,* with slight loss of way, kept on in pursuit of
the other ship and the two brigs, which had huddled together
as they fled. The sloop, however, had eased away toward the
southwest. Biddle let her go. As the weather continued squally,
he had to permit her to escape or lose the others. Ship and brigs
looked more valuable to him. All three hauled down their colors
simultaneously when the frigate began to overtake them.[22] They
proved a strange assortment.

The ship was the *Severn,* armed with eight 4-pounders, and
manned by a prize crew from the *True Briton.* She had sailed
from Jamaica under a Captain James Henderson in August,
laden with sugar, rum, ginger, and logwood, for London, but
had been taken by a North Carolina privateer, and a few days
later retaken by Captain Venture.

The larger brig was the *Charming Peggy,* Captain Philip
Lyon, which had sailed from Jamaica in company with the *True
Briton,* and was laden with 250 puncheons of rum for the British
army in New York.

The smaller brig was of French register—*L'Assumption,*
Andrew Laffont master. She had sailed from Martinique for
Charlestown with a cargo of salt, and had been captured by the

True Briton just a day or two before. Laffont and his crew, it was learned, were prisoners on the latter ship.[23]

Then Lieutenant Barnes came up with the *True Briton,* and Biddle discovered she was more valuable than any of the others. She was armed with twenty 6-pounders, and had a crew of seventy-four men. Her cargo, too, was rum for the British army —399 puncheons of it! [24]

It was a tremendous and rich haul, and the captain took every precaution to make sure that all four vessels would get in safely. Strong prize crews were placed on the *Severn* and *Charming Peggy,* and all navigators removed. Along with the officers from the *True Briton* came a number of disconsolate civilians who had taken passage in her from Jamaica. One was Charles Hamilton, Esquire, collector of Montego Bay, and identified as "a gentleman of a most amiable character." [25] Others were principally merchants of New York or Jamaica. Lieutenant McDougall took command of the *Severn,* and Midshipman Simeon Fanning, youngest brother of the *Randolph*'s third lieutenant, was sent prize master in the British brig.[26] Captain Laffont and his Frenchmen, released from the *True Briton,* manned their own brig.

With his first and second lieutenants in prizes along with sixty of his best men, Biddle had no alternative but to conclude the cruise and make for Charlestown, the *Randolph* acting as convoy for her prizes. The condition of the frigate's bottom also necessitated a prompt return so she could be graved. He was happy that he could show such success in so short a time. It rendered the early conclusion of the cruise more bearable.[27] He inquired regarding the sloop, which had escaped. She likewise had been laden with rum for the British army, but from the way she steered it was more likely that she would get into St. Augustine rather than New York. At any rate, there was nothing he could do about it.[28]

The captures had been made about thirty leagues southeast from Charlestown bar. The squally weather had ceased by evening, and the winds were propitious. Hence the *Randolph* and her covey of rum- and sugar-laden prizes reached the bar on Saturday morning, September 6. While awaiting pilots, Biddle graciously sent off his longboat, with John MacQueen as courier, to bear the good news to Charlestown.[29]

The tidings of Biddle's success, which MacQueen brought ashore late that Saturday afternoon, electrified Charlestown. Early Sunday morning there were reports that the *Randolph* and her prizes were already over the bar, and in Rebellion Road. Whether the sermons from the pulpits of St. Michael's, St. Philip's, and St. John's fell upon attentive ears that morning is doubtful. Certainly by afternoon the townsfolk were out in great numbers to greet the frigate as she ushered the two ships and two brigs through the harbor and into Cooper River.[30]

John Dorsius was one of the first to come aboard and extend his congratulations. He queried the captain as to the cargoes, and was informed they were principally rum and some sugar.

"I want you to libel in behalf of myself and the crew against both ships and the British brig," Biddle instructed him. "In the case of the True Briton, I intend to claim her entirely for the captors. But I will not lay claim for salvage of the French brig, as I am sure Congress will approve of me giving her up."

Dorsius looked puzzled.

"All right as to the Frenchie," he agreed, "but the True Briton is only a merchant ship."

"A merchant ship which acted like a cruiser," the captain replied. "This Captain Venture can produce no letter of marque commission, but he has taken a number of prizes since he left Jamaica. Morever, one of his passengers has informed me that before sailing he heard this same captain boast that he hoped to fall in with the Randolph off the Carolina coast. He's fortunate if we don't proceed against him for piracy."

"I'll tell you what I'll do," the agent said. "When the prizes are sold I'll pay you and your crew one half of the proceeds of the True Briton, and hold the other half until I can secure the opinion of Congress."

Whereupon Dorsius with his usual industry proceeded to file the libels in the Admiralty Court, inventory the cargoes, and arrange to have the *Randolph* hove down at the Hobcaw shipyard.[31] Until all this was done there was no occasion to advise the Marine Committee, so Biddle deferred his official report for a few days. We surmise some of those days were spent at Archdale Hall.

By September 12 the Continental agent was ready; so both he and the captain wrote that day, and sent the letters off by express. Biddle wasted few words on the late cruise, aside from naming the prizes and referring the Marine Committee to Dorsius for details as to their cargoes. Getting the frigate ready for another cruise was his primary interest.

"The Randolphs Bottom is very foul," he advised, "having lain in this Port the three worst Months in the Year since we Cleaned—And being apprehensive that the Worms will Ruin Her Bottom unless they are soon destroyed, I have thought Proper and am preparing to heave Her down."

He would be as expeditious as possible, he added, and hoped to be ready to execute any orders he might be sent by the return of the express. He concluded in the way that could be expected of him.

"I cannot omit telling You that My Officers have on every occasion given Me the greatest satisfaction," he said. "Two better Officers are not in the Service than Barnes and Mcdougall My first and second Leuts: And the Men I took from here behaved exceeding well." [32]

His praise was not confined to this letter. To friends in the north he wrote about his crew, singling out individuals whose relatives could take pride in them. One he mentioned specifically was Midshipman Mordecai Matlack, son of the secretary of the Pennsylvania Council of Safety. The lad, he said, "was much respected for his good behaviour." [33] Throughout Charlestown, at every telling of the cruise, he spoke of his satisfaction with all hands. Dorsius in his letter to Congress disclosed that "Capt Biddle says the Officers & People behaved well, when he engaged the True Briton." The agent was impressed more, however, by the value of the captures and the reward which would result to the captors.

". . . the Cargoes on b^d the three Prizes as far as has yet come to my knowledge," he wrote, "Consists of 702 Hhds

Rum, 215 Hhds & 74 Tierces Sugar, 7 hhds Coffee, 50 bags Ginger, 1 Tierce old Madeira and 11 Tons Logwood. Vessells & Cargoes are libelled & as soon as Condemned I shall make a Sale of them at Publick Vendue to the best advantage. I cant tell with any degree of Certainty what the Sales may Amount to, but judge it will be upwards of Sixty thousand Pounds Stg."

In concurring with Biddle that the frigate "is foul & must be hove down," he felt this would not detain her in port more than a month. Then with magnificent optimism he added:

"The Express I send by this will Return with all possible dispatch which may be in time to Receive the Instructions by Respecting the destination of the Randolph in her next Cruize." [34]

At Hobcaw, meanwhile, the *Randolph* had been stripped and her guns lifted out and deposited on shore by means of the main yard rigged as a derrick. One of the late passengers of the *True Briton,* who reached New York several months afterwards, insisted that the frigate had overset at Hobcaw, that "she lay full of mud the fifth of October, and there was little hopes of her floating again."

The report was half true. The *Randolph* had indeed capsized, but the accident was not as serious as the Britisher believed. Biddle told his brother James about it later.

"I have had a very narrow escape from a Fever that laid Violent hands on me soon after I came in to Port," he said. "And to Comfort Me in My distress the Randolph was Sunk in Careening and lay under water two Weeks before they could get Her up. I need not tell you that I felt much more concern on account of the Ship than for My own Safety." [35].

Condemnation of the prizes had been prompt and, as the sale of the prize goods began, it was realized that the single cruise would make comparatively wealthy men of every member of the crew.

"We have had hard fortune the first cruize," young Simeon Fanning wrote his mother and sisters on October 8, "but we have had better success the *last*. We were but six days out until we came across a fleet from Jamaica & took 2 ships . . . & 2 Brigs, which were richly laden with rum & sugar. I came in

Master of one of the Brigs— The ships and cargoes amounting to 90,000 £ Sterling."

He had hopes of being home during the winter, but was going to stay right in Charlestown for the prize money. Maybe then he would purchase a small vessel to sail north in. He was pretty confident his own share, as a midshipman, would be equal to about £1,000 sterling.[36]

Assuming Fanning's estimate of £90,000 was approximately correct, Biddle, who was entitled to one tenth of the whole, would net £9,000. Whether Fanning figured the whole or only half of the net proceeds of the *True Briton* in his total is not apparent. At any rate, when sales were completed toward the end of October and distribution made, the greater part of the money was expended in Charlestown. The captain and his officers invested largely in the securities of South Carolina. Lieutenant Joshua Fanning, for example, loaned the state £6,000 and received a certificate of indebtedness in return.[37]

Not so the seamen! These improvident gentry squandered their portions in all kinds of foolery, some of the particulars of which were long recalled in the city. A number of them paraded the streets, splendidly dressed, "with females ridiculously ornamented with jewelry." Others made dresses with large sheets of Continental paper money and hired carriages at any price, to take an airing like gentlemen. The prize story of all was told about one sailor who bought a horse to take a land cruise.

"The horse ran away with him," the chronicler recorded, "when Jack carried too much sail. Being owner as well as commander of the new craft, Jack concluded to go better found with ground tackle in his next cruise. He accordingly took on board a kedge anchor, secured the cable around the horse's neck as to the bow of his ship, and made sail, as before. The horse again ran away, and Jack soon brought him too, all standing, by casting anchor. The horse broke his neck in the fall, when Jack cooly took off the saddle, bridle, &c. and returned into port, saying that he had been cast away on a lee shore, and had lost his ship, but saved all the rigging." [38]

All this provided plenty of amusement for the residents of Charlestown and plenty of profit for the merchants of the city.

To Biddle, however, it brought assurance that when the time came for a new cruise, there would be no difficulty in manning the *Randolph*. After that brief September foray into the Atlantic, the frigate had suddenly gained the name of a lucky ship.[39]

Chapter XIV

Crusade

NEWS OF DISASTER IN THE NORTH REACHED CHARLES-town late in October, British frigates reappearing off the bar about the same time.[1] An express between Pennsylvania and South Carolina normally required about twenty days; the regular post at least a month.[2] Hence enemy warships, released after convoying Howe's transports safely up Chesapeake Bay to the Head of Elk, could arrive on the southern coast as quickly as the news of Brandywine, the capture of Philadelphia, and the battle in Germantown could travel overland. Nicholas Biddle, hearing the ill tidings, was glad his mother had gone to live with Edward Biddle's family in Reading and was safely away from the occupied city on the Delaware.[3]

Of more significance to Charlestonians, and the captain had almost begun to regard himself as one, was the renewal of the blockade. When the *Perseus* had preyed on shipping in the spring it had been bad enough, but now the enemy cruisers were more numerous. Their advent was most ill-timed from the viewpoint of President Rutledge and the Privy Council. Outward-bound shipping, chiefly for Europe, was ready to clear in large numbers. Quite a few ships were soon due from France with military supplies and clothing chiefly, on order by the government of South Carolina. There was little chance of any vessels getting into or out of port with the area beyond the bar patrolled by fast-sailing British frigates. Charlestown was easy to bottle up because of that selfsame bar which, while it kept the enemy out, delayed heavy-laden merchantmen who, entering or departing, had to wait for pilots or sometimes for a flood tide.[4]

To drive away the blockaders was a task beyond the so-called South Carolina navy, which in November, 1777, consisted of two small brigs, a schooner, a sloop, and several pilot boats.[5] Small wonder then that President Rutledge began to place his hopes in the frigate *Randolph*. Thoroughly graved, she was now being rerigged at Hobcaw. Both he and Biddle were pressing John Dorsius for speed; the Continental agent was doing his best. Not that Biddle had any vainglorious idea of going out singlehanded to tackle several British frigates. Always his orders had warned him against that. But weather conditions would not always permit the enemy ships to cruise together. Could he catch them apart, he had confidence in his ability to take or sink them, one at a time.[6]

Not until mid-November were the hostile craft identified as the frigates *Carysfort* and *Lizard*, of twenty-eight guns each; the *Perseus*, of twenty; and the brig *Hinchinbrook*, of six. We now know a lot more about them than Charlestown knew then. The three ships had been ordered south from the Chesapeake by Lord Howe to cruise off the South Carolina coast between Cape Romain and Port Royal Sound and intercept all shipping bound into or out of Charlestown. The *Hinchinbrook* was to join them from St. Augustine, where all four vessels were to send their prizes. However, as the *Hinchinbrook*'s masts were "too bad for her to keep at Sea," Captain Robert Fanshawe, of the *Carysfort*, senior officer on the station, employed her principally to bring fresh water from St. Augustine to the cruising frigates. Fanshawe was a determined soul, who, from prisoners taken, learned that Charlestown harbored "a Fleet of French and American shipping·laden and designed for different foreign ports in Europe," and who concentrated upon seeing they did not get to sea. By the end of November he had throttled the trade of the port until the wharves along Cooper River, and the anchorages below Shute's Folly were clogged with vessels laden with spoiling cargoes of rice, indigo, and tobacco.[7]

Meanwhile at Hobcaw the finishing touches were placed on the *Randolph* and Biddle ordered Lieutenant Barnes to bring her down into the harbor. Lieutenants McDougall and Fanning were placed in charge of enrolling a crew; it became apparent at once that seamen would quickly respond in sufficient numbers.

"The Randolph is rigged, with Her Guns & most of Her Stores on board," Biddle wrote to Robert Morris on November 23, "I have Recruiting Parties out and a Prospect of getting from Here in two or three weeks." [8]

Augmenting the effort to beat up a crew, the captain resorted to the *Gazette* and advertised for certain petty officers.

"WANTED immediately on board the Frigate *Randolph*," read one of these appeals, "two young gentlemen who can fill the office of Surgeon's Mate: Such, by making application on board said ship, will meet with proper encouragement."

Ever since his arrival in Charlestown in March, he had looked in vain for letters from his mother, his sisters, or his brother James. He poignantly expressed his yearning for word from them in a letter to the last-named begun on November 22.

"If you could form any Idea," he wrote, "of the unhappiness I feel at not hearing a single line from home [however, Charles had visited him] during the Many months that I have staid here You will I am sure favour me with one.

"If an express or Gentleman comes in from Pennsylvania My friends here tell me they hope all my Friends at home are well. And I am sick of Repeating that I do not get a line from any one there, They Naturally conclude I am a Person very little Esteemed or some one or other would surely take notice of me—These considerations together with an ardent desire I have of doing My duty made me on the first of Sep^t when the Pilot wished Me joy on being safe over the Bar of Charles Town burst into tears and cry God Bless You, Altho we struck twice in going over and (as I have since found) knocked off 11½ feet of the false keel."

The letter was not concluded for several days, and then at last the captain could acknowledge receipt of word from home. "Since I wrote the foregoing," he penned as a postscript, "I have Received a letter from You by Major [Pierce] Butler. It is the only one from any of the Family Since I left you." [9]

By December the frigate's complement was filled. Her roster showed more than 250 officers and men on board, a clear indication that the success of the September cruise had provided the needed spur. Under the lieutenants the men were being trained intensively with particular emphasis upon handling the great guns.

Biddle was ashore most of the time, spending his spare moments with Elizabeth Baker, but principally engaged in arranging necessary indents through John Dorsius and being supplied by Rutledge with latest intelligence about the enemy. The current advice placed all four of the blockaders cruising in concert off the bar. A large ship from Boston had been taken on December 8, and on the two subsequent days they had chased so close in shore that observers were sure there were pilots on board with intimate knowledge of the coast.[10]

In conference with Rutledge on the afternoon of December 11, the captain expressed his desire for action, remarking that he might not await Marine Committee instructions.

"My objective is to get to sea undetected," he explained; "so I expect to drop down into Rebellion Road and go out the first dark night that wind and tide are favorable."

"And then?" asked Rutledge.

"Then I propose to cruise along the coast," the captain continued, "keeping clear of the enemy as long as the frigates are in company. The Randolph is fleet, sir, and I'll defy them to catch me. Once they separate, I can deal with either of the twenty-eight-gun frigates, or the Perseus and Hinchinbrook together."

The president sprung his surprise—a plan that had been forming in his mind as the enemy menace to trade had developed. Said Rutledge:

"If the state of South Carolina engage two of the letter of marque ships now in port, say the Volunteer and General Moultrie, and add the state brig Notre Dame, will you accept the command of the armament, and proceed to clear the coast of the enemy ships of war?"

Before Biddle could reply, he continued eagerly: "All these vessels are ready for sea, Captain, but need crews. I have the assurance that private citizens will augment any bounty the State may grant, and that we can man them before the end of the year. In addition, the Privy Council will authorize detachments of the continental regiments to serve on board as marines." [11]

The captain considered. Because of the infrequency and uncertainty of the post, he had little hope of receiving orders from the Marine Committee for a long time. Yet if he pledged himself to Rutledge's proposal and contrary instructions arrived he would be in a quandary. The armament contemplated would be ample to deal effectively with the enemy cruisers, and the necessity of opening the port was self-evident. He weighed the matter carefully, and made his fateful decision.

"I will accept the command, Mr. President," he said, "and my sole request is that, if ever it becomes necessary, you justify me in the eyes of Congress." [12]

Rutledge convened the Privy Council on the morning of December 12, acquainted it with his plan for an armament, and informed it of Biddle's agreement to take command. The owners of the *Volunteer* and *General Moultrie* attended and agreed (perforce they could do no less) to place their ships at the service of the state on terms to be decided upon after each had been valued. Immediate instructions were sent to Edward Blake, first commissioner of the navy, advising him "That the Ships Volunteer & Gen¹ Moultrie are Engaged for, and it is intended to Order the Notre Dame on a Cruize." Blake was desired to "have those Vessels equipp'd with the utmost Expedition, & furnished with such articles as may be necessary for this Cruize, and that you will appoint a proper Person to value the Volunteer and Gen¹ Moultrie." [13]

The Privy Council resolved the same day to offer a bounty of ten dollars and monthly pay of twenty-one pounds to seamen entering on board any of the three vessels. This information, too, was conveyed to the navy board, after which the council's attention was directed to Rutledge's promise of marine detachments from the Continental regiments. [14] But here the council could only request, not demand. The troops were not under the authority of the state. The president, therefore, appealed directly to Major General Robert Howe, commanding all Continental forces in the Southern Department.

"The trade of this port being likely to suffer great injury from the vessels of war which have for some days past been in sight of the town," Rutledge set forth. "In order to clear the coast and protect the trade, Capt. Biddle has agreed to go on a cruize with the Randolph and several other vessels, engaged by the state, to be put under his command, but it being thought expedient that a number of marines should be embarked in the vessels, the council have advised, that you should be desired to order as many of the continental troops under your command as Capt. Biddle may apprehend to be necessary for this service, to be detached upon it. As I do agree in opinion with the Council, I do, therefore, and in pursuance of their advice, request that you will be pleased to give the necessary orders for this purpose." [15]

Howe instructed Brigadier General Moultrie to call a council of war the next day to determine whether detachments from the Continental troops could with propriety be sent upon the proposed expedition; if they could, what numbers could be spared; how long it would be prudent for them to be absent, and how many officers should accompany them.[16] The council of war listened, debated, and, while seeing no impropriety in sending the detachment requested, questioned how advisable it was. The reason was expressed tersely. The council was of opinion "that we have not men enough to defend the state should it be properly attacked." [17]

The findings were forwarded, Moultrie adding his endorsement approving the council of war's opinion. Back from Major General Howe came a prompt request that the officers reconsider, as he was "certain the military would be highly censured for not complying with the requisition of the Governor and Council." [18]

So the council was reconvened, but the officers stood to their guns.[19] They could not alter their former opinion, they pointed out, and they "would be unworthy of the commissions they hold if they could be induced by the dread of censure, or any other motives, to give an opinion contrary to their honor and conscience." Having thus salved both, they concluded by declaring "in the strongest terms, that they are ready and willing to obey orders." [20]

With this latest pronouncement, General Moultrie waited in person upon Rutledge and Biddle. The president listened impatiently and expressed his displeasure.

"The state questions the decision of the military in thwarting the armament we propose," he said coldly. "There are a number of vessels expected in every day, with military stores and other articles. All of these we are very much in want of. Unless the men-of-war are driven from our coast, these needed supplies cannot possibly get in. Moreover, General Moultrie, may I suggest that our vessels, by taking a short cruise, should be enabled to pick up a prize or two of some English ships outward bound to the West Indies, loaded with such stores as we want."

"How many men would be required?" Moultrie asked, purposely ignoring the president's anger.

Rutledge turned to Biddle for the answer.

"About 150 at the most," the captain explained. "A full company for the Randolph, and the remainder divided among the other vessels."

A good soldier, Moultrie was also somewhat of a diplomat. He sensed that if he persisted in a refusal, "the state might take it upon themselves," which would produce a clash between civil and military authority. That was certainly to be avoided. So, as the number of men requested was not large, he agreed to recommend to Major General Howe to grant the detachment.[21] The latter was in accord with Moultrie's change of mind, when the brigadier placed the matter again before him.

"The importance of protecting the trade of your state," he wrote sententiously (Howe being a North Carolinian), "from which almost all America, at present, derive their supplies, joined to the earnest request of the executive authority of the state, which I, as a citizen, ought ever to respect, and when possible, attend to, induces me to consent to furnish the 150 men desired by his excellency the president." [22]

By contrast with the hesitation of the military, the naval authorities moved spiritedly to carry out the Privy Council's desires. The first commissioner convened the navy board in extra meeting on the morning of December 13. A suitable person was selected to value the *Volunteer* and *General Moultrie,* and orders went forth promptly to Captain William Hall, of the brig *Notre Dame.* He should "Immediately Open a House of Rendezvous, under the direction of a proper Officer, to Enlist a Sufficient Number of Men (your Complement Eighty)." [23]

Meeting again on Monday morning, December 15, the commissioners received the valuations of the two ships. Instructions were issued to both Captain Philip Sullivan, of the *Volunteer,* and Captain Jacob Johnston, of the *General Moultrie,* to start recruiting, 120 men being specified as the size of each crew. Rutledge was informed of the progress, along with a request to furnish both captains with commissions as they might otherwise not "think themselves under the Direction of the Commissioners." [24]

That same day, to spur the recruiting, the Charlestown Insurance Company "at an Extraordinary Meeting" agreed to allow a bounty of ten dollars for each able seaman, up to three hundred, "who shall Enter in the Service of this State." [25] This bonus, along with the extra ten dollars already offered by the state, would have seemed sufficient to enroll all the hands necessary. Taking no chances, however, the Privy Council, on December 17, ordered an embargo on the port to be continued "until the Marine Expedition now fitting Out by the State be Ended, and the Cruise finished." [26]

Letters-of-marque commissions were ordered for Sullivan and Johnston that day, and the Privy Council resolved to add two more vessels to the armament—the brig *Fair American,* Captain Charles Morgan, with whom Biddle had had his unpleasant encounter in late August, and the brig *Polly,* Captain Hezekiah Anthony.[27] Both commanders were ordered to open rendezvous, Morgan to enroll eighty men, and Anthony ninety.[28]

By then the Privy Council had agreed to terms with all owners of the requisitioned vessels, namely, "that the Owners will equip them for a Cruise in the Public Service as long as may be

deemed necessary, The Public paying the running expence of the
Ship and such loss or damage as they may Sustain whilst in this
Service, the Public to Compleat the necessary number of Men
to Man them." [29]

As a final incentive to recruiting, the council, on December
20, added ten more dollars bounty, making the total bonus
thirty dollars, and the commissioners ordered one hundred
handbills printed and immediately distributed, thus:

Gentlemen Volunteers

Who are willing to Enter on Board the following Vessels in the Service
of this State now fitting upon an Expedition against the Enemies of
America, Shall be Entitled to a Bounty of Thirty Dollars P Man, and
such as are Inclined to serve the State for Six Months, Ten pounds more
and Twenty One pounds P Month wages upon applying to the Officers
at the Rendezvous—

Ship Volunteer of 20 Guns
Ship Gen Moultrie of 20 Guns—
Brigg Notre Dame of 16 Guns
Brigg Fair American 16 Guns
Brigg Polly . . . . 14 Guns [30]

Three days later, Captain Thomas Venture, late of the *True
Briton,* and six companions, broke out of Charlestown jail,
seized a small sailboat and made a successful escape to the British frigates.[31] Captain Fanshawe, of the *Carysfort,* on December 20, had "observed the Randolph Congress Frigate drop
down from Charles Town and join a large French Ship and a
Polacre in Rebellion Road." Now from Venture he had a definite account of the formation of "as great Naval Force" as the
port could provide, and of the embargo on shipping. The news
caused him to redouble his vigilance "to prevent the Fleet
getting out, or supplies going to them." He surmised that the
embargo indicated a want of seamen and refrained from making an overture he had contemplated for an exchange of prisoners.[32]

Actually, the departure of the *Randolph* from her berth off
Charlestown to an anchorage in Rebellion Road was with no
thought of an early sailing. Biddle had sent her there under
Lieutenant Barnes to avoid desertions, provide better room for

maneuvering and training, and prevent his own men from becoming dissatisfied through learning of the large bounties being
offered to man the state ships.

The captain himself continued on shore, counseling with
Rutledge, Vice-President Drayton, and First Commissioner
Blake, and conferring with the officers who would be under him
in command of the two ships and three brigs. It gave him an
opportunity to observe their respective abilities and compare
notes thereon with the state authorities.

On the day after Christmas the captains attended the navy
board, where Commissioner Blake urged them to expedite their
recruiting efforts and handed each a copy of Congressional resolves "Respecting the Provisions made for such persons, or
their Families as may be Killed or Maimed in the Sea or Land
Service of this State." [33] That night Captain Johnston resigned
command of the *General Moultrie*.[34]

Biddle's and Dorsius' letters of September 12 were read in
Congress at York, where the Continental Fathers had settled
down after being dispossessed of Philadelphia, on Friday,
October 3.[35] The journal for that day indicates no action upon
them, so it can be presumed they were turned over to the Marine
Committee. That body had dwindled to five members, all busily
engaged in many other activities, and, if the Committee's letter
book is any criterion, it issued no instructions or communications of any sort to anybody for a period of three weeks after
the receipt of the letters from Charlestown.[36]

Naval policy, however, had crystallized in Congress with the
growth of British sea power in American waters. It was expressed by the Committee of Foreign Affairs on October 6 in
a letter to the American Commissioners in Paris: "The marine
force of the enemy is so considerable in these seas, and so over-
proportionate to our infant navy, that it seems quite necessary
and wise to send our ships to distress the commerce of our
enemies in other parts of the world. For this purpose the marine
committee has already ordered some vessels to France under
your direction as to their future operations and more we expect
will be sent." [37]

Further instructions to Biddle were finally drafted by the

Marine Committee on October 24. As quickly as he could provide for the voyage he was to sail from Charlestown for France where his future procedure would be determined by the American Commissioners.

"For this purpose you are immediately on your arrival," the Marine Committee directed, "to send a trusty officer to acquaint the Commissioners of your arrival, and to receive their directions. Until you receive their answer it is left to your discretion and the intelligence you may collect of the enemies Cruizers whether to remain at your Port of arrival, or make a short Cruize, and repair for the reception of their answer to any other port."

After pointing out how he should replenish supplies for the *Randolph,* the committee advised him upon his conduct abroad.

"We would have you make as little shew as possible of being a Ship of Force, when you arrive, and during your stay in any Port of France," it cautioned, "and let your stay in Port be as short as possible. It is not necessary to direct a person of your discretion to be very cautious of communicating to any person, either in America or in France, what is your destination or what your orders."

There was a little more, regarding such goods as John Dorsius might wish to send abroad. The committee concluded its last orders for Nicholas Biddle with "Wishing you health & success We are Sir Yr. Friends & hble servants." [38]

Just when the letter went off for South Carolina is not evident. It may have been transmitted by Charles Biddle, who left Reading toward the end of October on a visit to Charlestown and would have passed through York on the way.[39] Or it may have been carried by Thomas Heyward, one of the South Carolina delegates, who secured leave of absence about that time to convey his family back south.[40] At any rate it could not have been received by Nicholas Biddle until some time after he had been irrevocably committed to the command of John Rutledge's naval armament. In the absence of any existing reference to it on the part of the captain, or his brother, or the South Carolina authorities, there are even possibilities it was never sent or had miscarried.

This latter contingent is borne out by Biddle's letter of November 23 to Robert Morris, previously referred to. On that day he stated specifically: "I have not Received any instructions from the Honble the Marine Committee since My cruise altho the Board of Commerce writes Mr. Dorsius word, that letters have been sent to me." [41]

Charles Biddle reached Charlestown on Friday, December 26, too late to spend Christmas with Nicholas. As we would assume the captain enjoyed a typical Southern holiday at Archdale Hall in the companionship of Elizabeth Baker, he probably was just as well satisfied to have the elder brother arrive a day late.

"When I arrived in Charlestown," wrote Charles Biddle later, "they were fitting out some vessels that were to sail with the Randolph to attack two frigates off the Bar. The day after my arrival, Mr. Drayton sent me a note informing me he had authority to offer me the command of a ship. . . . I returned him my thanks, and accepted the command." [42]

The ship was the *General Moultrie,* from which Captain Johnston had resigned two days before; Charles went on board the following Monday. As the fleet was reported ready to sail shortly, he expected to find his new command fully manned and outfitted. To his disappointment he discovered on board no more than fifty men, officers included, "and few of these seamen." While she was partly provisioned and had most of her warlike stores, he learned that her cartridge supply was low.[43] Before the day was done he sought out his brother to acquaint him with the true situation in the ship.

It was no news to Nicholas.[44] At the last minute it had been found that the matter of making and filling an adequate number of six-, four-, and three-pound cartridges for the state vessels had been miscalculated. The services of Captain Grimball's artillerymen were secured, and they were put to work producing 800 six-pound, 1,200 four-pound, and 200 three-pound cartridges.

"There are other delays as well," the captain said a bit gloomily. "The brig Polly needs more ballast. The Notre Dame is deficient in her supply of peas and rice. Then just today Mr.

Blake told me there is a shortage of 300 barrels of pork and fifty barrels of beef, which must be supplied before we can sail." [45]

"What would you advise?" Charles asked him. "I'd far rather go with you as a volunteer than become involved with the General Moultrie under present conditions."

"I would rather have you on board with me," the captain said, "and it is not too late to tender your resignation to Mr. Drayton."

Upon that advice Charles Biddle acted on January 6, 1778. To the vice-president of the Privy Council, officiating during Rutledge's absence upstate, he wrote a courteous note. Manned and fitted as the *General Moultrie* was, he felt he "could not acquire honor to my country or myself" in going out in command of her. Therefore, he would prefer serving with his brother as a volunteer and felt sure a suitable officer could be found to replace him on the state ship. [46]

"Capt Biddle has resigned the Command of the Ship Genl Moultrie," the clerk of the Privy Council informed the first commissioner of the navy board the following morning, adding that Mr. Blake was instructed "to appoint a proper person to Succeed to the Command of her." [47]

No successor was appointed. Captain Philip Sullivan of the *Volunteer,* who had found his ship also woefully undermanned and illy equipped, came forward with a proposal that solved the problem. The *General Moultrie,* he told the commissioners, was "a Much fitter Vessel for the present Intended Expedition than the Ship Volunteer," and could be "got ready for Sea Sooner." [48] As by then the commissioners had concluded it "impracticable that Men can be Obtained sufficient to Compleat the Complement for the Three Briggs & the Two Ships," they concurred, on January 8, and so recommended to the Privy Council. Next day the *Volunteer* was released to her owners, and Sullivan, with what hands he had recruited, was transferred to the *General Moultrie.* [49]

Biddle and Dorsius were seated in the latter's office on the afternoon of January 11, when a visitor was announced. There entered John Trevett, whom the captain had last seen when he sent him off from the *Andrew Doria,* in August, 1776, as prize master of the brigantine *Lawrence.* Biddle rose to greet his former lieutenant of marines in hearty fashion. He introduced Dorsius, and then asked what wind of fortune had blown John Trevett into Charlestown. The story was unfolded. For the past six months Trevett had been serving as lieutenant of marines on the sloop *Providence,* John Peck Rathbun commander. The captain would remember Rathbun, who had been a lieutenant on the *Providence* during the New Providence expedition.

"Certainly," Biddle agreed, "and I believe he was first lieutenant under Jones on the Alfred last fall, was he not?"

"That's right," said Trevett. "Congress commissioned him a captain in April and gave him the Providence. He's a Rhode Islander, like I am, and a good officer."

"And where is the sloop now?" Biddle asked.

"At Georgetown, having been chased in two days ago," Trevett continued. "We left New Bedford on a cruise, and a few days out sprung our bowsprit. So we stood to the southwest, intending for South Carolina. But when we ran in for Charlestown bar it was night time and we saw no pilot boat. So we lay off to await daylight, and a British privateer mistook us for a coasting sloop. We took her, but a couple of frigates gave us chase, and drove us so far to the eastward that we stood for Georgetown. The enemy prisoners were lodged in jail there, all but the captain. I escorted him down here, and delivered him to the Commissary of Prisoners this afternoon."

"You're the man I want," said Biddle. "I'm short a marine officer, and we're about to sail on an expedition where I need officers I can count upon."

"I've heard all about the armament, Captain Biddle," Trevett replied, "and I'd like to join you. But I'm pledged to Captain Rathbun. The sloop is getting in water and provisions at Georgetown right now, before we go take New Providence."

"Before you what?" exploded both auditors simultaneously.

"Take New Providence," repeated Trevett, as though it were the most casual of occurrences. "And we'd like to borrow a few of the Randolph's marines if you can spare them."

"Are you serious?" Dorsius inquired.

Trevett affirmed that he was dead serious and explained why. A merchant captain had lately arrived at Georgetown from New Providence and had informed Rathbun that a rich ship from Jamaica had put into Nassau in distress, and that she would be some time repairing.

"That ship is the same one we had a smart engagement with south of Sandy Hook some six months ago," he continued. "She killed our sailing master that day. So we think the time for retaliation has come, and we've a notion to kill two birds with one stone."

"What does Captain Rathbun propose?" asked Biddle.

"Go and take Fort Nassau first," was the explanation. "Then we shall have command of the town and harbor, and take what we please."

" 'Tis a bold, but most foolhardy plan," the captain commented. "Considering the odds against you, Mr. Trevett, it's downright presumptious. Do you remember what happened to you and Lieutenant McDougall on the Scotch transport, when you were greatly outnumbered?"

"I remember it well enough, Captain, but you will also remember the prisoners were safely landed in Virginia."

"I wish I could persuade your commander," Biddle continued, "to release you to go with me even if he will not relinquish his scheme."

"He's at the Coffee House, right now—came down from Georgetown with me," Trevett replied. "If he'll consent I'm willing to join you on the Randolph."

Whereupon Biddle and Trevett left John Dorsius and strode off to the coffee house, where after greetings and an exchange of pleasantries the captain came to the point.

"Mr. Trevett has been telling me of your proposal to take New Providence, Captain Rathbun. I presume you cannot be dissuaded?"

"No, Captain Biddle, my plans are well laid," Rathbun answered.

"Then may I borrow Lieutenant Trevett?" Biddle asked. "I need another lieutenant of marines, and Mr. Trevett has consented to accompany me if you will release him."

"I'm exceedingly sorry, Captain, but I have made an agreement with Mr. Trevett," was Rathbun's response, "and I will not give him up."

That put a finish to the conversation. Biddle arose, made his compliments to his fellow captain, and extended his hand to John Trevett.

"I am very sorry," he said simply, "for I shall never see you more."

He passed out into the darkness of a January twilight, and Rathbun and Trevett left next morning for Georgetown.[50]

Was it fears for Trevett's safety, or a premonition of his own fate, which provoked Nicholas Biddle's closing remark, "I shall never see you more"? He may have thought the lieutenant would not return from the attack on New Providence. On the other hand, his action the day afterwards has a different implication, for on January 12, 1778, he made his last will and testament.[51]

The expedition seemed upon the point of sailing. As a result of his cruises in the *Andrew Doria* and particularly the last brief one in the *Randolph,* he had amassed a modest fortune in prize money.[52] It was logical to provide against the "uncertainty of this transitory life," as sailors' wills so frequently stated. But there had been other times when he had sailed forth into danger and had made no such provisions for the eventualities of death at sea. This time, however, it was different. Added to forebodings of disaster, if such can be read into Trevett's account of that farewell, was a new sense of responsibility—to that girl at Archdale Hall to whom he had plighted his troth. For Elizabeth Baker was in his mind, as the will so clearly indicates.

Biddle's good friend and attorney, Joshua Ward, probably drew the instrument, which named Thomas Farr and Ward as executors, and which was direct and brief.

"I Give and Bequeath unto Elizabeth Elliott Baker Daughter of Richard Bohun Baker of the State of South Carolina, Esqr

the sum of Twenty five Thousand pounds lawful Currency of the said State." Thus it read, and continued: "And the remainder of my Estate whether real or personal I do bequeath unto my Mother Mary Biddle of the State of Pennsylvania— But in case of her Dying without a Will I desire that such sums of Money or property of what Kind soever as she may have received or have been entitled to receive be Equally divided between my Brothers James and Edward and my Sisters Lydia McFunn and Mary Biddle of the State of Pennsylvania."

Biddle signed. Two gentlemen, William Graham and David Warhamll, witnessed his signature, and Ward folded and filed the will in his office safe.[53] That afternoon, undoubtedly, the captain went out to Archdale Hall to make his farewells, for the expedition was to sail within three days.

Orders for the soldiers to be sent on board the fleet to serve as marines had been issued the day before—one company each from the First and Second regiments of the South Carolina line, a half company from the Fourth regiment, and a platoon from the Fifth. They were to be in readiness "to go on board the Vessels Drawn for." The instructions read:

"Each Regt. to provide their men with 18 Rounds each & 50 Rounds per man to be put into a Military Chest on board the Vessels they go in. The officers Commanding parties are to take Care to keep Good order and Discipline amongst their men And prevent them from getting into any Disputes with the Sailors, & assist the Cap^ts of the Vessels to the utmost of their power, in attacking the enemy." [54]

The captains and subalterns who were to command the different parties had already been selected "after a generous competition," as a general emulation pervaded the corps to have the honor of serving under Biddle's command.[55] They met on January 12 at the new barracks to draw for vessels,[56] and the coveted assignment to the *Randolph* was won by the company from the First regiment, commanded by Captain Joseph Ioor, with Lieutenant George Gray as his subaltern.[57] But the orders to go on board did not arrive, for something had interfered.

Captains Hall, Sullivan, Morgan, and Anthony attended upon the commissioners of the navy on the morning of Tuesday,

January 13. They could not possibly be ready for sea, said they, until the next spring tides, as "the Men on board each Vessel Ought to be Stationed & Trained some Little time before they sail." They had heard Biddle intended to proceed on Thursday, and it was beyond them to meet that date.[58]

Hence, when the captain returned to his Charlestown quarters on the afternoon of that day, it was to be presented with a long letter from Commissioner Blake. It outlined the reasons why the four captains could not be "properly fitted and Clear to proceed to Sea."

"As the Success of the Expedition will probably be attended with very great advantages to the Continent in General as well as this State in particular," Blake pointed out, "the Commissioners . . . therefore request as a particular favour that you will not Sail with the Ship Randolph, before the next spring Tides by which time the Gen¹ Moultrie, Notre Dame, Fair American and Polly will Certainly be fitt'd, Mann'd, Clear and ready to Sail." [59]

The spring tides were well-nigh a month away, yet what else could Biddle do but wait?

Chapter XV
The Last Cruise

FROM THE DECK OF HIS MAJESTY'S TWENTY-GUN SHIP *Perseus*, at anchor about five leagues eastward of Charlestown lighthouse, in the early morning hours of January 15, a great red glow was observed to suffuse the western sky. Through his glass Captain Keith Elphinstone could discern flames and smoke billowing aloft, and in his journal made this entry:

"At 4 A M Saw Charles Town on fire!" [1]

Two leagues further south lay the *Carysfort,* where a view of the harbor was obstructed by the low marshes of Morris Island. As the sky crimsoned in the distance, silhouetting the dark outline of the intervening land, Captain Robert Fanshawe, too, made a journal entry:

"At 5 perceived a very great fire in the N.W. w^h we immagine is in Charles Town." [2]

The fire was, indeed, in Charlestown—a spreading conflagration which started in a bakehouse in Union Street just below Queen, and was fanned by a strong winter wind blowing out of the northeast. [3] The dread cry of "Fire!" reached Charles Biddle and a group of cronies who had supped late and sat up later. They rushed through the streets, reaching the blazing kitchen just as a woman was brought out so badly burned that she died within a few minutes.

"Had there been any engines, it would have soon been put out," Charles Biddle related later, "but, as no water was near, the people did not know what to do." [4]

Flames thus raging unhampered were communicated to neighboring houses, while flying sparks ignited the roofs of dwellings in adjacent streets. All Charlestown southwest of

227

Queen and East Bay streets seemed doomed as the fire mounted in intensity, sending forth the vivid red glare which the enemy had sighted from five leagues distance at sea.[5]

With the blazing inferno seemingly out of control, Charles Biddle suddenly thought of the wife of Sailing Master Johnson, of the *Randolph,* whose home lay near by along the water front. She had followed her husband to Charlestown and had opened a little shop to supplement the wages of a sailing master. Mrs. Johnson was removing her goods when Charles reached the shop. He went promptly to her assistance. In one corner was a small cask with the head loosely resting upon it. Presuming it contained coffee or tea, he took it in his arms and started out. At the door a servant wench gasped in alarm.

"Lawzee, Master, watch what you're doin'," she whimpered. "Dat's gunpowder you're totin' out."

"The fire was falling fast near me, when she told me what I was carrying," Charles Biddle said in relating this experience subsequently. "So I covered the cask as well as I could with my coat, made my way to the waterside, and threw it in. If that girl hadn't informed me it was powder, I should certainly have been blown up." [6]

Out at Archdale Hall, meanwhile, Nicholas Biddle was awakened with word that a great fire was raging in Charlestown. Down the old Dorchester road the seventeen miles to the city he rode at breakneck speed, his way lighted by the glare of the ascending flames. When he reached the town gate, some time around daylight, he found the approaches guarded and patrols ranging the streets, while dull rumbles ahead indicated where houses were being blown up in the effort to check the red tide of destruction.[7]

All through that day the citizens and the military, aided by a landing party from the *Randolph,* fought a valiant fight, and as the wind died down succeeded in bringing the fire under control. But 252 houses, in one of which had been stored the books and papers of the Charlestown Library, had been destroyed; the devastated area extended from south of Queen Street to Granville's battery, and from Church Street eastward to the bay.[8]

Brigadier General Moultrie met the captain that afternoon and voiced a conviction that the fire had been the work of incendiaries.

"We have information that the men-of-wars' men have been in town almost nightly," he said. "Their boats are constantly reported in the harbor, and we have every reason to believe they were the instigators of this. It's high time they're driven away." [9]

To the latter statement Biddle subscribed heartily. He was not in a position to know, however, whether Moultrie's charges were true. Nor are we today, although a postscript which Captain Fanshawe of the *Carysfort* added to a letter written a little later to the Lords of the Admiralty, and which has come to light after a lapse of more than 150 years, tends to justify the darkest suspicions.

"Chas Town was sett on Fire on ye 15 Jany ab^t 20 minutes after 4 in ye morning," Fanshawe wrote in that postscript, "it burnt with tolerable effect." [10]

In the face of the great calamity which had descended upon the city, the final arrangements for the naval expedition received another setback. Some stores intended for the *General Moultrie, Notre Dame, Fair American,* and *Polly* had gone up in smoke when the fire swept down East Bay Street.[11] But the principal delay had been the need for all executive authority to concentrate upon the requirements of the homeless and destitute, those pitiful victims "worn down with fatigue, standing to watch over their property, covered with blankets, and shivering with cold." [12]

Nicholas Biddle realized it could not be otherwise and was reconciled to a further postponement of the cruise. Not so his brother Charles. The latter announced that he feared the fleet would rot in Charlestown Harbor, and he for one was not going to rot with it. Would Nicholas relieve him of his promise to sail as a volunteer? He was concerned in a letter-of-marque ship fitting out in New Bern, and he would like to set out for North Carolina to take command of her.

With Nicholas agreeable to the proposal, they parted a day

or two after the fire. To Charles, riding off northward on the Georgetown road, came no premonitions of the future. He did not sense then that, in taking an affectionate leave of his brother, he had spoken a last farewell. Nor did he realize that his decision was preserving his own life for a long and useful career.[13]

A week after the fire, Commissioner Blake called upon Nicholas Biddle with an optimistic report of progress. The four captains had appeared before the navy board the night before and had given assurances of being ready to sail in ten days.[14] It was time, therefore, to call for the men promised from the various regiments to serve as marines. The captain communicated with General Moultrie, suggesting the detachment for the *Randolph* be ordered on board first. On January 23, from Charlestown headquarters, Moultrie responded in General Orders, and significantly chose "Parole Randolph" as the password of the day.

"1 Capt 1 Subaltern, 2 Serj^{ts} & 48 Rank and file from the 1 Reg^t to go on Board the Randolph tomorrow morning as was order'd before," the orders read. "The Boats will be ready at the market wharf for them." [15]

In their trim black uniforms faced with red, Captain Ioor and his company of the South Carolina line's First regiment marched from the barracks to the Market wharf on the morning of January 24. Fifty strong, they embarked in boats from the *Randolph* and were rowed down the harbor and out into Rebellion Road. Lieutenant Barnes, commanding the frigate while Biddle was ashore, had arranged for quartering them— Captain Ioor and Lieutenant Gray with the officers on the main deck aft, the two sergeants with the ship's petty officers, and the privates forward with the crew.[16]

Three days later the remainder of the military detachment was ordered on board the state vessels—Captain John Blake, with a lieutenant, sergeant, and thirty-four rank and file of the Second regiment to the *General Moultrie;* Lieutenant Adrian Proveaux, a sergeant, and twenty-four privates from the Fourth regiment to the *Fair American;* Lieutenant William Blameyer, a sergeant, and fifteen privates from the Fifth regiment to the *Notre Dame,* and a lieutenant, sergeant, and

twenty-nine privates to the *Polly*.[17] That same day, after ordering a dozen hands from the *Notre Dame* to the *General Moultrie,* the commissioners of the navy directed the four captains to
take their vessels down into Rebellion Road and join the *Randolph*.[18]

Just when the little fleet was finally assembled in the Road
cannot be determined exactly. But it was probably February 5
before the last arrived. On that same day Commissioner Blake
delivered instructions to the state captains, and the clerk of the
navy board was sent down to "take an Exact List of all the Men
on board," and procure from each purser an account of provisions. That day also the board ordered:

"That the Captains of the different Vessels be directed to
go and remain on board, & see that the Men are Regularly
Quartered & Exercised at least twice Every day while they remain in port and that no more Men be enlisted for the present Expedition till the above [returns] are laid before the
Board." [19] The actual number then signed on for the ship and
three brigs at the thirty-dollar bounty figure was "Three
Hundred Men & upwards." [20]

For the last time Nicholas Biddle rode along the avenue lined
with live oaks, which led from the main entrance of Archdale
Hall to the Dorchester road. Behind him on the great brick
stairs leading up to the entrance a girlish figure waved a fond
farewell. To his right spread the green lawn of the estate, and
to his left lay the family burial ground where generations of
Bakers slept beneath myrtle-covered mounds. At the entrance
way he turned, lifted his hat in a gay salute, and then galloped
off to the southward, down the dusty road towards Charlestown, and forever out of the life of Elizabeth Elliott Baker.
It was February 5, 1778—the same day that had witnessed the
departure of the last vessel of the little fleet from its anchorage
in the harbor.[21]

Before the day was done the captain, too, was ready to go
down to Rebellion Road. He had held his last conference with
John Rutledge, who had wished him a successful cruise, and
with Edward Blake, who had deplored the delays which the
navy board had been unable to prevent. He had said farewell to

numerous friends and had accepted as volunteers several promising young Charlestonians, who were filled with martial ardor to sail with him. One of these was a Lieutenant Simons—Christian name missing—and the names of the others unfortunately have not been preserved for posterity.[22]

At the wharf the frigate's carpenter, Richard Fordham, who had been sent ashore a few days earlier to superintend the building of a ship's boat, saluted the captain and requested further orders. The boat was far from completion. Should he remain behind until it could be delivered to him or accompany the captain on board? Fordham had injured his leg some time before and was limping. Biddle considered, and then made a decision which the carpenter would relate for years to come.

"Better remain on shore, Mr. Fordham," he said. "That leg of yours needs attention even if the boat does not." [23]

Biddle stepped into the stern of the *Randolph*'s barge. A midshipman—maybe it was young Burrows, a Pennsylvania lad [24]—gave the order, "Let fall," and the men bent to their oars as the boat slipped steadily through the harbor and out into the Road. There the captain had a splendid opportunity to study his consorts, which lay at anchor along the route the barge took as it neared the frigate. Their appearance pleased him.

Largest of them all was the *General Moultrie*, of about 200-ton burden. Very deep waisted, and with a small head and an upright plain stern, she had a reputation from harbor maneuvering as easy to steer. She had been built in Charlestown for an armed ship and was ready for her maiden cruise, with a crew numbering 155 officers and men, including the detachment of infantrymen from the Second regiment. She was armed with twelve short 12-pounders, and six 4-pounders, all on the main deck, and a number of cohorns in her broad tops, being unusually high-rigged.

The three brigs were all of about the same burden, ranging from 130 to 160 tons. Most heavily armed of the trio was the state brig *Notre Dame,* with eighteen 4-pounders and numerous swivels. She was low-built, with a projecting figurehead and a plain stern with yellow moldings. On previous cruises she had proved a fast sailer. Her crew, including the soldiers from the Fifth regiment, totaled ninety-four officers and men.

Of somewhat less armament was the former privateer *Fair American,* with eight 4-pounders and six 6-pounders. She was a Bermuda-built brig, short and broad, but high-masted. Her roundhouse had been removed, giving her a light quarter-deck. With a small figurehead, and neither badges nor fashion pieces on the quarters, she looked not unlike most brigs, but sailed uncommonly well. On board her was a complement of ninety-nine.

Equal almost in armament with the *Fair American* was the *Polly.* Although pierced for eighteen guns, she showed but fourteen in her main battery, all of them 4-pounders. Low-built like the *Notre Dame,* she too was a prime sailer, and boasted a total crew of seventy-four.[25]

The four vessels looked trim and fit to the captain, and, from the way their crews manned the yards and cheered as the barge drove past, he augured well for the enthusiasm and discipline on board each of them.

On board the *Randolph* everything was shipshape, as he naturally expected it would be under his three excellent lieutenants. Lieutenant Barnes reported later that day upon the size and condition of the crew. There were 315 officers and men on board, including Captain Ioor's company and a number of gentleman volunteers.[26] The crew had been trained to the guns to a point close to perfection, Barnes declared with pride. The men were eager to get under way and confident of success. He hesitated a moment and then said, somewhat diffidently:

"You know, Captain, speaking of success, the last cruise made us all pretty wealthy men."

"I hope you haven't squandered it all," Biddle smiled.

"Hardly," Barnes grinned, "but we got talking—McDougall and Fanning and myself—and Fanning thought we ought to make our wills, like he did last December a year."

"An excellent idea," Biddle agreed. "I did the same myself less than a month ago."

"I wanted you to know about it," Barnes continued earnestly, "so if anything happens to me you'll notify Captain William

Pickles, an old shipmate of mine. He's my executor. You see, Captain, out in Tredeffryn township, Chester county, there's a young lady, Priscilla Walker, who's waiting for my return, and I want to be sure she's provided for."

"I see," Biddle nodded gravely, "but let's hope no such contingency arises."

Later McDougall embraced an opportunity to confide to the captain about his will. He had named his uncle, now Major General Alexander McDougall, as executor and principal beneficiary. Perhaps it gave Biddle a moment of unease—three wills all executed, as he learned, within a single week—his, Barnes's, and McDougall's. And Fanning's had been executed before that. Certainly not pleasant to contemplate at the beginning of a cruise! [27]

Most likely, however, Biddle brushed the thought aside and turned to the more urgent matter of orders for his captains. These were drafted in the cabin that night, and his clerk made fair copies for the four, who were called on board the following morning. They came promptly—Sullivan of the *General Moultrie,* Hall of the *Notre Dame,* Morgan of the *Fair American,* and Anthony of the *Polly*—and listened courteously and understandingly as he outlined his plans.

No copy exists today of those orders. We know they embraced first the destruction or dispersal of the British blockaders and then a cruise to the windward of the West Indies to intercept British merchantmen bound for Barbados, Antigua, Dominica, or Jamaica. We know also that the captain laid great emphasis upon the necessity for prompt obedience to signals, and proper precautions to be taken in engaging the enemy. In fact, at the foot of each order as it had been copied by the clerk, he wrote in his own hand an injunction which later took on somber significance.

"In case of coming to action in the night," warned Biddle, "be very careful of your magazine." [28]

Only the shallow depth of water on the bar, and contrary winds, held the armament within Rebellion Road. For more than a week there had been no sight of enemy ships. The way was clear to proceed to sea, without having to engage while

involved in negotiating the channel. But for day after day, even
as the tides rose higher each twenty-four hours, the wind continued out of the east. Then it veered around, and came the
awaited opportunity. On Thursday, February 14, one after another the vessels moved out, and "were over the bar by eight
o'clock on the morning." With them went a number of merchantmen—eighteen sail in all.[29]

From Charlestown two days later President Rutledge wrote
to the South Carolina delegates in Congress. He sketched the
tedious operations, which "like all our other works took up
more time than was expected." Unfavorable winds had added
to the delay, he explained, but the fleet had sailed at last.

"I hope Captain Biddle will have a good account of some of
the enemy's vessels," he concluded.[30]

Beyond the bar before noon of February 12 the last of the
pilots had been discharged, and the fleet stood due eastward
to give the merchantmen a good offing. Lookouts on the fighting vessels scanned the seas for a glimpse of enemy frigates,
but not even a slender stick was visible over the horizon in any
direction.[31] Prevalent opinion was that the British had forsaken
the blockade and sought safety elsewhere when spies reported
Biddle's armament as ready to sail. Such a belief was not only
erroneous, but an unwarranted reflection upon Captain Fanshawe of the *Carysfort*. It has existed, however, ever since that
February day long years ago.[32]

Actually the three enemy ships had been so glutted by prize
taking that it had become impossible to maintain any consistent
patrol of the area beyond the bar. Each prize sent to St. Augustine had required a prize crew, and added prisoners until the
shrinking complements of the vessels were equalled or exceeded
by the number of rebel and French seamen to be guarded. First
to be detached from the blockade had been the *Perseus*, which
had sailed for St. Augustine on January 22, "encumbered with
Prisoners," convoying several prizes, and much in need of
water. On February 3, the *Carysfort*, with "26 men Sick on
board, and Seven on shore, and 35 absent in prizes; 83 prisoners and encumbered with three foreign Vessels seized off

Charlestown," was forced to return to the base in East Florida.
The *Lizard* remained cruising.[33]

Perhaps it was just as well for that frigate of twenty-eight
guns that pursuit of likely prey on February 10 turned into a
long, stern chase. On the day Biddle's squadron put to sea, the
Lizard was many leagues distant, manning a prize and prevented by a strong northwest wind from "getting off the Bar
again for some Days." Otherwise her presence on blockading
duty might have spelled the end of one of His Majesty's ships
of war.[34]

With no enemy to destroy or disperse, the *Randolph* and her
consorts did not remain long upon the coast. On the second day
out, a prize was picked up—a dismasted ship from New England, which had been taken by a privateer and was proceeding
for St. Augustine. Biddle ordered the prize crew removed to
one of the brigs and, as the New Englander carried no cargo
and was unseaworthy, he directed that she be burned. Before
applying the torch to the disabled ship, six light guns and a few
stores were removed.[35]

Thereafter they continued east by south until in the proximity of Bermuda, and then south by east. Ten more days found
them to windward of Antigua, and the captain plotted his course
more easterly, passing north of Barbados, and running along
the thirteenth parallel of latitude—in the path of the trade
between Great Britain and her West India islands.

British merchantmen, however, were conspicuous by their
absence. Frequently in the ensuing week, sails were sighted, but
each time when the quarry was overhauled she proved to be a
neutral—a Dutchman from or to St. Eustatius or Saba, or a
Frenchman from or to Martinique or Guadeloupe.[36] Biddle was
disappointed by the barrenness of the cruise and disturbed at the
growing possibility of heavy British ships being sent out in quest
of them. As the Americans had spoken so many merchantmen,
it was a foregone conclusion that news of their presence in the
waters to windward of Barbados would soon reach English
ears. Biddle voiced his views to Captain John Blake, who had
come aboard from the *General Moultrie* and, with Captain Ioor,

was dining with him on the afternoon of March 4. They had been discussing their continuous bad luck, and Biddle had listened while the army officers deplored the lack of action.

"We have been cruising here for some time, gentlemen, and we have been unfortunate," he admitted. "However, as you desire some excitement, may I remind you we have spoken a number of vessels, who will give information, no doubt, and presently we may expect the enemy out looking for us."

"Reports in Charlestown were that the British ships in the West Indies were chiefly light cruising frigates," Captain Blake pointed out.

"There are probably one or two ships of the line on the West Indies station," the captain replied. "My old ship, the Portland, I have heard is at Antigua."

"And what is her rating?" Blake asked.

"Sixth class, with fifty guns mounted on two decks," Biddle said, "and I would not like to meet her. But I think myself a match for any ship that mounts her guns on one deck." [37]

The conversation was interrupted by a midshipman who entered the cabin to report that the *Polly* had just taken a prize— a small schooner from New York bound for Grenada. The capture had been without effort. The schooner had mistaken the squadron for a British force—no flags had been flying to identify the ships otherwise—and had sailed unsuspectingly to within hailing distance of the hindmost brig, the *Polly*.[38]

Later in the day, having examined the prize, Biddle decided to man her as a fleet tender. He detached ten men from the *Randolph* under Midshipman Simeon Fanning.[39] These ten were a master's mate, Philip Treglohn; [40] and nine seamen, including one Caleb Idelet, of whom more later.[41] A few hands were added from the other vessels, and young Fanning was given command. His brother, Joshua, who had been on the sick list ever since the fleet had sailed from Charlestown, wished him good luck as he went over the side to the schooner. But for Joshua and Simeon only ill luck lay ahead.[42] With the departure of the detachment of 10, there remained on board the *Randolph* 305 officers and men.[43]

On the afternoon of Saturday, March 7, three days after the capture of the schooner, the squadron was sailing on a wind and standing to the northward about sixty leagues due east of Barbados. The cruise had continued barren of results, but an end came to monotony with a shrill cry from the masthead:

"Sail ho!"

"Where away?" sang out the officer of the deck.

"Four points off the starboard bow," was the answer, "but too distant to make her out."

Word was passed to Biddle, who appeared promptly on the quarter-deck. His decision was to investigate; so he ordered the course changed nearer to the wind then blowing out of the northeast. From the *Randolph*'s deck, signal flags arose, directing her consorts to haul their wind and stand after the flagship.[44] Obediently, one after the other they bore up, the *General Moultrie* off the frigate's quarter to leeward, the three brigs and the schooner tender spread out astern. By best estimate the distant sail had been nine leagues off when first sighted, and it was a full hour before she was visible from the quarter-deck.[45] The captain studied her intently through his telescope.

"She's a ship, and seems to be standing our way," he said, passing the glass to Lieutenant Barnes. The latter kept it glued to his eye for a long observation, and then nodded in confirmation.

"Either a big merchantman, or an English frigate," was his comment.

"We'll know quickly enough once she sights us," Biddle stated.[46]

Thereafter they waited and watched while another hour ticked away. The faint March sun was low in the western sky, and visibility was becoming increasingly poor. But the ship was continuing her course toward them and in the fading light seemed to be spreading more canvas.[47]

"She's looking for a fight, gentlemen," the captain told the little knot of officers surrounding him. "And whatever her rating we'll give her that satisfaction."

His brown eyes glanced approvingly about him. The *Randolph*'s crew was spoiling for action. To a man there was every confidence in the outcome, and, since the first hail from the mast-head, an eager air of expectancy had permeated the ship.

"You may beat to quarters, Mr. Barnes," Biddle said quietly, and as the drums rolled he watched the hands springing to their stations with more alacrity than he had ever witnessed in the King's navy. "They'll do," he thought to himself, and again turned his attention to the oncoming enemy, speculating as to her size, and figuring her as a twenty- or perhaps twenty-eight-gun frigate.[48]

But what was rushing down upon them out of the northeast was no frigate! The enemy was a sixty-four-gun ship of the line, the *Yarmouth,* Captain Nicholas Vincent, out of Antigua on a cruise against the American rebels. It was after five o'clock that fateful Saturday afternoon when the lookouts on the *Yarmouth* discovered six sail in the southwest quarter, and bore down on them "steering for the headmost and largest ship." [49] Vincent had not a doubt but that they were "American privateers," and he had singled out the *Randolph* as his particular quarry.[50]

Then the sun set and, in the dim afterglow around seven o'clock, Biddle determined to heave to and wait his opponent. The *Randolph*'s mizzen topsail was laid to the mast, and she turned slowly to windward. Promptly the *General Moultrie,* about 150 yards astern and to leeward, followed suit. This maneuver carried her to windward of the *Notre Dame.* Captain Hall, being unable to pass the ship and get into the *Randolph*'s wake, laid his maintopsail to the mast so the *General Moultrie* would shoot ahead. The *Fair American* and *Polly,* further to leeward, brought about in a confused tack which took them far off the course toward the west, and the schooner tender followed them.[51]

In darkness illuminated only by a moon, which, a few days past its first quarter, hung low in the western sky, the *Yarmouth* hauled by the wind to parallel the *General Moultrie,* and fired a warning gun. As she swept abreast, she hailed:

"Who are you?"

"The Polly," called Captain Sullivan.

"Where are you from?" the insistent voice asked.

"From New York!" Sullivan answered, and with no further attention to the *General Moultrie* the sixty-four-gun ship stood on after the *Randolph*.

"My God!" gasped Captain John Blake as she passed. "A twodecker!" [52]

On the *Notre Dame,* astern of the *General Moultrie,* Captain Hall also had caught a glimpse of a high poop, and a flag flying from her foretop masthead. He too realized they had caught a Tartar, but pluckily continued his efforts to get under the stern of the enemy.[53]

From the quarter-deck of the *Randolph,* Biddle had heard the stranger hail the *General Moultrie* and in the dimness noted her huge bulk as she bore down upon him. They were close—scarcely two ships' lengths apart—when a voice called out of the night:

"Who are you? Hoist your colors, or we'll fire into you!"

Gunport lids had been triced up. The thirteen 12-pounders in the port battery were loaded and run out, the gunners waiting behind each with matches burning. On the quarter-deck the six-pounders were ready, and Biddle knew the forecastle guns were likewise only waiting his order to fire. He turned to Lieutenant Barnes.

"Give him an answer and open fire!" he said quietly. At the same time a quartermaster hauled the Grand Union to the gaff.

Barnes's voice rang out, clear as a bell and so distinct as to be heard on the *General Moultrie* astern.

"This is the Continental frigate Randolph!" [54]

Simultaneously the twelve- and six-pounders spoke—a thunderous discharge which punctuated the silent night. The *Yarmouth* answered while the echoes of the first broadside were still reverberating between the two ships.[55] Thereafter the two were joined in a continuous roar—a terrific engagement in which, according to one eyewitness, "the Randolph appeared to fire four or five broadsides to the Yarmouth's one." [56] They were, said another observer, "so near as to throw their hand grenades from their tops upon each other's decks." [57]

In the early moments the advantage lay with the *Randolph.* Her broadsides had shot away the *Yarmouth*'s mizzen topmast and bowsprit, and her guns, grenades, and marines' musketry fire had killed a British lieutenant and four men and wounded twelve others.[58]

On the lee quarter, the *General Moultrie* fired three successive broadsides in the general direction of the engagement, the last of which, as the enemy had shot so much ahead, probably struck the frigate. Captain Blake had induced Sullivan to stop such indiscriminate firing, pointing out that "instead of Assisting we are firing into the Randolph." The *General Moultrie's* captain then made sail to try to get ahead and engage on the bow.[59] The *Notre Dame* had succeeded in discharging a broadside of her puny 4-pounders into the stern of the *Yarmouth,* as the battle opened, but the *Fair American* and *Polly* had not yet come within range.[60]

It was all the *Randolph's* fight, and singlehanded Biddle and his gallant crew were putting up a magnificent scrap. The crash of the great guns was almost incessant. Each sweating, straining gun crew was serving its weapon with masterful precision . . . load . . . run out . . . aim . . . fire . . . recoil . . . swab out . . . reload . . . run out . . . aim . . . fire . . . On forecastle and quarter-deck the marines, including the South Carolina infantrymen, were directing their musketry fire into the enemy's tops, trying to pick off the men hurling hand grenades on the *Randolph's* deck. On forecastle and quarter-deck also, the 6-pounders were being fired with even greater rapidity than the great guns on the gun deck below. The frigate, as an awed chronicler related, was "fighting at a most infernal rate." [61]

Almost a quarter hour had elapsed since the opening broadside when Biddle was wounded. Either a musket ball or a flying splinter struck him in the thigh. He fell, blood gushing from his leg, but had struggled to a sitting position before any of his officers could reach him.

" 'Tis only a slight touch," he insisted as they would have carried him below. "Send me a surgeon's mate, and a chair from my cabin. I'll stay right here."

The chair was brought and he was lowered into it. A surgeon's mate came hastily up from the cockpit; he bent down, examined the wound and began to dress it.

One of the crew of the nearest 6-pounder had seen the captain fall, heard him protest he was not seriously wounded and, before turning back to the gun, rendered silent homage to the courage of his commander. Thus, propped in a chair on the quarter-deck, encouraging his crew to victory, Nicholas Biddle died.

For at that moment the *Randolph* blew up! [62]

Chapter XVI
Aftermath

BECAUSE SHE LAY TO WINDWARD, AND DESPITE THE
narrow space separating them, the *Yarmouth* escaped destruction when her enemy blew into a million pieces. The
terrific concussion momentarily stunned the entire personnel of
the big sixty-four-gun ship. In its wake a deluge of debris from
the vanished *Randolph* rained down upon the decks, hurtling
through sails and rigging, tearing the canvas to shreds and sev-
ering stays, backstays, shrouds, and ratlines. A heavy timber
descended upon the topgallant sail, which was then on the cap,
and stuck there. Another beam, six feet long, crashed upon the
poop. The truck on the flagstaff at the main topgallant masthead was carried away. An American ensign, the Grand Union
flag of "thirteen stripes," rolled up and not so much as singed,
blew in upon the forecastle. The whole ship was covered with
parts of the lost frigate.[1]

By the time the *Yarmouth* had been cleared and could make
a little sail, the rest of the American squadron was vanishing
into the night. She tried a halfhearted pursuit; first of two vessels disappearing southward, and then of a third which had
borne away before the wind. But the risk of masts and remaining rigging was too great and she hove to, handed her sails, and
spent the next twenty-four hours making repairs and burying
her dead.[2]

Fortunate it was for the *General Moultrie*, the three brigs,
and the prize schooner that the *Yarmouth* had sustained such
damage. Otherwise they would have had slight opportunity to
escape; particularly the *General Moultrie*, as Captain Sullivan

had lost his head when the *Randolph* exploded. He rushed up to Captain Blake, repeating over and over again, "What shall we do?"

"Consult our own safety and get away from here as fast as we can," Blake replied vehemently.

At the tiller, the helmsman, also in a blue funk, added his cries to those of the captain.

"It's impossible to get off, sir," he wailed. "The ship is now aboard us." Then turning to Sullivan he implored, "Captain, may I haul down the flag?"

"Aye, do what you will," Sullivan responded, but again Blake interposed.

"Look here, Captain, whether the colors are up or down is of no consequence," he pointed out. "Nobody can see a flag in this darkness. Why not encourage the people to make sail, and at least try to get away?"

Sullivan ran down to the main deck, while the helmsman, still badly frightened, continued his cries.

"Unless you remove him," Blake said to the sailing master, "we'll probably be taken."

So the man was kicked from the tiller, the master took it himself, and, as the sails were sheeted home, the *General Moultrie* got under way and fled southward.[3]

On the *Fair American,* which had just come within range when disaster overtook the *Randolph,* Captain Morgan thought it had been the enemy which had blown up. He bore away to inquire how Captain Biddle was, and had the trumpet in his hand, ready to hail, when he discovered his mistake. The *Fair American* promptly made sail southward in the wake of the *General Moultrie.*[4]

Both Captain Hall in the *Notre Dame* and Captain Anthony in the *Polly,* along with Midshipman Fanning in the prize schooner, sought safety to the westward, clapping on all the sail their respective vessels could carry.[5]

The dim moon faded behind the clouds and black silence of night descended upon that spot fifty leagues east of Barbados where Nicholas Biddle and his valiant crew had perished.

But not all were lost. Four men in the gun crew of a quarter-deck six-pounder, dazed by the devastating impact, glimpsed the ship disintegrating about them as a mighty force hurled them clear of the shattered timbers that had been the *Randolph*. They plumped into the cool salt water and fought their way gasping to the surface. Darkness hemmed them in. Debris fell around them upon the sea to be succeeded by a vast stillness, punctuated only by their own splashing efforts to keep afloat.

By strange coincidence the four men had been blown through the air in parallel arcs. They had emerged from their involuntary dives almost as near each other as they had been a few minutes before on the frigate. One had found a long spar. His labored panting, as he hauled himself waist-high, guided the others to him. Only after all were clinging to it did they clear their bemused minds and take stock of their situation.[6]

The four seamen were Alexander Robinson, John Carew, Hans Workman, and Bartholomew Bourdeau[7]—identified in the newspapers later simply as "a Scotchman, a Frenchman, a Spaniard and a Dane." [8] From their actual names it would seem some poetic license had been taken by the gentlemen of the West India press.

All four were young and hardy and excellent swimmers. With the instincts of self-preservation strong in their breasts they set out to improve their precarious perch. Around them bobbed much shattered lumber and somehow, with the spar as a nucleus, they fashioned a crude raft, lashing it together with what broken lengths of rope they found floating on the surface. One of them salvaged a blanket and tossed it on the float. Then all four scrambled on board as the tropical dawn broke around them. For as far as their eyes could see the ocean was empty.

Thus for four days and nights the quartet of seamen floated on the waves, "buried alive as it were under the vault of Heaven." Occasional squalls struck them, and they sucked eagerly of the rain water retained by the saturated blanket. They had no food, but their thirst was satisfied and the pangs of hunger were easier to bear when not accompanied by parched throats. Only their feet bothered them, as the raft was constantly awash and the salt water caused toes and ankles to swell.

On the morning of March 12 they sighted off in the southeast a vessel, which loomed rapidly larger. They stripped the shirts from their backs and waved frantically. The vessel drew abreast and hove to. A boat was lowered and they were saved! [9]

The ship which took them from the raft was none other than the *Yarmouth!* She was continuing her cruise, and had been chasing a distant sail when her masthead lookout spotted an object on the water to starboard.[10] Momentarily Captain Vincent gave over pursuit, hauled his wind and, by the help of his spy glass, "discovered four men that seemed to be standing in the water, for what supported them was not at first visible." [11]

"At ½ past 9 shortend Sail and hoisted a Boat out," reads the *Yarmouth*'s log, "and brot on board 4 Men who were on a piece of a wreck." [12]

They climbed the ladder to the main deck of the sixty-four unaided. Three of them appeared but little the worse for their experience, but the Frenchman, Bourdeau, showed signs of collapse.[13] They were not hungry, they explained, but very, very sleepy. Humanely Captain Vincent refrained from immediate questioning, but ordered a basin of tea and a hammock for each. Later they told him who they were and where they came from. But they could offer no idea of what had caused the *Randolph* to blow up.[14] Meanwhile, as her lower rigging was still slack and her masts in danger, the *Yarmouth* headed for Barbados, where she anchored on the afternoon of March 14.[15]

For Captain Vincent and his crew the decision to stop and pick up the four men carried with it an unexpected reward. His Majesty's government allowed head money to the crew of a British ship which sank or captured a rebel vessel of war—£5 for each man in the enemy crew. But the government required proof positive which, in the case of the *Randolph,* could not have been supplied without the evidence of the survivors.[16] Bourdeau was too ill to be interrogated by the Chief Justice of His Majesty's Court of Common Pleas of the Island of Barbados, who came on board on March 16. The other three were examined, however, and swore to a lengthy document identi-

DESTRUCTION OF THE *RANDOLPH*, MARCH 7, 1778. From
an old English woodcut. Courtesy, Navy Department.

fying themselves as "late Seamen on Board the Privateer Ship called the Randolph, whereof [blank] Beedle was Captain and Commander." Their affidavit concluded: "And that at the Time the said Ship Randolph was Blown up . . . there were Actually on Board the said Ship Three Hundred and five Men including Officers and Seamen." [17]

Before the year was done the commissioners of His Majesty's navy paid £1,525 "Bounty to the Yarmouth for destroying the Randolph an American Privateer." [18]

First word of the tragedy to reach Charlestown was brought in by Simeon Fanning, who arrived on March 29 with the captured schooner. He carried a number of letters from Captain Hall of the *Notre Dame*—one to John Dorsius and another to John Rutledge as president of the Privy Council. The youthful midshipman, still grieving at the death of his brother, his captain, and his shipmates, delivered the first missive to the Continental agent and added his own eyewitness story. [19] The whereabouts of the *General Moultrie* and *Fair American* he knew not. He had not seen them afterwards. He had parted with the *Notre Dame* and *Polly* after several days, Captains Hall and Anthony having determined to continue cruising. [20] Dorsius described the disaster in a letter which he sent express to the Marine Committee. [21]

The letter for Rutledge, however, reached other hands, for Rawlins Lowndes had succeeded the former as president of the Privy Council.

"The melancholy news of the loss of the Randolph," wrote Lowndes to Congress, "has reached us by the Prize Master of a Small Schooner from New York which was captured by poor Biddle—he was witness of the dreadful scene when the Randolph blew up in the Engagement." Continuing, he quoted at length from Captain Hall's account. Apparently unaware of Biddle's plan, approved by Rutledge, to cruise against the West India trade as well as drive the blockaders from the Carolina coast, he concluded with a lament: "His taking so large a circuit was incompatible in my opinion with his destination, and the Views of Goverm^t and has left us now without any Recourse from the Evil, which we every day feel the effect of." [22]

We do not know who carried the dire tidings to Archdale Hall. Nor have we any account of how the shock of her great loss affected Elizabeth Elliott Baker. Perhaps, even in dark despair, she clung to some faint hope that first reports might be erroneous or exaggerated; that Nicholas Biddle may have been among those saved. If so, in little more than a fortnight came confirmation of the tragedy, with details that swept away all possibility that her captain had survived. It was a dispatch in the *South Carolina Gazette,* quoting a letter of March 21 from St. Eustatius:

"Advices from Barbados mention, that it was the Yarmouth of 64 guns, that engaged our fleet on March 7 . . . that 4 sailors of the Randolph's crew had been picked up on part of the wreck, some days after she blew up." [23]

On April 18 the *General Moultrie* and *Fair American* arrived, but Captains Sullivan and Morgan could add nothing new to the few meager details. The *Randolph* had disappeared in a gigantic explosion, and her consorts had fled the scene. Undoubtedly a spark had reached the frigate's magazine, but how it had happened no one could hazard a guess. The two captains shook their heads and expressed wonderment that even four men had come alive from that frightful blast.[24]

The first account of the loss of the *Randolph* reached Charles Biddle at New Bern, North Carolina, on April 22, and struck him with stunning force.

"I could get no sleep for several nights," he wrote later, "and, as some of the fleet had returned to Charlestown, I was determined to go there and inquire into the particulars of the unfortunate accident."

Accompanied by Major John Lucas, of the Georgia line, he set off from New Bern filled with "many melancholy reflections," and a mischief-making landlady at Charlestown added fuel to his somber thoughts. This dame drew him aside and whispered about an affair that "had given her a great deal of pain." Captain Morgan, at a recent dinner, said she, had proposed a toast reflecting very much on Captain Biddle.

Charles Biddle, feeling "a gloomy pleasure at the thought of calling him out," sent Major Lucas with a challenge to Morgan to meet him with pistols at the earliest possible date. Within an hour Lucas was back and Morgan with him. The latter denied any such toast had been offered.

"My toast was, 'More wisdom to those at the head of our navy,' " he explained. "I meant it for those who fitted out our ships. No man ever loved and esteemed another more than I did your brother. I would have risked my life at any time to serve him."

So earnest was Morgan, who offered to take oath under his own hand to the truth of his statement, that Charles Biddle believed him. Commenting later, Charles remarked: "Had I known what was long afterwards told me respecting the conduct of Sullivan, I should have sent Lucas to him."

Then, having called at Archdale Hall to offer what solace he could to the grieving Elizabeth, he prepared to return to New Bern and the outfitting of his ship.[25] Before departure, however, he sat in Joshua Ward's office and heard his brother's will read. A few days later the executors served notice in the Charlestown newspapers that "All Persons having any demands against the estate of the late Capt. Nicholas Biddle, are desired to call for payment." [26]

Simeon Fanning, anxious to return north, had delayed to settle the affairs of his dead brother. By July he had negotiated with Edward Rutledge to pay him $2,500 in return for which he conveyed title to Rutledge for the money Joshua Fanning had loaned to the state of South Carolina.[27] Then, accompanied by the sailor, Caleb Idelet, he set off from Charlestown. Simeon never reached home. For some time nothing was heard of him. Then a relative found Idelet at Chincoteague, Virginia. The former sailor, well dressed and in funds, stammered out a story which no one believed, but which no one could disprove. Simeon Fanning, said he, had become overheated, drunk some cold water, and died suddenly in North Carolina on the northward journey! [28]

Long before this, however, the whole Continent had learned

of the tragedy off Barbados. The British in New York had the news on April 12.[29] It reached Howe's forces occupying Philadelphia a week later.[30]

At York, where Congress sat in session, the express from South Carolina arrived on April 24.[31] Rumor and report had preceded it by a few days.[32] The secretary of the Marine Committee notified Robert Morris "of the Melancholy News of the Randolph Frigate having blown up, and every Soul belonging to her perished . . . Had it not been for the unhappy Accident, they would in all probability have taken the british Ship, as they had shot away her Bowsprit, Mizzen Top Mast, and otherwise much damaged her." [33]

A few days later, at Reading, Mary Biddle heard of the death of her beloved son and bowed in grief.

"I submit with resignation to thy holy will," she prayed, "and beseech thee in thy mercy to grant the affliction which thou hath permitted to fall on me may purify my soul." [34]

There was consolation, she told those who called to comfort her: "He was one of the best of young men and died in the service of his country." [35]

Through the years since 1778 there have been countless conjectures as to why the *Randolph* blew up, and what might have been the course of American naval history had Nicholas Biddle been spared. No answer can ever be found for either question. That he was brave to excess, skilled in his profession, the beau ideal of a naval officer, his deeds, as recounted, bear strong testimony. That, when he fell at the age of twenty-seven, his country lost a gallant captain goes without saying. But, in the grim tragedy of his passing, he provided the American navy with its first great tradition—to die fighting!

And that, for the bold heart of Nicholas Biddle, would have been honor enough.

Appendix A
Poems in Memoriam

TWO POEMS were written during the American Revolution in memory of Nicholas Biddle and the *Randolph*. In each there appears poetic license and inaccuracy.

One, written by William Scull and dedicated "to the Memory of my Beloved Cousin Capt. Nich. Biddle," was first published in the *New Jersey Gazette,* on December 13, 1780.

The other, by Philip Freneau, was issued in a pamphlet in 1781 by Francis Bailey of Philadelphia, and then included in subsequent editions of the poet's collected works in 1786, 1795, and 1809.

VERSES to the Memory of Capt. Nicholas Biddle, of the *Randolph,* Frigate of 32 guns, blown up in an engagement with the *Yarmouth,* a British Man of War of 64 guns.

WHAT dread explosion rends the distant skies!
What sulph'rous flames in spiral volumes rise!
The *Randolph* swims no more!—Modest and brave,
The virtuous Biddle finds an early grave.
O gallant youth! what monument of praise
Can thy afflicted, grateful country raise?
When Britain's tyrant o'er the Atlantic waves,
Pour'd forth his num'rous hosts of armed slaves,
Their master's bloody dictates to fulfil,
And bend a free-born people to his will,
Thy gen'rous soul disdain'd luxurious rest!
Thy country's wrongs inflam'd thy manly breast.
Repeated laurels gather'd on the main,
Increase thy glory, not thy warmth restrain!
Tho' beauty, with alluring, virtuous charms,
In softest accents woo'd thee to her arms,

Thy country's love, and love of martial fame,
The gentler passions of the soul o'ercame;
And bade thee hope to see thy wish complete,
"On equal terms the British flag to meet
"Pluck naval honors from the *Briton*'s brow,
"Or dauntless sink to ocean's caves below!"
Such was thy wish, o much lov'd gentle youth,
Pattern of friendship, and unblemish'd truth;
Such was thy wish!—mysterious Heav'n deny'd
Deserv'd success to crown thy noble pride!
O'er pow'r'd by double force, the trembling main
Beheld thy ship, th' unequal fight sustain;
Amaz'd beheld the British bands retire,
Confus'd and falling at thy dreadful fire!
E'en their proud chief, in that destructive hour,
Confess'd thy naval skill and thund'ring pow'r!
Too soon, alas! too soon the wrapping flame
The *Randolph* seiz'd, and spar'd the *Briton*'s shame!
Mounting in air, amidst his warlike crew,
To Heav'n's blest seats heroick Biddle flew;
There swell'd America's immortal band,
Heroes who dy'd to save their native land;
All haste to bind the youthful warrior's brow,
With wreaths whose verdure shall forever glow!

W[ILLIAM] S[CULL]

On the Death of Captain Nicholas Biddle Commander of
the *Randolph* Frigate Blown up near Barbados, 1776 [*sic*].

What distant thunders rend the skies,
What clouds of smoke in columns rise,
  What means this dreadful roar?
Is from his base Vesuvius thrown,
Is sky-topt Atlas tumbled down,
  Or Etna's self no more!

Shock after shock torments my ear;
And lo!—two hostile ships appear,

Red Lightnings round them glow:
The *Yarmouth* boasts of sixty-four,
The *Randolph* thirty-two—no more—
  And will she fight this foe!

The *Randolph* soon on Stygian streams
Shall coast along the land of dreams,
  The islands of the dead!
But Fate, that parts them on the deep,
May save the Briton yet to weep
  His days of victory fled.

Say, who commands that dismal blaze,
Where yonder starry streamer plays?
  Does Mars with Jove engage!
'Tis Biddle wings those angry fires,
Biddle, whose bosom Jove inspires,
  With more than mortal rage.

Tremendous flash!—and hark, the ball
Drives through old *Yarmouth,* flames and all;
  Her bravest sons expire;
Did Mars himself approach so nigh,
Even Mars, without disgrace, might fly
  The *Randolph*'s fiercer fire.

The Briton views his mangled crew,
"And shall we strike to thirty-two?—
  (Said Hector, stained with gore)
"Shall Britain's flag to these descend—
"Rise, and the glorious conflict end,
  "Britons, I ask no more!"

He spoke—they charged their cannon round,
Again the vaulted heavens resound,
  The *Randolph* bore it all,
Then fixed her pointed cannon true—
Away the unwieldy vengeance flew;
  Britain, thy warriors fall.

The *Yarmouth* saw, with dire dismay,
Her wounded hull, shrouds shot away,
   Her boldest heroes dead—
She saw amidst her floating slain
The conquering *Randolph* stem the main—
   She saw, she turned—and fled!

That hour, blest chief, had she been thine,
Dear Biddle, had the power divine
   Been kind as thou wert brave;
But Fate, who doomed thee to expire,
Prepared an arrow tipt with fire,
   And marked a watery grave,

And in that hour, when conquest came,
Winged at his ship a pointed flame,
   That not even he could shun—
The battle ceased, the *Yarmouth* fled,
The bursting *Randolph* ruin spread,
   And left their task undone!

[Philip Morin Freneau]

Appendix B
Muster Rolls

Complete muster rolls for the brig *Andrew Doria* have been found, but none for the frigate *Randolph*. From correspondence, journals, wills, and other documents a partial roster for the latter vessel has been pieced together. In the course of her various cruises, the *Andrew Doria*'s muster rolls account for a total complement of 154 officers and men. The partial list for the *Randolph* provides the names of forty-nine of her crew. Painstaking research has revealed no more.

Muster Roll of the Brig *Andrew Doria*
December, 1775–October, 1776

Quality	Name	Entered	Remarks
Captain	Nicholas Biddle	Dec. 9, 1775	
1st Lieut.	James Josiah	Dec. 11, 1775	Taken in *Crawford,* June 12, 1776
2d Lieut.	Elisha Warner	Dec. 11, 1775	To 1st Lieut., June 18, 1776
3d Lieut.	John McDougall	Dec. 11, 1775	To 2d Lieut., June 18, 1776
Master	Benjamin Dunn	Dec. 11, 1775	To 3d Lieut., June 18, 1776
Lieut. Mar.	Isaac Craig	Nov. 1775	To Capt. Mar., June 18, 1776
Lieut. Mar.	John Trevett	Apr. 19, 1776	
Surgeon	Thomas Kerr	Dec. 1775	Left sick at New London, Apr. 9, 1776
Gunner	Alexander McKenzie	Dec. 1775	
Boatswain	William Darby	Dec. 1775	To sloop *Providence,* Feb. 12, 1776
Boatswain	Joseph Shields	Feb. 12, 1776	
Pilot	Edward Latham	Apr. 24, 1776	
M. Mate	Philip Brown	May 1776	To Master, June 18, 1776
M. Mate	William Moran	Dec. 1775	
M. Mate	John Margeson	Dec. 1775	To sloop *Providence,* May, 1776

Quality	Name	Entered		Remarks
M. Mate	John Dent	Dec.	1775	
Midship.	William Reynolds	Dec.	1775	
Midship.	William Lamb	Dec.	1775	
Midship.	Dennis Leary	Dec.	1775	
Midship.	Evan Bevan	Dec.	1775	Taken in *Crawford,* June 12, 1776
Carpenter	David Edminston	Dec.	1775	
Cook	William Johnston	Dec.	1775	
Surg. Mate	Michael Jennings	Dec.	1775	
Capt. Clerk	John Young	Dec.	1775	
Steward	Elias Rohl	Dec.	1775	
Cooper	William Kennedy	Dec.	1775	
Boat. Mate	John Nowland	Dec.	1775	
Boat. Mate	John Dennis	Feb. 14,	1776	
Boat. Mate	Lawrence Meadows	May	1776	
Boat. Mate	Richard Willson	May	1776	
Carp. Mate	William Green	Jan. 6,	1776	Run, Feb. 10; retaken Feb. 14, 1776
Cook's Mate	John Mackee	Dec.	1775	
Gun. Mate	John Webb	Jan. 6,	1776	Run, Jan. 15, 1776
Gun. Mate	Daniel Harper	May	1776	
Gun. Yeoman	Bartholomew Moore	Dec.	1775	
Qtr. Gunner	Edward Kirk	Dec.	1775	Taken in *Crawford,* June 12, 1776
Qtrmaster	Alex. Livingston	Dec.	1775	
Yeoman	Benjamin Simpson	Jan. 6,	1776	Run, Jan. 20, 1776
Seamen	William Adams	Dec.	1775	
	John Anderson	July	1776	
	James Angus	Dec.	1775	
	Edward Barrett	Jan. 6,	1776	Discharged same day, "unfit for duty"
	Michael Brady	Dec.	1775	
	James Brown	April	1776	From a prize
	Jasper Chamberlin	April	1776	From a prize
	John Chisnell	Jan. 18,	1776	
	John Christian	Dec.	1775	
	Robert Cockran	July	1776	
	Thomas Connor	June	1776	
	Jacob Cook	Dec.	1775	
	Nicholas Cooney	Dec.	1775	
	George Cowell	July	1776	
	James Crosby	Dec.	1775	
	Arthur Dancey	Jan. 6,	1776	Run, Jan. 12, 1776
	George Dickson	July	1776	
	Samuel Dobbins	Dec.	1775	
	James Duffen	Dec.	1775	
	Joseph Elding	Feb. 12,	1776	
	James Evans	Dec.	1775	

Quality	Name	Entered		Remarks
	John Farrell	Dec.	1775	Left sick at New London, Apr. 9, 1776
	Thomas Fisher	June	1776	
	Robert Floreman	Jan. 6,	1776	Run, Jan. 15, 1776
	—— Gardner	May	1776	
	Bernard Garland	Jan. 14,	1776	
	John George	June	1776	
	John Gordon	Jan. 6,	1776	Run, Jan. 12, 1776
	John Green	Dec.	1775	Left sick at New London, Apr. 9, 1776
	James Hayse	July	1776	
	James Heath	Jan. 6,	1776	Run, Jan. 15; retaken Jan. 26, 1776
	William Henderson	Dec.	1775	
	William Hughes	Jan. 14,	1776	
	David Ignew	Dec.	1775	Left sick at New London, Apr. 9, 1776
	Thomas Johnston	Dec.	1775	Left sick at New London, Apr. 9, 1776
	George Kelley	Jan. 18,	1776	
	Robert Kennedy	Dec.	1775	Died at New London, April, 1776
	—— Lawton	May	1776	
	John Lee	Dec.	1775	
	George McAdams	Dec.	1775	
	George McCain	Jan. 16,	1776	
	John McCoy	Dec.	1775	
	James McGuire	Jan. 14,	1776	
	David McKenzie	June	1776	
	Jeremiah Mahaney	Feb. 12,	1776	
	Peter Miller	Dec.	1775	
	William Milton	Dec.	1775	Left sick at New London, Apr. 9, 1776
	John Moise	Jan. 18,	1776	
	Samuel Moore	Jan. 6,	1776	Run, Jan. 12, 1776
	Malitia Nye	May	1776	Taken in *Crawford*, June 12, 1776
	John Patten	Feb. 12,	1776	Left sick at New London, Apr. 9, 1776
	John Pindor	July	1776	
	William Blake Russell	May	1776	Taken in *Crawford*, June 12, 1776
	Michael Smith	Dec.	1775	
	Samuel Smith	Dec.	1775	Left sick at New London, Apr. 9, 1776
	James Swan	Dec.	1775	Left sick at New London, Apr. 9, 1776
	George Sweeney	Dec.	1775	

Quality	Name	Entered	Remarks
	John Sweeney	Feb. 4, 1776	Left sick at New London, Apr. 9, 1776
	Jerry Towhig	Dec. 1775	
	Thomas Warren	Dec. 1775	
	William West	Feb. 12, 1776	Left sick at New London, Apr. 9, 1776
	William Wilding	Dec. 1775	
	James Willson	Jan. 18, 1776	Run, Jan. 28, 1776
Landsman	Daniel Duffy	June 1776	
Boys	Frank Gould	May 1776	Taken in *Crawford*, June 12, 1776; escaped, July 27, 1776 and rejoined
	John McCormick	May 1776	
	William Robertson	May 1776	
Negroes	John Cook	May 1776	From a prize
	Dick	April 1776	From a prize
	Dragoon	April 1776	From a prize

Marines

Quality	Name	Entered	Remarks
Sergeant	Thomas Vernon Turner	Dec. 1775	Died at sea, March 31, 1776
Sergeant	Robert Hunter	Dec. 1775	Left sick at New London, Apr. 9, 1776
Sergeant	Robert Kearns	Dec. 1775	
Sergeant	Jonathan Seaton	May 1776	
Armorer	Samuel Johnson	Dec. 9, 1775	
Drummer	Robert McPharlin	May 30, 1776	From Scotch transport
Piper	Donald McCoy	May 30, 1776	From Scotch transport
Privates	Robert Anderson	Dec. 1775	Left sick at New London, Apr. 9, 1776
	John Broomfield	Dec. 22, 1775	Died at New London, April, 1776
	Andrew Campbell	Dec. 1775	
	James Campbell	Dec. 18, 1775	
	John Campbell	Dec. 1775	
	David Clark	Dec. 9, 1775	
	Patrick Crafford	Dec. 9, 1775	Left sick at New London, Apr. 9, 1776
	Isaac Dewees	Dec. 15, 1775	
	Francis Dowie	Dec. 1775	
	Henry Frazer	Dec. 10, 1775	
	John Frazie	Dec. 22, 1775	Left sick at New London, Apr. 9, 1776
	John Garrigues	Dec. 1775	Left sick at New London, Apr. 9, 1776

Quality	Name	Entered	Remarks
	John Glackner	June 1776	
	Cornelius Grimes	Dec. 1775	
	Samuel Harvey	Dec. 12, 1775	Left sick at New London, Apr. 9, 1776
	John Harwood	Jan. 6, 1776	Run the same day
	Simon Harwood	Dec. 13, 1775	Left sick at New London, Apr. 9, 1776
	Thomas Harwood	Jan. 6, 1776	Run the same day
	William Haslip	Dec. 13, 1775	
	Henry Jarett	Dec. 18, 1775	
	Patrick Kenney	Dec. 18, 1775	
	Edmond Lee	Dec. 15, 1775	
	William Lock	Dec. 12, 1775	Left sick at New London, Apr. 9, 1776
	John McNeal	Dec. 9, 1775	
	James Molesworth	Dec. 1775	Left sick at New London, Apr. 9, 1776
	Archibald Neilson	Dec. 22, 1775	
	Timothy O'Hara	Feb. 12, 1775	
	Richard Owens	Dec. 13, 1775	Left sick at New London, Apr. 9, 1776
	Charles Parker	Dec. 1775	Run, February, 1776
	John Porrett	Dec. 9, 1775	
	Andrew Scott	Dec. 11, 1775	
	William Skilling	Dec. 9, 1775	Left sick at New London, Apr. 9, 1776
	James Stevenson	Dec. 11, 1775	Discharged Dec. 19, 1775
	William Steward	Dec. 10, 1775	
	Benjamin Tate	Dec. 10, 1775	
	John Treasey	May 1776	
	Thomas Watson	Dec. 1775	Left sick at New London, Apr. 9, 1776
	James White	Dec. 13, 1775	Left sick at New London, Apr. 9, 1776 [a]
	James Williams	Dec. 13, 1775	

[a] Many more were landed sick at New London, but all eventually rejoined the *Andrew Doria* except those definitely listed as left there on April 9, 1776.

Partial Muster Roll of the Frigate *Randolph*
October, 1776–March 7, 1778

Quality	Name	Entered	Remarks
Captain	Nicholas Biddle	Oct. 11, 1776	Lost in ship
1st Lieut.	William Barnes	Aug 13, 1776	Lost in ship
2d Lieut.	John McDougall	Oct. 11, 1776	Lost in ship
3d Lieut.	Joshua Fanning	Oct. 11, 1776	Lost in ship

Quality	Name	Entered	Remarks
Master	Robert Johnson	Oct. 11, 1776	Lost in ship
Capt. Mar.	Samuel Shaw	June 25, 1776	Lost in ship
1st. Lt. Mar.	Franklin Reid	June 25, 1776	Resigned, Dec. 1776
2d Lt. Mar.	Panatiere de la Fal-conniere	Sept. 12, 1776	Sent under arrest to Congress, Sept. 1, 1777
Surgeon	Thomas Hore	Oct. 11, 1776	Lost in ship
Carpenter	Richard Fordham	Oct. 11, 1776	Left at Charlestown, Feb. 12, 1778
Pilot	Henry Tudor	Dec. 1, 1776	Left ship at Delaware capes, Feb. 6, 1777
Midship.	Simeon Fanning	Jan. 10, 1777	Sent in prize, March 5, 1778
Midship.	John McPherson	Nov. 1776	Wounded, discharged Sept. 10, 1777
Midship.	Peter Bocquet	Nov. 1776	Lost in ship
Midship.	Mordecai Matlack	Nov. 1776	Lost in ship
Midship.	——— Burrows	Nov. 1776	Lost in ship
M. Mate	William Irringston	Nov. 1776	Lost in ship
M. Mate	John Rogers	Nov. 1776	Left ship in March, 1777
M. Mate	Philip Treglohn	Dec. 7, 1776	Sent in prize, March 5, 1778
Volunteer	John MacQueen	Aug. 1777	For cruise; left ship Sept. 6, 1777
Volunteer	James Budd		Lost in ship
Volunteer	——— Simons	Jan. 24, 1778	Lost in ship
Seamen	Thomas Ellison	Nov. 1776	Lost in ship
	Bernard Garland	Nov. 1776	Lost in ship
	Joseph Barry	Nov. 1776	Lost in ship
	Alexander Leyburn	Nov. 1776	Lost in ship
	Thomas Tivy	Nov. 1776	Lost in ship
	William Connolly	Nov. 1776	Lost in ship
	Jeremiah Twig	Nov. 1776	Lost in ship
	Thomas Saunders Pascho	Nov. 1776	Lost in ship
	Dennis McCarthy	Nov. 1776	Lost in ship
	David Bigs	Nov. 1776	Lost in ship
	Hans Workman	Nov. 1776	Saved from wreck, Mar. 12, 1778
	John Carew	Nov. 1776	Saved from wreck, Mar. 12, 1778
	Alexander Robinson	Nov. 1776	Saved from wreck, Mar. 12, 1778
	Bartholomew Bourdeau	Nov. 1776	Saved from wreck, Mar. 12, 1778
	Caleb Idelet	Nov. 1776	Sent in prize, March 5, 1778
	Joseph Frost	Feb. 3, 1777	Deserted, April, 1777
	Joseph Berry	Feb. 3, 1777	Deserted, April, 1777

Quality	Name	Entered		Remarks
Landsmen	Edward Rowin	Nov.	1776	Deserted, Jan. 18, 1777
	Edward Higgins	Nov.	1776	Deserted, Jan. 18, 1777
Marines	Angus Cameron	July	1776	Deserted, Aug. 1776
	Philip Mulholand			Deserted, Jan. 15, 1777
	Neil Faran			Deserted, Jan. 15, 1777
	John Clements			Deserted, Jan. 15, 1777
	Thomas McNamie			Deserted, Jan. 15, 1777
	Henry Spear			Deserted, Jan. 18, 1777

First South Carolina regiment

Captain	Joseph Ioor	Jan. 24, 1778	Lost in ship
Lieutenant	George Gray	Jan. 24, 1778	Lost in ship

Bibliography

In listing the printed and manuscript materials consulted, I have endeavored to enhance the value of the bibliography by citing the principal materials used.

Printed Documents and Document Collections

DeSaussure, Wilmot G. (comp.). *The Names as far as can be ascertained of the officers who served in the South Carolina Regiments in the Revolution* (Charleston, 1886).

Egle, William Henry (comp.). *Pennsylvania Archives,* Third Series, 30 vols. (Harrisburg, 1897), XXV, XXVI.

Force, Peter (comp.). *American Archives,* Fourth Series, 6 vols. (Washington, 1837–46).

———— (comp.). *American Archives,* Fifth Series, 3 vols. (Washington, 1848–53).

Ford, Worthington Chauncey (ed.). *Journals of the Continental Congress, 1775–78,* 34 vols. (Washington, 1905–1908).

Hazard, Samuel (ed.). *Pennsylvania Colonial Records,* 16 vols. (Harrisburg, 1851–53), X, XI, "Minutes of the Pennsylvania Committee and Council of Safety relating to the Pennsylvania and Continental navies."

———— (comp.). *Pennsylvania Archives,* First Series, 12 vols. (Harrisburg, 1852–56), IX, "Memorial of Isaac Craig."

Hoadly, C. F. (ed.). *Public Records of the Colony of Connecticut,* 15 vols. (Hartford, 1890), XV, "Minutes of Council of Safety."

Linn, John Blair (comp.). *Pennsylvania Archives,* Second Series, 19 vols. (Harrisburg, 1879).

Montgomery, Thomas L. (comp.). *Pennsylvania Archives,* Fifth Series, 8 vols. (Harrisburg, 1906), I, "Pennsylvania seamen sent to Continental vessels"; IV, "Pension application of John McPherson."

Smith, Joseph Jencks (ed.). *Civil and Military Lists of Rhode Island* (Providence, 1901).

Wharton, Francis (ed.). *The Revolutionary Diplomatic Correspondence of the United States,* 6 vols. (Washington, 1889).

Biographies and General Works of History

Barney, Mary. *Biographical Memoir of the Late Commodore Joshua Barney* (Boston, 1832).

Clarke, James Stanier and McArthur, John. *The Life and Services of Admiral Lord Nelson* (London, 1839).

Etting, Frank M. *The Philadelphia Tea Party of 1773* (Philadelphia, 1873).

Field, Edward. *Esek Hopkins* (Providence, 1898).

Freneau, Philip Morin. *On the Death of Captain Nicholas Biddle* [Pamphlet issued by Francis Bailey] (Philadelphia, 1781).

Frost, John. *The Book of the Navy* (New York, 1842).

————. *Picture Book of the Commodores* (New York, 1845). The Nicholas Biddle sketch is taken in entirety from the *Port Folio* biography.

Johnson, Joseph. *Traditions and Reminiscences Chiefly of the Revolution in the South* (Charleston, 1851).

Lee, Sidney (ed.). *Dictionary of National Biography,* XV (London, 1909).

McCrady, Edward. *The History of South Carolina* (New York, 1901).

Miller, John C. *Origins of the American Revolution* (Boston, 1943).

Rogers, Ernest E. *Connecticut's Naval Office at New London during the War of the American Revolution* (New London, 1933).

Sands, Robert C. *Life and Correspondence of John Paul Jones* (New York, 1830).

Scharf, John Thomas and Westcott, Thomas. *History of Philadelphia* (Philadelphia, 1884).

Stryker, William S. *The Battles of Trenton and Princeton* (Boston, 1898).

Waldo, S. Putnam. *Biographical Sketches of Distinguished American Naval Heroes in the War of the Revolution* (Hartford, 1823). The sketch of Nicholas Biddle is largely a rewrite of the *Port Folio* biography.

Wilson, Thomas. *The Biography of the Principal American Military and Naval Heroes* (New York, 1817). This is the first complete rewrite of the *Port Folio* biography.

Printed Diaries and Collections of Letters

Adams, Charles Francis (ed.). *Letters of John Adams addressed to his wife,* 2 vols. (Boston, 1841).

———— (ed.). *The Works of John Adams,* 10 vols. (Boston, 1856).

Beck, Alverda S. (ed.). *The Correspondence of Esek Hopkins, Commander-in-Chief of the United States Navy,* Rhode Island Historical Society publication (Providence, 1933). This work contains two letters from Nicholas Biddle, dated May 21 and June 28, 1776.

———— (ed.). *The Letter Book of Esek Hopkins, Commander-in-Chief of the United States Navy, 1775–1777,* Rhode Island Historical Society publication (Providence, 1932).

Biddle, James S. (ed.). *Autobiography of Charles Biddle, Vice-President of the Supreme Executive Council of Pennsylvania, 1745–1821* (Philadelphia, 1883). This work contains invaluable source material on Nicholas Biddle's family, early voyages and shipwreck, and on Charles Biddle's efforts to learn more details of the loss of the *Randolph.*

Burnett, Edmond O. (comp.). *Letters of Members of the Continental Congress,* 5 vols. (Washington, 1921–31).

Deas, Anne Izard (ed.). *Correspondence of Mr. Ralph Izard of South Carolina* (New York, 1844).

Duane, William (ed.). *Extracts from the Diary of Christopher Marshall* (New York, 1835).

Ford, Worthington Chauncey (ed.). *Warren-Adams Letters, Being chiefly a correspondence among John Adams, Samuel Adams, and James Warren,* 2 vols. (Boston, 1917 and 1925).

Henkels, Stan V. (comp.). *The Confidential Correspondence of Robert Morris.* Catalogue No. 1183 (Philadelphia, 1917).

———— (comp.). *David N. Newbold Autograph Collection* [catalogue] (Philadelphia, 1928).

Littell, John Stockton (ed.). [Alexander] *Graydon's Memoirs of his Own Times with Reminiscences of the Men and Events* (Philadelphia, 1846).

Moore, Frank (comp.). *Materials for History* (New York, 1861). This work contains correspondence of Henry Laurens, 1777–78.

Moultrie, William. *Memoirs of the American Revolution so far as it relates to the States of North and South Carolina and Georgia* (New York, 1802).

Neeser, Robert Wilden (ed.). *The Despatches of Molyneux Shuldham,*

Vice-Admiral of the Blue and Commander-in-Chief of His Britannic Majesty's Ships in North America, January–July, 1776, Naval History Society publication (New York, 1913). This work includes "A Journal of a Cruse In the Brig Andrew Doria Nicholas Biddle Esqr. Commander from ye. Port of Philadelphia, Begun January 4th, 1776."

Nicolas, Sir Nicholas Harris (ed.). *The Dispatches and Letters of Vice Admiral Lord Viscount Nelson* (London, 1895).

Paullin, Charles Oscar (ed.). *Out-Letters of the Continental Marine Committee and Board of Admiralty, August, 1776–September, 1780,* Naval History Society publication (New York, 1914). This work includes sailing orders and instructions to Nicholas Biddle and letters to the Continental agents in Charleston, South Carolina.

Phipps, Constantine John. *A Voyage Towards the North Pole Undertaken by His Majesty's Command, 1773* (Dublin, 1775).

Salley, A. S., Jr. (ed.). *Journal of the Commissioners of the Navy of South Carolina, October 9, 1776–March 1, 1779* (Columbia, S. C., 1912).

———— (comp.). *Marriage Notices in the* South Carolina Gazette *and its Successors* (Albany, 1902).

Sparks, Jared (ed.). *Letters to George Washington,* 4 vols. (Boston, 1853).

Willard, M. W. (ed.). *Letters of the American Revolution* (Boston, 1925).

Periodicals

Almon, J. (ed.). *The* Remembrancer *or Impartial Repository of Public Events* (London, 1775–78).

Connecticut Historical Society Collections (Hartford), "Correspondence of Silas Deane, 1774–1776," II (1870).

Maryland Historical Society Publications, Archives of Maryland (Baltimore), "Journal and Correspondence of the Council of Maryland, April 1, 1778–October 26, 1779," XXI (1901).

Pennsylvania Magazine of History and Biography (Philadelphia). William John Potts. "Du Simitiere, Artist, Antiquary, and Naturalist . . . ," XIII (1889–90); "Autobiographical Sketch of the Life of Gen. John Burrows, of Lycoming Co., Penna.," XXXIV (1910); Joseph Jackson. "A Philadelphia Schoolmaster of the Eighteenth Century," XXXV (1911); "Journal of Captain John Ferdinand Dalziel Smyth, of the Queen's Rangers," XXXIX

(1915); "Letters of Montfort Browne, John Browne and Thomas Atwood, Relative to the New Providence Expedition," XLIX (1925).

Poor Richard's Almanack (Philadelphia, 1753), American Philosophical Society.

Port Folio (Philadelphia), "Biographical Memoirs of the Late Captain Nicholas Biddle," II, iv (1809). This is the first printed account of Biddle's life, presumably prepared by his brother Charles, and the basis of various biographical sketches appearing in the ensuing century. Volume II, v (1809), contains the article, "To Readers and Correspondents." This is a eulogy of the Nicholas Biddle biography in the previous issue, which "will challenge a comparison with the best biographies of foreign birth."

Rhode Island Historical Magazine (Newport), "Journal of John Trevett, 1775–80," VI, VII (1886–87).

Rhode Island Historical Society Collections (Providence), "Correspondence of Nicholas Cooke," VI (1867). This work contains a letter from Nicholas Biddle to Governor Cooke, July 26, 1776.

Rhode Island Historical Society Publications (Providence), "Papers of William Vernon and the Navy Board, 1776–1794," VIII (1900–1901).

South Carolina Historical and Genealogical Magazine (Charleston), I (1900), III (1902), XIV (1913), XXI–XXIV (1920–23). These various articles relate to Archdale Hall and the Baker family. "Order Book of the South Carolina Line," VII (1906). Volume X (1909) contains a letter from Rawlins Lowndes to Henry Laurens, March 30, 1778, regarding the loss of the *Randolph*.

Southern Literary Messenger (Richmond), "The Virginia Navy of the Revolution," (1857).

U.S. Naval Institute Proceedings (Annapolis), Edward Biddle, "Captain Nicholas Biddle (Continental Navy) 1750–1778," No. 175 (1917). This article quotes from a number of letters written by Nicholas Biddle, the originals of which, bound in a small volume, are in the estate of Edward Biddle, Philadelphia.

Newspapers

Boston *Gazette* (1776).

Hartford *Connecticut Courant and Hartford Weekly Intelligencer* (1778).

Philadelphia *Dunlap's Pennsylvania Packet, or the General Advertiser* (1778).

Charlestown *Gazette of the State of South Carolina* (1777, 1778).

Boston *Independent Chronicle* (1776).

Trenton *New Jersey Gazette* (1780), "Verses to the Memory of Captain Nicholas Biddle."

Newport *Mercury* (1776).

New York *Gazette and the Weekly Mercury* (1778).

Edenton *North Carolina Gazette* (1777, 1778).

Philadelphia *Pennsylvania Gazette* (1763–78).

Philadelphia *Pennsylvania Journal & Weekly Advertiser* (1766, 1777).

Philadelphia *Pennsylvania Ledger, or the Philadelphia Market-Day Advertiser* (1778).

London *Public Advertiser* (1772, 1773).

Charlestown *South Carolina and American General Gazette* (1777, 1778).

Charlestown *South Carolina Gazette* (1766).

Philadelphia *Town's Pennsylvania Evening Post* (1776–78).

London *Westminster Journal and London Political Miscellany* (1776–78).

Map and Ship Plans

"A Chart of the Atlantic Ocean. London. Printed for Robt Sayer. Map & Printseller. N° 53, in Fleet Street, as the Act directs 20 Feby 1775."

"A Chart of the British Channel; Comprehending the Southern Coasts of England and Wales; with the Coast of France, from Dunkirk to the River of Nantes. By *Thomas Jefferys* Geographer to the King. London. Published by Robert Sayer N° 53 in Fleet Street, as the Act directs 20 Feby 1775."

"A Chart of the Delaware Bay and River. By *Mr. Fisher* of Philadelphia, 1776."

"A Map of the Province of South Carolina with all the Rivers, Creeks, Bays, Inletts, Islands . . . Humbly inscribed to the Honble Lawlins [sic] Lowndes Esq Speaker & the rest of the Members of the Honble the Commons House of Assembly of the Province by their most Obed^t & faithfull Servt Jam^s Cook. Publish'd according to Act of Parliament June 7,th 1773, and Sold by H. Parker in Cornhill." Henry Clinton Papers, University of Michigan Library, Ann Arbor.

Charts of West Indies and various sections of the Atlantic coast of North America. Navy Department, Hydrographic Office, Washington.

Randolph, Continental frigate. Sheer, body, and half breadth plans from the Navy Department, Washington.

Manuscripts and Manuscript Collections

"A remarkable instance of the lives of four men being providentially saved," [broadside], *ca.* 1779, New York Public Library, New York City.

Bank of North America Papers, Instructions from Robert Morris to Nicholas Biddle, *ca.* 1776, Historical Society of Pennsylvania, Philadelphia.

John Barry Papers, W. Horace Hepburn Private Collection, Philadelphia.

Charles Biddle Letter Book, "List of persons with whom I was related or well acquainted with who have departed the world I hope for a better"; rough draft of memoir of Captain Nicholas Biddle, Historical Society of Pennsylvania, Philadelphia.

Nicholas Biddle Letters, Estate of Edward Biddle, Philadelphia. This collection comprises some twenty letters written by Biddle, several documents in his handwriting, a number of letters to him, and muster rolls of the *Andrew Doria*. The letters apparently were collected originally by his brother James, and were filed for safekeeping either by James or Charles Biddle in the Berks County Courthouse, Pennsylvania, and then forgotten. They were discovered, in 1880, among some old and dusty papers in a rubbish room adjoining the main courthouse entrance, and returned to the family. The Library of Congress bound the papers for the family in 1916, and Edward Biddle used extracts from some of the letters in preparing the article on Nicholas Biddle which appeared in *U.S. Naval Institute Proceedings* in 1917. After Edward Biddle's death the volume was mislaid and was not rediscovered until 1948, when it was found among his estate papers. This invaluable collection was then made available for this biography through the kindness and courtesy of Edward Biddle's executors.

British Admiralty Papers, Account General, Miscellanea, Class 43, Head money vouchers for crew of the *Yarmouth;* Admirals' Dispatches, Leeward Islands; Captains' Letters, Robert Fanshawe and Nicholas Vincent; "Captains' Logs," Class 51, *Carysfort, Cerberus, Glasgow, Lizard, Perseus, Portland, Roebuck, Seaford, Yarmouth;* Class 55, *Carcass Bomb, Racehorse;* "Masters' Logs," Class 52, *Carysfort, Yarmouth;* Muster Rolls, Class 36, *Carcass Bomb, Cerberus, Portland, Seaford, Racehorse, Yarmouth;* Secretary, In Letters, High Court of Admiralty, Miscellanea, "Log Book for the Wasp"; Public Records Office, London.

British Colonial Office, Vol. 28, Public Records Office, London.

Committee to Transact Continental Business at Philadelphia Letter Book, Library of Congress, Washington.

Papers of the Continental Congress, Vol. 58, Esek Hopkins correspondence; Vol. 78, letters of Nicholas Biddle and John Dorsius from Charlestown; Vol. 137 and Appendix, letters of Robert Morris, Library of Congress, Washington.

Data on position of the moon on March 7, 1778, U.S. Naval Observatory, Washington.

Ferdinand J. Dreer Autograph Collection, American Navy, Nicholas Biddle receipt, May 10, 1769; Fanning Papers, Simeon Fanning to his mother, October 8, 1777, Richard Fordham affidavit, December 7, 1821, Historical Society of Pennsylvania, Philadelphia.

Peter Force Transcripts, Library of Congress, Washington.

Benjamin Franklin Papers, Joseph Galloway to Franklin, April 23, 1771, American Philosophical Society, Philadelphia.

Simon Gratz Autograph Collection, American Navy of Revolution, Captains of Pennsylvania fleet to Committee of Safety, October 12 and 30, 1775; Nicholas Biddle to Peter Long, ca. 1775, Historical Society of Pennsylvania, Philadelphia.

Private Collection of the late Mrs. John Drayton Grimke, papers relative to the family of Richard Bohun Baker, and to Archdale Hall, Charleston, South Carolina.

Joshua Humphreys Book of Ship Dimensions, "Dimentions of the Randolph and other documents relating to that frigate," Joshua Humphreys Papers, Historical Society of Pennsylvania, Philadelphia.

John Paul Jones Manuscripts, Library of Congress, Washington.

Miscellaneous Naval Papers and Manuscripts, U.S. Naval Academy Museum, Annapolis.

Marine Committee Letter Book, Library of Congress, Washington.

Thomas Penrose Note Book, "Dementions of Ship Randolph Masts & Yards," Historical Society of Pennslyvania, Philadelphia.

Revolutionary Papers, Pennsylvania State Library, Harrisburg.

Charles Roberts Autograph Collection, Naval Committee to Esek Hopkins, January 4, 1776; "Indent of Sundry Slops Wanted for the Randolph Frigate," November 19, 1776, Haverford College Library, Haverford, Pennsylvania.

Franklin Delano Roosevelt Manuscript Collection, Nicholas Biddle to Robert Morris, November 23, 1777, Roosevelt Memorial Library, Hyde Park, New York.

Nathaniel Shaw, Jr., Papers and Account Books, Yale University Library, New Haven.

Society Collection, George Lux to Edward Burd, October 2, 1775; "Philadelphia Directory, 1767–1768," compiled from newspapers; "Military Stores & Ammunition put on board the Gondolas," *ca.* 1775, Historical Society of Pennsylvania, Philadelphia.

George Washington Papers, Library of Congress, Washington.

John Fanning Watson Manuscript Annals, "Incidents of the war and its calamities to a family—best known to the author," Historical Society of Pennsylvania, Philadelphia.

Abraham Whipple Papers, Burton Historical Collection, Detroit Free Library.

Will Book R, 1778, 1779, Wills of Joshua Fanning and members of the crew of the *Randolph,* Register of Wills Office, Philadelphia.

Will Books, 1774–79, Wills of Nicholas Biddle, John McDougall, and William Barnes, Charleston Free Library, Charleston.

Charles Willing Papers, letters relating to Captain Walter Sterling, Historical Society of Pennsylvania, Philadelphia.

Samuel W. Woodhouse Collection, Day Book of Charles Wharton, 1775–83, containing chandlery supplied for the *Andrew Doria, Franklin,* and *Randolph;* commissioners of the navy in account with the frigate *Randolph,* Historical Society of Pennsylvania, Philadelphia.

Notes

Chapter I

[1] James S. Biddle (ed.), *Autobiography of Charles Biddle, Vice-President of the Supreme Executive Council of Pennsylvania, 1745–1821* (Philadelphia, 1883), 15, 20. This work is hereafter cited as *Charles Biddle's Autobiography.*

[2] Joseph Jackson, "A Philadelphia Schoolmaster of the Eighteenth Century," *Pennsylvania Magazine of History and Biography* (Philadelphia), XXXV (1911), 315–33.

[3] "Biographical Memoirs of the late Captain Nicholas Biddle," *Port Folio* (Philadelphia), II, iv (October, 1809). This work is hereafter cited as *"Port Folio* Biography." Nicholas Biddle's endorsement on a bill of John Laurence to Mary Biddle, June 9, 1761, in David McNeely Stauffer's extra-illustrated copy of John Thomas Scharf and Thomas Westcott's *History of Philadelphia* (Philadelphia, 1884), VI, 488.

[4] "Sailings for Quebec, Outward and Cleared," *Pennsylvania Gazette,* April 19, 26, 1764; "Inward Entries," *ibid.,* August 30, 1764; *"Port Folio* Biography."

[5] Biddle (ed.), *Charles Biddle's Autobiography,* 15, 20, 368.

[6] *Pennsylvania Gazette,* August 23, 1764.

[7] Extract of a letter from Mrs. William Biddle to Mrs. George Lux, undated, Biddle (ed.), *Charles Biddle's Autobiography,* 2, 3.

[8] Nicholas Biddle's endorsement on bill of John Laurence to Mary Biddle, June 9, 1761; *Pennsylvania Gazette,* March 10, 1763.

[9] Memorandum of Mrs. Mary Biddle, 1775, Biddle (ed.), *Charles Biddle's Autobiography,* 241, 242.

[10] *Ibid.,* 36–78.

[11] *Ibid.,* 1.

[12] *Ibid.,* 2; Christ Church Records, Philadelphia.

[13] Extract of a letter from Mrs. William Biddle to Mrs. George Lux, undated, Biddle (ed.), *Charles Biddle's Autobiography,* 2, 3.

[14] Biddle (ed.), *Charles Biddle's Autobiography,* 370, 389, 390; John Blair Linn (comp.), *Pennsylvania Archives,* Second Series (Harrisburg, 1879), II, 557, 558, 607; Thomas L. Montgomery (comp.), *Pennsylvania Archives,* Fifth Series (Harrisburg, 1906), I, 63, 89, 99, 108, 113, 129, 179, 265, 314. These works are hereafter cited as *Pa. Arch.*

[15] Memorandum of Mrs. Mary Biddle, 1775, Biddle (ed.), *Charles Biddle's Autobiography,* 241, 242.

[16] Linn (comp.), *Pa. Arch.,* II, 550.

[17] *Ibid.,* 542–51.

[18] Biddle (ed.), *Charles Biddle's Autobiography,* 15, 16.

[19] *Pennsylvania Gazette,* August 30, October 4, 1764.

[20] Biddle (ed.), *Charles Biddle's Autobiography,* 15.

[21] *Ibid.,* 16.

[22] *Ibid.,* 17.

[23] *Ibid.,* 18.

[24] *Ibid.,* 19.

[25] In his *Autobiography,* Charles Biddle describes the negro revolt, the killing of the settler Cook, and the cruel execution of Marlborough as occurring during a subsequent voyage under Captain William McFunn. News of the revolt and of Cook's death, however, was contained in an article printed in the *Pennsylvania Gazette,* September 5, 1765. It had been imparted by Captain Naesmith upon the return of the *Ann and Almack* to Philadelphia.

[26] *Pennsylvania Gazette,* September 5, 12, 1765.

[27] Biddle (ed.), *Charles Biddle's Autobiography,* 20.

Chapter II

[1] *Pennsylvania Gazette,* September 26, 1765.

[2] Biddle (ed.), *Charles Biddle's Autobiography,* 20, 23.

[3] For the most comprehensive review of the Stamp Act agitation, see John C. Miller, *Origins of the American Revolution* (Boston, 1943) 109–64.

[4] "Philadelphia Directory, 1767–1768," manuscript compiled from newspapers, Society Collection, Historical Society of Pennsylvania, Philadelphia; Memorandum of Mrs. Mary Biddle, 1775, Biddle (ed.), *Charles Biddle's Autobiography,* 241, 242.

[5] "List of persons with whom I was related or well acquainted with who have departed the world I hope for a better," Charles Biddle Letter Book, 125–51, Historical Society of Pennsylvania, Philadelphia; Biddle (ed.), *Charles Biddle's Autobiography,* 25; "Outward Entry," *Pennsylvania Gazette,* October 24, 1765.

[6] Biddle (ed.), *Charles Biddle's Autobiography,* 20, 21.

[7] The account of the shipwreck is told in great detail, *ibid.,* 22–28. This seems to be the sole source and was used in part in the *"Port Folio* Biography," and in Edward Biddle's brief article, "Captain Nicholas Biddle (Continental Navy), 1750–1778," in *U.S. Naval Institute Proceedings* (Annapolis), No. 175 (1917). This latter article is hereafter cited as "Edward Biddle Memoir."

[8] *South Carolina Gazette,* Monday, July 28–Monday, August 4, 1766.

[9] *Ibid.,* Monday, August 18–Monday, August 25, 1766; Biddle (ed.), *Charles Biddle's Autobiography,* 29.

[10] *Pennsylvania Journal & Weekly Advertiser,* July 3, 1766.

[11] Mrs. William Biddle to Mrs. George Lux, undated, Biddle (ed.), *Charles Biddle's Autobiography,* 2, 3.

[12] *"Port Folio* Biography"; Linn (comp.), *Pa. Arch.,* II, 557; XVI, 486, 490, 494; "Memo of Broᵗ Nicholas," in handwriting of James Biddle (1731–97), The Letters of Captain Nicholas Biddle, 1771–1778, Edward Biddle estate. This collection is hereafter cited as Nicholas Biddle Letters.

[13] Nicholas Biddle receipt, May 10, 1769, Ferdinand J. Dreer Autograph Collection, Naval Officers, I, Historical Society of Pennsylvania, Philadelphia.

[14] Biddle (ed.), *Charles Biddle's Autobiography,* 109.

[15] *Ibid.,* 37–90.

[16] "Philadelphia Directory, 1767–1768."

[17] *"Port Folio* Biography."

[18] Description from Charles Willson Peale portrait.

[19] "Warrants of land in County of Berks," William Henry Egle (comp.), *Pennsylvania Archives,* Third Series (Harrisburg, 1897), XXVI, 245. This work is hereafter cited as *Pa. Arch.*

[20] Charles Biddle Letter Book, 89, 90; rough draft of memoir of Nicholas Biddle, Historical Society of Pennsylvania, Philadelphia. This draft is hereafter cited as Charles Biddle's Rough Draft.

Chapter III

[1] *Pennsylvania Gazette,* November 15, 22, and 29, 1769.

[2] Biddle (ed.), *Charles Biddle's Autobiography,* 50; *Pennsylvania Gazette,* March 28, 1771.

[3] *"Port Folio* Biography"; "Edward Biddle Memoir."

[4] Joseph Galloway to Benjamin Franklin, April 23, 1771, Benjamin Franklin Papers, III, 50, American Philosophical Society, Philadelphia.

[5] *Pennsylvania Gazette,* April 11, 18, and 25, 1771; Nicholas Biddle to James Biddle, June 28, 1777, Nicholas Biddle Letters.

[6] Muster Table, H.M.S. *Seaford,* 1771, British Admiralty, Class 36, No. 7678, Public Records Office, London.

[7] Charles Willing Papers, Historical Society of Pennsylvania, Philadelphia.

[8] Muster Table, H.M.S. *Seaford,* 1771; Nicholas Biddle to James Biddle, July 13, 1771, Nicholas Biddle Letters.

[9] "Journal of H.M.S. *Seaford,"* June 22–August 8, 1771, British Admiralty, Class 51, No. 879, Public Records Office, London.

[10] "Edward Biddle Memoir"; *"Port Folio* Biography"; "Journal of H.M.S. *Seaford,"* August 13, 1771; Muster Table, H.M.S. *Portland,* 1771–72, British Admiralty, Class 36, No. 7471, Public Records Office, London.

[11] "Proceedings of His Majesty's Ship Portland," August 14–17, 1771, British Admiralty, Class 51, No. 710, Pt. ii, Public Records Office, London. These proceedings are hereafter cited as *"Portland* Journal."

[12] *Ibid.,* August 18–September 25, 1771; Muster Table, H.M.S. *Portland.*

[13] Muster Table, H.M.S. *Portland,* 1771–72; Biddle (ed.), *Charles Biddle's Autobiography,* 99.

[14] *"Portland* Journal," September 26, 1771.

[15] *Ibid.,* September 27–November 23, 1771.

[16] "Supernumeraries born for Victuals only by Order of Adml Pye," November 24, 1771, Muster Table, H.M.S. *Portland,* 1771–72.

[17] *"Portland* Journal," November 24, 1771.

[18] *Ibid.,* November 25–December 11, 1771.

[19] *Ibid.,* December 12–20, 1771.

[20] *Ibid.,* December 26, 1771.

[21] "A Log Book kept on Board his Majesty's Ship Portland," January 27, 1772, British Admiralty, Class 52, No. 1917, Pt. iii, Public Record Office, London; *"Portland* Journal," January 27–29, 1772.

[22] *Dictionary of National Biography,* XV (London, 1909), 564–65, contains a biography of Sir Ralph Payne which states that he had a good figure, and was popular in the Leeward Islands, "but his language was turgid and wonderfully verbose."

23 *"Portland* Journal," January 31, June 15, 1772; Nicholas Biddle to James Biddle, May 14, 1772, Nicholas Biddle Letters.

24 Nicholas Biddle to Charles Biddle, June 16, 1772, "Edward Biddle Memoir"; Nicholas Biddle Letters.

25 *"Portland* Journal," June 17–July 3, 1772.

26 Nicholas Biddle to James Biddle, July 6, 1772, "Edward Biddle Memoir."

27 *"Portland* Journal," August 4, 1772.

28 *Ibid.,* August 5–September 20, 1772; "Extract of a letter from Portsmouth," September 20, 1772, London *Public Advertiser,* September 22, 1772.

29 "Extract of a letter from Portsmouth," September 22, 1772; *ibid.,* September 24, 1772.

30 "Extract of a letter from Portsmouth," September 29, 1772; *ibid.,* October 1, 1772; "Ship News, Deal," October 1, 1772; *ibid.,* October 3, 1772; *"Portland* Journal," September 28–October 4, 1772.

31 *Ibid.,* October 5–13, 1772.

32 "A Log Book kept on Board his Majesty's Ship Portland," October 13, 1772; Muster Table, H.M.S. *Portland,* 1771–72.

33 *"Port Folio* Biography."

Chapter IV

1 Nicholas Biddle to Lydia McFunn, October 20, 1772, "Edward Biddle Memoir."

2 *"Port Folio* Biography."

3 Constantine John Phipps, *A Voyage Towards the North Pole Undertaken by his Majesty's Command, 1773* (Dublin, 1775), 10. This work is hereafter cited as *Phipps' Journal.*

4 London *Public Advertiser,* May 24, 1773.

5 "Edward Biddle Memoir."

6 *Phipps' Journal,* 13, 15.

7 Muster Table, H.M.S. *Carcass,* 1773, British Admiralty, Class 36, No. 7567, Public Records Office, London.

8 *"Port Folio* Biography."

9 *Phipps' Journal,* 11, 12.

10 Muster Table, H.M.S. *Carcass,* 1773.

11 *Ibid.*

12 *Phipps' Journal,* 20.

13 Muster Table, H.M.S. *Carcass,* 1773; *"Port Folio* Biography"; Sir Nicholas Harris Nicolas (ed.), *The Dispatches and Letters of Vice Admiral Lord Viscount Nelson* (London, 1895), 1–3.

14 Nicholas Biddle's copy of the log was lost with him in the *Randolph. "Port Folio* Biography."

15 *Phipps' Journal,* 19.

16 "A Journal of the Proceedings of his Majesty's Sloop Carcass on a Voyage of Discovery towards the North Pole," June 3, 4, 1773, British Admiralty, Class 55, No. 12, Public Records Office, London. This journal is hereafter cited as *"Carcass* Log."

17 *Ibid.,* June 6–11, 1773; *Phipps' Journal,* 22, 23.

18 *Ibid.,* 23, 24; London *Public Advertiser,* June 4, 1773.

19 *"Carcass* Log," June 14–16, 1773.

[20] *Ibid.*, June 17, 1773.

[21] *Ibid.*, June 18–23, 1773; *Phipps' Journal*, 24–29.

[22] *Phipps' Journal*, 30, 31.

[23] "Carcass Log," June 29, 30, 1773.

[24] *Phipps' Journal*, 33, 34.

[25] *Ibid.*, 39–41; "Carcass Log," July 4–7, 1773.

[26] *Phipps' Journal*, 42–44.

[27] "Carcass Log," July 10–12, 1773.

[28] *Ibid.*, July 26, 1773.

[29] *Ibid.*, July 31, 1773.

[30] *Phipps' Journal*, 62, 63.

[31] *Ibid.*, 64; "Carcass Log," August 3, 4, 1773.

[32] "Carcass Log," August 5, 1773; James Stanier Clarke and John McArthur, *The Life and Services of Admiral Lord Nelson* (London, 1839), 21, 22.

[33] *Phipps' Journal*, 65.

[34] *Ibid.*, 66, 67.

[35] "Carcass Log," August 7, 1773.

[36] *Phipps' Journal*, 68.

[37] *Ibid.*, 69; "Carcass Log," August 8, 9, 1773.

[38] "Carcass Log," August 10, 1773.

[39] *Ibid.*, August 11, 12, 1773; *Phipps' Journal*, 70.

[40] *Phipps' Journal*, 71–74.

[41] *Ibid.*, 75.

[42] "Carcass Log," September 10, 1773.

[43] *Ibid.*, September 11, 1773.

[44] Skeffingham Lutwidge to Philip Stephens, September 18, 1773, "Carcass Log" enclosure.

[45] *Phipps' Journal*, 76.

[46] London *Public Advertiser*, September 23, 1773.

[47] Nicholas Biddle to Lydia McFunn, October 18, 1773, "Edward Biddle Memoir"; Nicholas Biddle Letters.

[48] Charles Biddle's Rough Draft; Muster Table, H.M.S. *Carcass*, 1773.

[49] London *Gazateer and New Daily Advertiser*, March 19, 1774.

[50] "Port Folio Biography."

Chapter V

[1] Frank M. Etting, *The Philadelphia Tea Party of 1773* (Philadelphia, 1873); "Port Folio Biography"; Newport *Mercury*, May 16, June 27, and July 25, 1774.

[2] Biddle (ed.), *Charles Biddle's Autobiography*, 389, 390.

[3] Miller, *Origins of the American Revolution*, 355–76.

[4] Biddle (ed.), *Charles Biddle's Autobiography*, 390.

[5] "Warrants of Land in Northumberland County," Egle (comp.), *Pa. Arch.*, XXV, 66, 67; Nicholas Biddle to James Biddle, October [?] 1774, Nicholas Biddle Letters.

[6] Biddle (ed.), *Charles Biddle's Autobiography*, 75.

[7] Worthington Chauncey Ford (ed.), *Journals of the Continental Congress, 1775–78* (Washington, 1905–1908), June 3, 1775, II, 79–80. This work is hereafter cited as *Journal of Congress*.

[8] Charles Biddle's Rough Draft.

9 Samuel Adams to James Warren, June 10, 1775, Worthington Chauncey Ford (ed.), *Warren-Adams Letters* (Boston, 1917), I, 55.

10 J. Almon (ed.), *The* Remembrancer *or Impartial Repository of Public Events* (London, 1775), 167, 168.

11 John Adams to James Warren, July 26, 1775, Ford (ed.), *Warren-Adams Letters*, I, 92.

12 Ford (ed.), *Journal of Congress*, August 1, 1775, II, 235–39.

13 Biddle (ed.), *Charles Biddle's Autobiography*, 420.

14 "Minutes of Pennsylvania Committee of Safety," June 30, 1775, Samuel Hazard (ed.), *Pennsylvania Colonial Records* (Harrisburg, 1851–53), X, 280. This work is hereafter cited as *Pa. Col. Rec.*

15 *Ibid.*, July 6, 1775, pp. 283, 284.

16 *Ibid.*, July 15, 19, 26, 1775, pp. 287, 288, 291.

17 Josiah Quincy to George Washington, October 31, 1775, Jared Sparks (ed.), *Letters to George Washington* (Boston, 1853), I, 75.

18 "Minutes of Pennsylvania Committee of Safety," July 6, 11, 1775, Hazard (ed.), *Pa. Col. Rec.*, X, 284–86.

19 *Ibid.*, July 17, August 4, 1775, pp. 288, 298.

20 The captains' commissions were dated: Dougherty, July 17; Rice, July 18; and Alexander, July 24, 1775, *ibid.*, 335.

21 *Ibid.*, August 1, 1775, p. 296.

22 *Ibid.*, August 23, 24, 1775, p. 314.

23 *Ibid.*, July 11, August 29, 1775, pp. 304, 305, 327.

24 *Ibid.*, August 4, 14, 1775, pp. 298, 305.

25 William Duane (ed.), *Extracts from the Diary of Christopher Marshall* (New York, 1835), August 28, 1775.

26 "Military Stores & Ammunition put on Board the Gondolas," undated mss., Historical Society of Pennsylvania, Philadelphia.

27 "Minutes of Pennsylvania Committee of Safety," August 28, 29, 1775, Hazard (ed.), *Pa. Col. Rec.*, X, 315–27.

28 *Ibid.*, September 1, 1775, p. 329.

29 Duane (ed.), *Extracts from the Diary of Christopher Marshall*, August 24, 1775.

30 "Minutes of Pennsylvania Committee of Safety," September 15, 1775, Hazard (ed.), *Pa. Col. Rec.*, X, 335, 336.

31 Biddle (ed.), *Charles Biddle's Autobiography*, 393.

32 "Minutes of Pennsylvania Committee of Safety," September 2, 1775, Hazard (ed.), *Pa. Col. Rec.*, X, 330.

33 *Ibid.*, July 8, 1775, p. 284; "Ship Chandlery for the *Franklin*," October 16, 30, 1775, Day Book of Charles Wharton, Samuel W. Woodhouse Collection, Historical Society of Pennsylvania, Philadelphia.

34 Josiah Quincy to George Washington, October 31, 1775, Sparks (ed.), *Letters to George Washington*, I, 75.

35 "John Adams' Diary," September 28, 1775, Charles Francis Adams (ed.), *Works of John Adams* (Boston, 1856), II, 429.

36 Duane (ed.), *Extracts from the Diary of Christopher Marshall*, September 28, 1775.

37 "Minutes of the Pennsylvania Committee of Safety," October 9, 1775, Hazard (ed.), *Pa. Col. Rec.*, X, 361.

[38] *Ibid.,* October 30, 1775, p. 384.

[39] *Ibid.,* October 9, 1775, p. 361.

[40] "The Memorial of the Captains belonging to the Pennsylvania Fleet," October 12, 1775, Simon Gratz Autograph Collection, American Navy of Revolution, Historical Society of Pennsylvania, Philadelphia.

[41] "Minutes of the Pennsylvania Committee of Safety," October 24, 1775, Hazard (ed.), *Pa. Col. Rec.,* X, 380, 381.

[42] *Ibid.,* October 23, 1775, pp. 379, 380.

[43] "The Memorial of the Captains employed in the Provincial Armed Boats," October 30, 1775, Simon Gratz Autograph Collection, American Navy of Revolution.

[44] "Minutes of the Pennsylvania Committee of Safety," October 23, 1775, Hazard (ed.), *Pa. Col. Rec.,* X, 378.

[45] *Ibid.,* November 2, 1775, pp. 388, 389.

[46] Nicholas Biddle to Peter Long, *ca.* 1775, Simon Gratz Autograph Collection, American Navy of Revolution.

[47] "Minutes of the Pennsylvania Committee of Safety," November 17, 1775, Hazard (ed.), *Pa. Col. Rec.,* X, 405.

[48] "Military Stores & Ammunition put on Board the Gondolas."

[49] *"Port Folio* Biography."

[50] Ford (ed.), *Journal of Congress,* October 13, 30, November 2, 25, 30, 1775, III, 291–94, 311–12, 315–19, 370–76, 392–94; "Autobiography of John Adams," C. F. Adams (ed.), *Works of John Adams,* III, 11, 12; Naval Committee to Dudley Saltonstall, November 27, 1775, Museum Collection, U.S. Naval Academy, Annapolis. Stephen Hopkins to Esek Hopkins, November 6, 1775, Alverda S. Beck (ed.), *The Correspondence of Esek Hopkins* (Providence, 1933), 3. This work is hereafter cited as *Hopkins' Correspondence.* Solomon Drowne to William Drowne, December 27, 1775, *Pennsylvania Magazine of History and Biography,* XLVIII (1932), 247, 248.

[51] *"Port Folio* Biography."

[52] "Minutes of the Pennsylvania Committee of Safety," December 9, 1775, Hazard (ed.), *Pa. Col. Rec.,* X, 425.

[53] "Muster roll of Armed Boat *Franklin,* 1775," Linn (comp.), *Pa. Arch.,* I, 313.

Chapter VI

[1] "Autobiography of John Adams," C. F. Adams (ed.), *Works of John Adams,* III, 11, 12.

[2] Charles Biddle's Rough Draft.

[3] "Stephen Hopkins Esqr. for Brigt. Andrew Doria fitted for a Vessel of War," Wharton and Humphreys, Ship Yard Accounts, 1773–95, Joshua Humphreys Papers, Historical Society of Pennsylvania, Philadelphia.

[4] "Memorial of John Barry to Pennsylvania House of Assembly [1783]," W. Horace Hepburn Private Collection, Philadelphia.

[5] "State of the Rebel Marine forces [1775]," Robert Wilden Neeser (ed.), *The Despatches of Molyneux Shuldham, Vice-Admiral of the Blue and Commander-in-Chief of His Britannic Majesty's Ships in North America* (New York, 1913), 122, 123. This work is hereafter cited as *Shuldham's Despatches.*

[6] "Autobiography of John Adams," C. F. Adams (ed.), *Works of John Adams,* III, 11, 12.

⁷ "State of the Rebel Marine forces [1775]," Neeser (ed.), *Shuldham's Despatches*, 122, 123.

⁸ "Extract of a letter from Philadelphia," December 6, 1775, M. W. Willard (ed.), *Letters on the American Revolution* (Boston, 1925), 232. E. P. to Earl of Dartmouth, December 20, 1775, Peter Force (comp.), *American Archives*, Fourth Series (Washington, 1837–46), IV, 358–63. This work is hereafter cited as *Force*, and, unless otherwise specified, the Fourth Series has been used.

⁹ Intelligence enclosure No. 2 in Molyneux Shuldham to Philip Stephens, March 8, 1776, Neeser (ed.), *Shuldham's Despatches*, 116.

¹⁰ "State of the Rebel Marine forces [1775]," *ibid.*, 122, 123.

¹¹ "Autobiography of John Adams," C. F. Adams (ed.), *Works of John Adams*, III, 11, 12; "Minutes of the Pennsylvania Committee of Safety," December 8, 1775, Hazard (ed.), *Pa. Col. Rec.*, X, 424.

¹² "State of the Rebel Marine forces [1775]," Neeser (ed.), *Shuldham's Despatches*, 122, 123.

¹³ Stephen Hopkins to Esek Hopkins, November 6, 1775, Beck (ed.), *Hopkins' Correspondence*, 3.

¹⁴ Edward Field, *Esek Hopkins* (Providence, 1898), 134.

¹⁵ Rhode Island Committee to Nicholas Cooke, December 2, 1775, *Rhode Island Historical Society Collections* (Providence), VI (1867), 138.

¹⁶ Rhode Island Delegates to Nicholas Cooke, December 2, 1775, Simon Gratz Autograph Collection.

¹⁷ John Paul Jones to President of Congress, December 7, 1779, Papers of the Continental Congress, Library of Congress, Washington, Vol. 168, II, 107–20. Whether the Grand Union flag was raised on December 3 or December 7, 1775, has long been in dispute. A letter from B. P. to the Earl of Dartmouth, December 20, 1775, states "the 3d instant, the Continental flag on board the Black Prince [*Alfred*] opposite Philadelphia was hoisted." Jones, in the letter of December 7, 1779, referred to above, states, "It is this day four years since I had the honor to receive my first Commission as the Senior of the first Lieutenants in the Navy. . . . I hoisted with my own hands the Flag of Freedom the first time that it was displayed on board the Alfred on the Delaware." It is quite possible that, knowing his commission was forthcoming, Jones might have anticipated its receipt by assuming his post as executive officer of the *Alfred* on December 3, 1775. A letter from Philadelphia of December 6, 1775, printed in M. W. Willard, *Letters on the American Revolution*, 231–34, strengthens this assumption by a passage which reads, "The Black Prince, a fine vessel . . . carries a flag, and mounts twenty to thirty twelve and sixteen pounders. . . ." However, in support of the December 7 claim for the event, another letter from Philadelphia, also dated December 6, 1775, and published in the *Westminster Journal and London Political Miscellany*, January 13, 1776, states the fleet is "to be commanded by one Hopkins, who was to hoist his flag on board the ship called the Black Prince."

¹⁸ Naval Committee to Dudley Saltonstall, November 27, 1775, Museum Collection, U.S. Naval Academy, Annapolis.

¹⁹ Commission of Abraham Whipple, December 8, 1775, Abraham Whipple Papers, Burton Historical Collection, Detroit Free Library.

²⁰ "Autobiography of John Adams," C. F. Adams (ed.), *Works of John Adams*, III, 11, 12.

²¹ "Memorial of Captain Isaac Craig, February 21, 1782," Samuel Hazard

(comp.), *Pennsylvania Archives,* First Series (Harrisburg, 1852–56), IX, 497–99. This work is hereafter cited as *Pa. Arch.*

[22] "Minutes of the Pennsylvania Committee of Safety," December 11, 1775, Hazard (ed.), *Pa. Col. Rec.,* X, 426.

[23] "Journal of John Trevett, 1775–80," *Rhode Island Historical Magazine,* (Newport), VI, July, 1885. This work is hereafter cited as "Trevett."

[24] "Arrangement of officers in the Continental Fleet," undated, but prior to June, 1776, Beck (ed.), *Hopkins' Correspondence,* 84, 85.

[25] Ford (ed.), *Journal of Congress,* December 5, 13, 1775, III, 405–408, 425–27.

[26] "Extracts from minutes of the Naval Committee of Congress," December 18, 19, 1775, Linn (comp.), *Pa. Arch.,* I, 601.

[27] "Minutes of the Pennsylvania Committee of Safety," December 20, 1775, Hazard (ed.), *Pa. Col. Rec.,* X, 433.

[28] Ration tables in "Rules for the Regulation of the Navy of the United Colonies," Ford (ed.), *Journal of Congress,* November 28, 1775, III, 383.

[29] "Minutes of the Pennsylvania Committee of Safety," December 19, 1775, Hazard (ed.), *Pa. Col. Rec.,* 432.

[30] "A Journal of a Cruse In the Brig Andrew Doria," January 17, 1776, Neeser (ed.), *Shuldham's Despatches,* 275.

[31] "Minutes of the Pennsylvania Committee of Safety," December 23, 1775, Hazard (ed.), *Pa. Col. Rec.,* X, 435.

[32] "Extract of a letter from Philadelphia," December 27, 1775, *Force,* IV, 468.

[33] "Muster Roll of Captain Isaac Craig's Company of Marines," December 19, 1775, *Pennsylvania Magazine of History and Biography,* XII (1888–89), 350, 351.

[34] "Minutes of the Pennsylvania Committee of Safety," December 23, 27, 1775, Hazard (ed.), *Pa. Col. Rec.,* X, 435–37.

[35] John Hancock to Commanding Officer of Pennsylvania Battalion, December 2, 1775, *Force,* IV, 154; "Orderly Book, First Pennsylvania Battalion," December 2, 3, 1775, Linn (comp.), *Pa. Arch.,* X, 49.

[36] Ford (ed.), *Journal of Congress,* November 28, 1775, III, 378–89.

[37] *Ibid.,* November 28, 1775.

[38] *"Port Folio* Biography."

[39] Ford (ed.), *Journal of Congress,* December 22, 1775, III, 443–45. The lieutenants who resigned were Richard Stansbury and Daniel Vaughan. Those omitted from the list, in addition to Josiah, were Jonathan Maltbie and Elisha Hinman.

[40] *Ibid.*

[41] "Intelligence received from Philadelphia the 12th December 1775," enclosure C in Molyneux Shuldham to Philip Stephens, January 19, 1776, Neeser (ed.), *Shuldham's Despatches,* 43.

[42] Solomon Drowne to William Drowne, December 27, 1775, *loc. cit.,* 247, 248.

[43] Intelligence from Philadelphia, January 4, 1775, enclosed in Molyneux Shuldham to Philip Stephens, March 8, 1776, Neeser (ed.), *Shuldham's Despatches,* 120.

[44] Ford (ed.), *Journal of Congress,* December 19, 1775, III, 436–37.

[45] "Minutes of the Pennsylvania Committee of Safety," December 20, 1775, Hazard (ed.), *Pa. Col. Rec.,* X, 433; Pennsylvania Committee of Safety to County Committees, December 30, 1775, Hazard (comp.), *Pa. Arch.,* IV, 694.

46 "Minutes of the Pennsylvania Committee of Safety," January 5, 1776, Hazard (ed.), *Pa. Col. Rec.*, X, 447.

47 Silas Deane to Elizabeth Deane, December 27, 1775, *Connecticut Historical Society Collections* (Hartford), II (1870), 346.

48 "Du Simitiere, Artist, Antiquary, and Naturalist . . . ," *Pennsylvania Magazine of History and Biography*, XIII (1889–90), 341–75.

49 "Minutes of the Pennsylvania Committee of Safety," January 1, 1776, Hazard (ed.), *Pa. Col. Rec.*, 441, 442.

50 News dispatch from New Bern, North Carolina, February 9, 1776, *Force*, IV, 964, 965.

51 Intelligence from Philadelphia, January 4, 1776, Neeser (ed.), *Shuldham's Despatches*, 120.

52 "A Journal of a Cruse In the Brig Andrew Doria," January 4, 1776, Neeser (ed.), *Shuldham's Despatches*, 275.

53 Order of the Naval Committee of Congress, January 4, 1776, Enclosure No. 5 in Molyneux Shuldham to Philip Stephens, March 8, 1776, *ibid.*, 124.

54 *Ibid.*, 275.

55 Biddle (ed.), *Charles Biddle's Autobiography*, 82.

56 Intelligence from Philadelphia received the beginning of January, 1776, Enclosure No. 2 in Molyneux Shuldham to Philip Stephens, March 8, 1776, Neeser (ed.), *Shuldham's Despatches*, 119.

57 Naval Committee to Esek Hopkins, January 5, 1776, Beck (ed.), *Hopkins' Correspondence*, 23, 24; Naval Committee to Esek Hopkins, January 5, 1776 (Operational Instructions), Papers of the Continental Congress, Vol. 58, p. 239.

58 "Edward Biddle Memoir."

59 *"Port Folio* Biography."

60 "Trevett."

61 "A Journal of a Cruse In the Brig Andrew Doria," January 17, 1776, Neeser (ed.), *Shuldham's Despatches*, 275.

62 Timothy Matlack to Esek Hopkins [January 15, 1776], Beck (ed.), *Hopkins' Correspondence*, 30, 31.

63 "A Journal of a Cruse In the Brig Andrew Doria," January 17, 1776, Neeser (ed.), *Shuldham's Despatches*, 275; "Private Intelligence from Philadelphia 13th. Feby. 1776," Enclosure No. 10, in Molyneux Shuldham to Philip Stephens, March 8, 1776, *ibid.*, 131.

64 Josiah Bartlett to John Langdon, February 3, 1776, William Whipple Correspondence, Peter Force Transcripts, I, 83, Library of Congress, Washington; "A Journal of a Cruse In the Brig Andrew Doria," January 17, 1776, Neeser (ed.), *Shuldham's Despatches*, 275; "A List of the Seamen and Landsmen that Came out of the Capes of the Deliware [*sic*] in the Fly," Beck (ed.), *Hopkins' Correspondence*, 42, 43.

65 Ford (ed.), *Journal of Congress*, January 16, 1776, IV, 57–61. Lieutenant Hacker was appointed to command the *Fly* on January 20, 1776, Esek Hopkins to Marine Committee, June 19, 1776, Alverda S. Beck (ed.), *The Letter Book of Esek Hopkins* (Providence, 1932), 71–73. This work is hereafter cited as *Hopkins' Letter Book*.

66 Nathaniel Falconer to Esek Hopkins, January 30, 1776, Beck (ed.), *Hopkins' Correspondence*, 33, 34.

[67] "A Journal of a Cruse In the Brig Andrew Doria," February 11, 1776, Neeser (ed.), *Shuldham's Despatches*, 275.

[68] Esek Hopkins to John Hancock, April 8, 1776, Beck (ed.), *Hopkins' Letter Book*, 46–48; Naval Committee to William Stone, January 10, 1776, Beck (ed.), *Hopkins' Correspondence*, 28.

[69] "Private Intelligence from Philadelphia 13th Feby 1776," Neeser (ed.), *Shulham's Despatches*, 131.

[70] "*Port Folio* Biography."

[71] Naval Committee to Esek Hopkins, January 5, 1776, Papers of the Continental Congress, Vol. 58, p. 239.

[72] "Fragment of Esek Hopkins' testimony before Congress," undated, Beck (ed.), *Hopkins' Correspondence*, 56, 57.

[73] Naval Committee to Esek Hopkins, January 18, 1776, *ibid.*, 31, 32.

[74] Joseph Jencks Smith (ed.), *Civil and Military Lists of Rhode Island* (Providence, 1901), 703–704, containing the commissioned and warrant personnel of the five vessels; Nicholas Biddle to Lydia McFunn, February 14, 1776, Nicholas Biddle Letters.

[75] "Signals for the American Fleet," Beck (ed.), *Hopkins' Letter Book*, 40–44; another copy in Beck (ed.), *Hopkins' Correspondence*, 17–20.

[76] "Orders given the Several Captains in the Fleet at Sailing from the Capes of Delaware Febry 1776," Beck (ed.), *Hopkins' Letter Book*, 44.

[77] "Edward Biddle Memoir."

[78] Esek Hopkins to Nicholas Cooke, April 8, 1776, Beck (ed.), *Hopkins' Letter Book*, 49; "A Journal of a Cruse In the Brig Andrew Doria," February 18, 1776, Neeser (ed.), *Shuldham's Despatches*, 275.

Chapter VII

[1] "A Journal of a Cruse In the Brig Andrew Doria," February 18, 1776, Neeser (ed.), *Shuldham's Despatches*, 275.

[2] "Arrangement of Officers and Men, of the Marines, onboard the American Fleet," undated, Beck (ed.), *Hopkins' Correspondence*, 85.

[3] "Officers onboard the A. Doria," undated, *ibid.*, 84.

[4] "*Port Folio* Biography."

[5] Esek Hopkins to the Naval Committee, April 8, 1776, Beck (ed.), *Hopkins' Letter Book*, 46–48.

[6] "A Journal of a Cruse In the Brig Andrew Doria," February 19, 1776, Neeser (ed.), *Shuldham's Despatches*, 275.

[7] Robert C. Sands, *Life and Correspondence of John Paul Jones* (New York, 1830). This work is hereafter cited as *Sands*.

[8] "A Journal of a Cruse In the Brig Andrew Doria," March 1, 1776, Neeser (ed.), *Shuldham's Despatches*, 275.

[9] *Sands*, 35.

[10] Esek Hopkins to the Naval Committee, April 8, 1776, Beck (ed.), *Hopkins' Letter Book*, 46–48. The description of the island of New Providence is from the map facing page 14 in Edward Field, *Esek Hopkins* (Providence, 1898).

[11] John Paul Jones to Joseph Hewes, April 14, 1776, John Paul Jones Manuscripts, Library of Congress, Washington.

[12] "A Journal of a Cruse In the Brig Andrew Doria," March 1–3, 1776, Neeser

(ed.), *Shuldham's Despatches,* 275; Esek Hopkins to the Naval Committee, April 8, 1776, Beck (ed.), *Hopkins' Letter Book,* 46–48.

[13] "A Journal of a Cruse In the Brig Andrew Doria," March 3, 1776, Neeser (ed.), *Shuldham's Despatches,* 275.

[14] *Sands,* 35.

[15] "Signals for the American Fleet," Beck (ed.), *Hopkins' Letter Book,* 40–44.

[16] *Sands,* 36.

[17] "A Journal of a Cruse In the Brig Andrew Doria," March 3, 1776, Neeser (ed.), *Shuldham's Despatches,* 275, 276.

[18] Thomas Atwood to the Earl of Dartmouth, March 22, 1776, *Pennsylvania Magazine of History and Biography,* XLIX (1925), 361–66.

[19] "Extract of a letter from the Captain of Marines on Board the Ship Alfred," April 10, 1776, *Force,* V, 846, 847.

[20] "Copy of the Manifesto sent Onshore at New Providence," March 3, 1776, Beck (ed.), *Hopkins' Letter Book,* 44.

[21] Thomas Atwood to the Earl of Dartmouth, March 22, 1776, *loc. cit.,* 361–66.

[22] "Extract of a letter from the Captain of Marines on Board the Ship Alfred," April 10, 1776, *Force,* V, 846, 847; "Inventory of Stores &c. taken at Fort Nassau—March 3, 1776," Beck (ed.), *Hopkins' Correspondence,* 35.

[23] Montfort Browne to George Germain, November 5, 1776, *Pennsylvania Magazine of History and Biography,* XLIX (1925), 352–57; "A Journal of a Cruse In the Brig Andrew Doria," March 3, 1776, Neeser (ed.), *Shuldham's Despatches,* 276.

[24] "Trevett."

[25] "A Journal of a Cruse In the Brig Andrew Doria," March 6, 1776, Neeser (ed.), *Shuldham's Despatches,* 276; "Log Book for the Wasp," March 9, 1776, British High Court of Admiralty, Miscellanea, 733, 10, Public Records Office, London.

[26] Esek Hopkins to the Naval Committee, April 8, 1776, Beck (ed.), *Hopkins' Letter Book,* 46–48; "Extract of a letter from the Captain of Marines on Board the Ship Alfred," April 10, 1776, *Force,* V, 846, 847.

[27] "Log Book for the Wasp," March 11, 1776.

[28] "A Journal of a Cruse In the Brig Andrew Doria," March 16, 1776, Neeser (ed.), *Shuldham's Despatches,* 276.

[29] Esek Hopkins to the Naval Committee, April 8, 1776, Beck (ed.), *Hopkins' Letter Book,* 46–48.

[30] *Port Folio* Biography."

[31] "A Journal of a Cruse In the Brig Andrew Doria," March 11–16, 1776, Neeser (ed.), *Shuldham's Despatches,* 276.

[32] Montfort Browne to George Germain, November 5, 1776, *loc. cit.,* 352–57.

[33] "A Journal of a Cruse In the Brig Andrew Doria," March 17, 1776, Neeser (ed.), *Shuldham's Despatches,* 277.

[34] "Orders given the Several Captains at Sailing from New Providence, March 18th, 1776," Beck (ed.), *Hopkins' Letter Book,* 45.

[35] *Port Folio* Biography"; "Account of Nathaniel Shaw, Jr., with Esek Hopkins for 'boarding out the Sickest of his people,'" Nathaniel Shaw Papers, Book 39, p. 4, Yale University Library, New Haven.

[36] "A Journal of a Cruse In the Brig Andrew Doria," March 19–24, 1776,

Neeser (ed.), *Shuldham's Despatches,* 278–80; "Log Book for the Wasp," March 19–24, 1776.

[37] "A Journal of a Cruse In the Brig Andrew Doria," March 25–27, 1776, Neeser (ed.), *Shuldham's Despatches,* 281, 282.

[38] *Ibid.,* March 28–April 3, 1776, pp. 282–85.

[39] *Ibid.,* April 4, 1776, pp. 286, 287.

[40] Esek Hopkins to the Naval Committee, April 8, 1776, Beck (ed.), *Hopkins' Letter Book,* 46–48.

[41] "A Journal of a Cruse In the Brig Andrew Doria," April 5, 1776, Neeser (ed.), *Shuldham's Despatches,* 286, 287.

[42] Molyneux Shuldham to Philip Stephens, April 25, 1776, *ibid.,* 207, 208; "Extract of a letter from the Captain of Marines on Board the Ship Alfred," April 10, 1776, *Force,* V, 846, 847.

[43] Esek Hopkins to the Naval Committee, April 8, 1776, Beck (ed.), *Hopkins' Letter Book,* 46–48.

[44] "A Journal of a Cruse In the Brig Andrew Doria," April 6, 1776, Neeser (ed.), *Shuldham's Despatches,* 286, 287.

[45] *Ibid.;* Nicholas Biddle to Charles Biddle, May 2, 1776, Nicholas Biddle Letters.

[46] "Extract of a letter from the Captain of Marines on Board the Ship Alfred," April 10, 1776, *Force,* V, 846, 847.

[47] Captain David Hawley's account of the engagement between the American fleet and the *Glasgow,* Hartford *Connecticut Courant,* May 20, 1776.

[48] "Remarks on board his Majesty's Ship Glasgow Saturday the 6th. day of April 1776," Neeser (ed.), *Shuldham's Despatches,* 180, 181.

[49] "A Journal of a Cruse In the Brig Andrew Doria," April 6, 1776, *ibid.,* 286, 287; John Paul Jones to Joseph Hewes, April 14, 1776, John Paul Jones Manuscripts.

[50] Abraham Whipple to Esek Hopkins, April 30, 1776, Beck (ed.), *Hopkins' Correspondence,* 42, 43; "Remarks on board his Majesty's Ship Glasgow Saturday the 6th. day of April 1776," Neeser (ed.), *Shuldham's Despatches,* 180, 181.

[51] John Paul Jones to Joseph Hewes, April 14, 1776, John Paul Jones Manuscripts.

[52] "A Journal of a Cruse In the Brig Andrew Doria," April 6, 1776, Neeser (ed.), *Shuldham's Despatches,* 286, 287; Abraham Whipple to Esek Hopkins, April 30, 1776, Beck (ed.), *Hopkins' Correspondence,* 42, 43; Captain David Hawley's account of the engagement between the American fleet and the *Glasgow,* *Connecticut Courant,* May 20, 1776.

[53] Captain David Hawley's account of the engagement between the American fleet and the *Glasgow, Connecticut Courant,* May 20, 1776.

[54] *Ibid.*

[55] Esek Hopkins to the Naval Committee, April 8, 1776, Beck (ed.), *Hopkins' Letter Book,* 46–48.

[56] "A Journal of a Cruse In the Brig Andrew Doria," April 8, 1776, Neeser (ed.), *Shuldham's Despatches,* 290, 291.

[57] "A List of the Kill'd & Wounded On Board the Brigantine Cabot," Beck (ed.), *Hopkins' Correspondence,* 37.

[58] John Paul Jones to Joseph Hewes, April 14, 1776, John Paul Jones Manuscripts.

[59] Esek Hopkins to the Naval Committee, April 8, 1776, Beck (ed.), *Hopkins' Letter Book*, 46–48.

[60] John Paul Jones to Joseph Hewes, April 14, 1776, John Paul Jones Manuscripts.

[61] Esek Hopkins to the Naval Committee, April 8, 1776, Beck (ed.), *Hopkins' Letter Book*, 46–48.

[62] "A Journal of a Cruse In the Brig Andrew Doria," April 7, 8, 1776, Neeser (ed.), *Shuldham's Despatches*, 290, 291.

[63] Nicholas Biddle to James Biddle, May 10, 1776, Nicholas Biddle Letters.

Chapter VIII

[1] New London news dispatch, April 12, 1776, *Connecticut Courant*, April 15, 1776.

[2] "To Expences of a Hospitole on shore £562 . . 14 . . o. To Expences boarding the Sickest of the people, £113 . . 13 . . 6," "Account of Nathaniel Shaw, Jr., with ship *Alfred*, 1776," Nathaniel Shaw Papers, Book 39, p. 4.

[3] Esek Hopkins to the Marine Committee, May 1, 1776, Beck (ed.), *Hopkins' Letter Book*, 54–56.

[4] "Account of Nathaniel Shaw, Jr., with Esek Hopkins, for 'boarding out the Sickest of his people,' " Nathaniel Shaw Papers, Book 39, p. 4.

[5] *"Port Folio* Biography."

[6] "A Journal of a Cruse In the Brig Andrew Doria," April 9, 1776, Neeser (ed.), *Shuldham's Despatches*, 290, 291.

[7] "Account of Nathaniel Shaw, Jr., with the brig *Andrew Doria*, 1776," Nathaniel Shaw Papers, Book 39, p. 7.

[8] "A Journal of a Cruse In the Brig Andrew Doria," April 9, 10, 1776, Neeser (ed.), *Shuldham's Despatches*, 290, 291.

[9] *Ibid.*, April 11, 12, 1776, pp. 290–93.

[10] Nathaniel Shaw, Jr., to Richard Henry Lee, June 27, 1779, Ernest E. Rogers, *Connecticut's Naval Office at New London* (New London, 1933), 323, 324.

[11] "A Journal of a Cruse In the Brig Andrew Doria," April 12, 1776, Neeser (ed.), *Shuldham's Despatches*, 292, 293.

[12] Nathaniel Shaw, Jr., to Esek Hopkins, June 13, 1776, Rogers, *Connecticut's Naval Office at New London*, 281, 282.

[13] "A Journal of a Cruse In the Brig Andrew Doria," April 12, 13, 1776, Neeser (ed.), *Shuldham's Despatches*, 292, 293.

[14] Nathaniel Shaw, Jr., to Esek Hopkins, June 13, 1776; Esek Hopkins to Nathaniel Shaw, Jr., June 5, 1776, Rogers, *Connecticut's Naval Office at New London*, 113, 281, 282.

[15] Esek Hopkins to the Marine Committee, May 22, 1776, Beck (ed.), *Hopkins' Letter Book*, 60–62.

[16] *Id.* to Stephen Hopkins, June 8, 1776, *ibid.*, pp. 64–66.

[17] *Id.* to the Marine Committee, May 1, 1776, *ibid.*, pp. 54–56.

[18] "A Journal of a Cruse In the Brig Andrew Doria," April 15–19, 1776, Neeser (ed.), *Shuldham's Despatches*, 292, 293; "Trevett."

[19] John Paul Jones to Joseph Hewes, April 14, 1776, John Paul Jones Manuscripts.

[20] "A Journal of a Cruse In the Brig Andrew Doria," April 19, 1776, Neeser (ed.), *Shuldham's Despatches*, 292, 293.

21 Esek Hopkins to Stephen Hopkins, April 21, 1776, Beck (ed.), *Hopkins' Letter Book,* 52.

22 "A Journal of a Cruse In the Brig Andrew Doria," April 20, 1776, Neeser (ed.), *Shuldham's Despatches,* 294, 295.

23 *Ibid.,* April 21–25, 1776, pp. 294, 295.

24 Esek Hopkins to Nicholas Biddle, April 25, 1776, Beck (ed.), *Hopkins' Letter Book,* 53.

25 "A Journal of a Cruse In the Brig Andrew Doria," April 26–May 1, 1776, Neeser (ed.), *Shuldham's Despatches,* 294, 295; Nicholas Biddle to Lydia McFunn, April 26, 1776, Nancy Biddle to Nicholas Biddle, June 26, 1776, Nicholas Biddle Letters.

26 "A Journal of a Cruse In the Brig Andrew Doria," May 2, 3, 1776, Neeser (ed.), *Shuldham's Despatches,* pp. 294, 295.

27 "Account of Nathaniel Shaw, Jr., with the brig *Andrew Doria,* 1776," Nathaniel Shaw Papers, Book 39, p. 7.

28 *Ibid.,* Book 39, p. 7.

29 "Account of Nathaniel Shaw, Jr., to sale of prize schooner *John and Joseph,*" Nathaniel Shaw Papers, Book 39, p. 36.

30 "A Journal of a Cruse In the Brig Andrew Doria," May 4, 5, 1776, Neeser (ed.), *Shuldham's Despatches,* 294–97.

31 *Ibid.,* May 6, 1776, pp. 296, 297.

32 Abraham Whipple to Esek Hopkins, April 30, 1776, Beck (ed.), *Hopkins' Correspondence,* 42, 43.

33 "Proceedings of a Court-Martial on Abraham Whipple, Commander of the Columbus," May 6, 1776, Papers of the Continental Congress, Vol. 58, p. 259.

34 Esek Hopkins to John Paul Jones, May 7, 1776, John Paul Jones Manuscripts.

35 "Proceedings of a Court-Martial on John Hazard, Commander of the Sloop Providence," May 8, 1776, Papers of the Continental Congress, Vol. 58, p. 263.

36 *Sands,* 37.

37 "A Journal of a Cruse In the Brig Andrew Doria," May 12, 1776, Neeser (ed.), *Shuldham's Despatches,* 296, 297.

38 Esek Hopkins to Nicholas Biddle, May 12, 1776, Beck (ed.), *Hopkins' Letter Book,* 57, 58.

39 *Id.* to Elisha Hinman, May 12, 1776, *ibid.,* 58; Nicholas Biddle to James Biddle, May 10, 1776, Nicholas Biddle Letters.

40 "A Journal of a Cruse In the Brig Andrew Doria," May 13–15, 1776, Neeser (ed.), *Shuldham's Despatches,* 296, 297.

41 *Ibid.,* May 16–20, 1776, pp. 296–99.

42 Newport *Mercury,* May 13, 1776; *Pennsylvania Gazette,* May 29, 1776.

43 "A Journal of a Cruse In the Brig Andrew Doria," May 20, 1776, Neeser (ed.), *Shuldham's Despatches,* 298, 299.

44 *Ibid.,* May 21, 1776, pp. 298, 299.

45 Libel against sloop *Two Friends,* Newport *Mercury,* May 27, 1776.

46 "A Journal of a Cruse In the Brig Andrew Doria," May 21, 1776, Neeser (ed.), *Shuldham's Despatches,* 298, 299.

47 "Remarks on Tuesday May 21st 1776 [on board sloop *Two Friends*]," bound loose leaf in "A Journal of a Cruse In the Brig Andrew Doria," *ibid.,* 289.

48 Nicholas Biddle to Esek Hopkins, May 21, 1776, Beck (ed.), *Hopkins' Correspondence,* 49.

49 Newport *Mercury,* May 27, 1776.

50 *"Port Folio* Biography."

51 "A Journal of a Cruse In the Brig Andrew Doria," May 22–26, 1776, Neeser (ed.), *Shuldham's Despatches,* 298, 299.

52 *Ibid.,* May 27–29, 1776, pp. 298–301; "Extract of a letter from Newport," June 21, 1776, *Pennsylvania Ledger,* June 29, 1776.

53 "A Journal of a Cruse In the Brig Andrew Doria," May 29, 1776, Neeser (ed.), *Shuldham's Despatches,* 300, 301.

54 "Authentic Account of the Fate of the Scotch Expedition from Clyde," London *Public Advertiser,* September 16, 1776.

55 "A Journal of a Cruse In the Brig Andrew Doria," May 29, 1776, Neeser (ed.), *Shuldham's Despatches,* 300, 301; "List of Scotch Prisoners taken back of Long Island," enclosed in Nathanael Greene to George Washington, June 24, 1776, *Force,* VI, 1055.

56 "List of Scotch Prisoners taken back of Long Island," *Force,* VI, 1055; "A Journal of a Cruse In the Brig Andrew Doria," May 30, 1776, Neeser (ed.), *Shuldham's Despatches,* 300, 301; "Trevett."

57 "Supernumeraries Born for Victuals," Muster Table, H.M.S. *Cerberus,* British Admiralty, Class 36, No. 7731, Public Records Office, London.

58 "A Journal of a Cruse In the Brig Andrew Doria," May 30, 1776, Neeser (ed.), *Shuldham's Despatches,* 300, 301.

59 "Trevett."

60 "List of Scotch Prisoners taken back of Long Island," *Force,* VI, 1055; Nicholas Biddle to James Biddle, June 16, 1776, Nicholas Biddle Letters.

61 News dispatch from Newport, June 17, 1776, *Pennsylvania Gazette,* June 26, 1776.

62 "Trevett."

63 "List of Scotch Prisoners taken back of Long Island," *Force,* VI, 1055; "Supernumeraries born for Victuals," Muster Table, H.M.S. *Cerberus.*

64 "A Journal of a Cruse In the Brig Andrew Doria," June 1–11, 1776, Neeser (ed.), *Shuldham's Despatches,* 300–305.

65 Molyneux Shuldham to Philip Stephens, July 8, 1776, *ibid.,* 273.

66 News dispatch from Newport, June 17, 1776, *Pennsylvania Gazette,* June 26, 1776.

67 Esek Hopkins to Nathanael Greene, June 20, 1776, Beck (ed.), *Hopkins' Letter Book,* 73, 74; Nicholas Biddle to James Biddle, June 16, 1776, Nicholas Biddle Letters.

68 News dispatch from Providence, June 22, 1776, *Pennsylvania Gazette,* July 3, 1776.

69 Libel of Nicholas Biddle against arms, etc., taken in the Scotch transports, Newport *Mercury,* July 18, 1776.

70 News dispatch from Gwynn Island, Virginia, June 26, 1776, London *Public Advertiser,* August 7, 1776.

71 "Trevett."

72 News dispatch from Williamsburg, Virginia, June 22, 1776, *Force,* VI, 983.

73 "Trevett"; news dispatch from Williamsburg, June 22, 1776, *Pennsylvania Gazette,* July 3, 1776.

74 "Trevett."

75 Ford (ed.), *Journal of Congress,* December 5, 1776, VI, 1006–1008.

76 "Captain's Log, H.M.S. *Cerberus,*" June 11, 12, 1776, British Admiralty, Class 51, No. 181, pt. v, Public Records Office, London.

77 "Supernumeraries born for Victuals," Muster Table, H.M.S. *Cerberus.*

78 Molyneux Shuldham to Philip Stephens, July 6, 1776, Neeser (ed.), *Shuldham's Despatches,* 273.

79 Charles Pond to George Washington, June 19, 1776, *Force,* VI, 974.

80 Nathanael Greene to George Washington, June 24, 1776, *ibid.,* 1055.

81 Charles Pond to George Washington, June 19, 1776, *ibid.,* 974.

82 *Pennsylvania Evening Post,* June 22, 26, 1776.

83 Ford (ed.), *Journal of Congress,* December 5, 1776, VI, 1006–1008.

Chapter IX

1 Esek Hopkins to the Marine Committee, June 19, 1776, Beck (ed.), *Hopkins' Letter Book,* 71–73.

2 *Id.* to Nicholas Biddle and Abraham Whipple, June 16, 1778, *ibid.,* 68, 69.

3 *Id.* to Nicholas Biddle, June 17, 1776, *ibid.,* 69.

4 *Id.* to Nicholas Biddle, June 18, 1776, *ibid.,* 70; Nicholas Biddle to James Biddle, June 16, 1776, Nicholas Biddle Letters.

5 "Extract of a letter from Newport," June 21, 1776, *Pennsylvania Ledger,* June 29, 1776.

6 News dispatch from Providence, June 22, 1776, *Pennsylvania Gazette,* July 3, 1776; "Captain's Log, H.M.S. *Cerberus,*" June 20, 1776.

7 "Extract of a letter from Newport," June 21, 1776, *Pennsylvania Ledger,* June 29, 1776.

8 Esek Hopkins to Nathanael Greene, June 20, 1776, Beck (ed.), *Hopkins' Letter Book,* 73, 74.

9 Ford (ed.), *Journal of Congress,* May 22, 1776, IV, 374–83.

10 *Ibid.,* June 13, 1776, V, 436–39.

11 John Hancock to Esek Hopkins, June 14, 1776, *Force,* VI, 885, 886.

12 Esek Hopkins to Nicholas Biddle, June 20, 1776, Beck (ed.), *Hopkins' Letter Book,* 74, 75.

13 *Id.* to Stephen Hopkins, June 8, 1776, *ibid.,* 64–66.

14 *Id.* to Abraham Whipple, June 20, 1776, *ibid.,* 74.

15 *Id.* to Nicholas Biddle, June 20, 1776, *ibid.,* 74, 75.

16 Nicholas Biddle to Esek Hopkins, June 28, 1776, Beck (ed.), *Hopkins' Correspondence,* 56.

17 Ford (ed.), *Journal of Congress,* June 6, 1776, V, 420–24.

18 William Whipple to John Langdon, July 16, 1776, Peter Force, *American Archives,* Fifth Series (Washington, 1848–53), I, 368. This work is hereafter cited as *Force,* Fifth Series.

19 News dispatch from New London, June 28, 1776, *Connecticut Courant,* July 1, 1776.

20 Libel against ship *True Blue,* June 24, 1776, Newport *Mercury,* June 24, 1776.

21 "Minutes of the Pennsylvania Committee of Safety," July 5, 1776, Hazard (ed.), *Pa. Col. Rec.,* X, 632.

[22] "Account of Nathaniel Shaw, Jr., with the Brig *Andrew Doria*, August, 1776," Nathaniel Shaw Papers, Book 39, p. 7.

[23] Nicholas Biddle to Esek Hopkins, June 28, 1776, Beck (ed.), *Hopkins' Correspondence*, 56.

[24] Newport *Mercury*, July 22, 1776.

[25] Esek Hopkins to the Marine Committee, September 1, 1776, Beck (ed.), *Hopkins' Letter Book*, 75, 76.

[26] Ford (ed.), *Journal of Congress*, July 2–4, 1776, V, 506–18; Nicholas Biddle to Esek Hopkins, July 22, 1776, Nicholas Biddle Letters.

[27] *Pennsylvania Gazette*, July 31, 1776.

[28] Nicholas Biddle to Nicholas Cooke, July 26, 1776, "Correspondence of Nicholas Cooke," *Rhode Island Historical Society Collections* (Providence), VI (1867), 159.

[29] Newport *Mercury*, July 15, 1776.

[30] "Extract of a letter from New York," July 29, 1776, *Pennsylvania Evening Post*, August 3, 1776.

[31] News dispatch from Newport, August 5, 1776, *Pennsylvania Gazette*, August 14, 1776.

[32] News dispatch from Newport, July 29, 1776, *ibid.*, August 7, 1776.

[33] "Captain's Log, H.M.S. *Cerberus*," July 26, 1776.

[34] Nathaniel Shaw, Jr., to Robert Morris, July 31, 1776, Rogers, *Connecticut's Naval Office at New London*, 286.

[35] "Captain's Log, H.M.S. *Cerberus*," July 26, 1776.

[36] *Ibid.*, July 27, 1776; Nathaniel Shaw, Jr., to Robert Morris, July 31, 1776, Rogers, *Connecticut's Naval Office at New London*, 286.

[37] News dispatch from Providence, August 3, 1776, Boston *New England Chronicle*, August 8, 1776; "Nathaniel Shaw, Jr.'s account with the Andrew Doria's prize, the ship *Nathaniel & Elizabeth*, 1776," Nathaniel Shaw Papers, Book 38, p. 39.

[38] Nathaniel Shaw, Jr., to Robert Morris, July 31, 1776, Rogers, *Connecticut's Naval Office at New London*, 286.

[39] Newport *Mercury*, July 29, 1776.

[40] John Hancock to George Washington, August 8, 1776, *Force*, Fifth Series, I, 832.

[41] Extracts from Muster Tables of H.M.S. *Cerberus* between July 1 and August 31, 1776.

[42] Newport *Mercury*, July 29, 1776.

[43] John Hancock to George Washington, August 8, 1776, *Force*, Fifth Series, I, 832.

[44] *"Port Folio* Biography."

[45] Ford (ed.), *Journal of Congress*, August 7, 1776, V, 635–36.

[46] George Washington to Richard Howe, August 17, 1776, George Washington Papers, Library of Congress, Washington.

[47] Richard Howe to George Washington, August 19, 1776, *Remembrancer* (London), IV (1776), 57.

[48] "A just account of the treatment which Mr. Josiah, first Lieut. of the Continental brig And. Doria received while a prisoner," *Pennsylvania Evening Post*, April 29, 1777.

[49] Ford (ed.), *Journal of Congress*, July 11, 1776, V, 539–45.

[50] "Extract from the Minutes of the Marine Committee, March 27, 1777," Peter Force Transcripts.

[51] "Trevett"; Lydia McFunn to Nicholas Biddle, July 12, 1776, Nicholas Biddle Letters.

[52] Esek Hopkins to the Marine Committee, September 1, 1776, Beck (ed.), *Hopkins' Letter Book*, 75, 76.

[53] Newport *Mercury*, August 12, 1776.

[54] Esek Hopkins to the Marine Committee, September 10, 1776, Beck (ed.), *Hopkins' Letter Book*, 79, 80.

[55] News dispatch from Philadelphia, September 18, 1775, *Force*, Fifth Series, II, 378.

[56] News dispatch from Newport, September 13, 1776, Boston *Independent Chronicle*, September 19, 1776.

[57] Libel of Nicholas Biddle against negro slaves taken in prizes, *Pennsylvania Evening Post*, November 12, 1776.

[58] *Ibid.; New England Chronicle*, September 12, 1776; news dispatch from Philadelphia, September 18, 1776, *Force*, Fifth Series, II, 378.

[59] "Trevett."

[60] Esek Hopkins to the Marine Committee, September 10, 1776, Beck (ed.), *Hopkins' Letter Book*, 79, 80; Marine Committee to Daniel Tillinghast, October 30, 1776, Marine Committee Letter Book, Library of Congress, Washington, 14.

[61] Libel of Nicholas Biddle against negro slaves taken in prizes, *Pennsylvania Evening Post*, November 12, 1776; news dispatch from Philadelphia, September 18, 1776, *Force*, Fifth Series, II, 378.

[62] News dispatch from Newport, September 13, 1776, *Independent Chronicle*, September 19, 1776.

[63] Libels filed in behalf of Esek Hopkins, Newport *Mercury*, September 23, 1776.

[64] "Extract from the Minutes of the Marine Committee, March 27, 1777," Peter Force Transcripts.

[65] "Captain's Log, H.M.S. *Cerberus*," September 11, 12, 1776.

[66] News dispatch from Newport, September 16, 1776, *Pennsylvania Gazette*, September 25, 1776. "Master's Log, H.M.S. *Cerberus*," September 12, 13, 1776, British Admiralty, Class 52, No. 1650, Public Records Office, London.

[67] "*Port Folio* Biography."

[68] *Pennsylvania Gazette*, September 18, 1776.

[69] Revolutionary Papers, V, 53, Pennsylvania State Library, Harrisburg.

[70] Biddle (ed.), *Charles Biddle's Autobiography*, 98.

Chapter X

[1] The frigates still on the ways were the *Congress* and *Montgomery*, building at Poughkeepsie on the Hudson, and the *Effingham*, building at Philadelphia, "Minutes of New York Committee of Safety," October 29, 1776, *Force*, Fifth Series, III, 275; *Pennsylvania Packet*, January 4, 1777.

[2] Ford (ed.), *Journal of Congress*, April 17, 1776, IV, 289–91.

[3] Josiah Bartlett to John Langdon, September 23, 1776, *Force*, Fifth Series, II, 459, 460; William Whipple to John Langdon, October 26, 1776, *ibid.*, 1248.

[4] "*Port Folio* Biography."

[5] Ford (ed.), *Journal of Congress*, October 10, 1776, VI, 860–66.

[6] Richard Henry Lee to Samuel Purviance, Jr., October 11, 1776, *Force,* Fifth Series, II, 989; Josiah Bartlett to John Langdon, October 15, 1776, *ibid.,* 1063.

[7] Ford (ed.), *Journal of Congress,* October 10, 1776, VI, 860–66.

[8] Revolutionary Papers, V, 53.

[9] William Whipple to John Langdon, July 16, 1776, *Force,* Fifth Series, I, 368.

[10] "Account of Commissioners for Naval Stores with the Frigate Randolph," Samuel W. Woodhouse Collection.

[11] Joseph Johnson, *Traditions and Reminiscences Chiefly of the Revolution in the South* (Charleston, 1851), 117. This work is hereafter cited as *Johnson.*

[12] Commissioners for Building Philadelphia Frigates to Commissioners of Naval Stores, January 9, 1776, Papers of the Continental Congress, Vol. 78, XXIV, 331.

[13] "Dimentions of the Randolph . . . Frigate," Joshua Humphreys' Book of Ship Dimensions, 163, 164, Historical Society of Pennsylvania, Philadelphia.

[14] "Dementions of Ship Randolph Masts & Yards," Thomas Penrose Note Book, Historical Society of Pennsylvania, Philadelphia.

[15] Ford (ed.), *Journal of Congress,* August 13, 1776, V, 649–52; Ship Register of Philadelphia, Linn (comp.), *Pa. Arch.,* 549, 555, 559.

[16] John Fanning Watson Manuscript Annals, 435, Historical Society of Pennsylvania, Philadelphia.

[17] Advertisement for deserters from Captain Samuel Shaw's company of Marines, *Pennsylvania Evening Post,* August 13, 1776.

[18] Ford (ed.), *Journal of Congress,* June 25, 1776, V, 477–80.

[19] Advertisement for deserters from Captain Samuel Shaw's company of Marines, *Pennsylvania Evening Post,* August 13, 1776; advertisement for deserters from the *Randolph, ibid.,* January 21, 1777.

[20] Ford (ed.), *Journal of Congress,* September 9, 1776, V, 747–48; Nicholas Biddle to Robert Morris, September 1, 1777, Papers of the Continental Congress, Vol. 78, II, 237.

[21] William Moultrie to Robert Howe, March 11, 1777, William Moultrie, *Memoirs of the American Revolution* (New York, 1802), 190, 191. This work is hereafter cited as *Moultrie.*

[22] "Account of Commissioners for Naval Stores with the Frigate Randolph," Samuel W. Woodhouse Collection.

[23] William Hooper to Joseph Hewes, November 16, 1776, Edmond O. Burnett (ed.), *Letters of Members of the Continental Congress* (Washington, 1921–31), II, 155.

[24] "Account of Commissioners for Naval Stores with the Frigate Randolph," Samuel W. Woodhouse Collection.

[25] Ford (ed.), *Journal of Congress,* October 4, 1776, V, 847.

[26] *Ibid.,* October 14, 1776, VI, 869–75.

[27] Libel of Nicholas Biddle against negro slaves taken in prizes, *Pennsylvania Evening Post,* November 12, 1776.

[28] *"Port Folio* Biography."

[29] Description from Charles Willson Peale portrait.

[30] Ford (ed.), *Journal of Congress,* November 14, 1776, VI, 950–51.

[31] William Hooper to Joseph Hewes, November 16, 1776, Burnett (ed.), *Letters of Members of the Continental Congress,* II, 155.

[32] "Account of Commissioners for Naval Stores with the Frigate Randolph," Samuel W. Woodhouse Collection.

[33] "Indent of Sundry Slops Wanted for the Randolph Frigate," November 19, 1776, Charles Roberts Autograph Collection, Haverford College Library, Haverford, Pennsylvania.

[34] Richard Henry Lee to Samuel Purviance, November 24, 1776, *Force,* Fifth Series, III, 826, 827.

[35] George Washington to President of Congress, December 1, 1776, "half after 7 p.m.," *ibid.,* 1028.

[36] News dispatch from Philadelphia, November 28, 1776, *ibid.,* 890; Nathanael Greene to Nicholas Cooke, December 4, 1776, *ibid.,* 1071, 1072.

[37] Ford (ed.), *Journal of Congress,* November 30, 1776, VI, 993–96.

[38] *Ibid.,* December 12, 1776, VI, 1024–27.

[39] John Cadwalader to George Washington, December 15, 1776, *Force,* Fifth Series, III, 1229, 1230. "John Barry's Memorial to the Pennsylvania Assembly," *ca.* 1783, W. Horace Hepburn Collection; "Forces Collected in Burlington County," 1776, William S. Stryker, *The Battles of Trenton and Princeton* (Boston, 1898), 433; news dispatch from Boston, January 16, 1777, London *Public Advertiser,* April 3, 1777.

[40] Robert Morris to President of Congress, December 23, 1776, *Force,* Fifth Series, III, 1370–72.

[41] William Duane (ed.), *Extracts from the Diary of Christopher Marshall,* December 3, 1776.

[42] *Ibid.,* December 2, 1776.

[43] Ford (ed.), *Journal of Congress,* December 2, 1776, VI, 998–1001.

[44] *Ibid.,* December 7, 1776, VI, 1009–12.

[45] William Ellery to Nicholas Cooke, December 10, 1775, *Force,* Fifth Series, III, 1148, 1149.

[46] Henry Fisher to Pennsylvania Council of Safety, December 11, 1776, Hazard (comp.), *Pa. Arch.,* V, 99, 100.

[47] Ford (ed.), *Journal of Congress,* December 12, 1776, VI, 1024–27.

[48] Robert Morris to President of Congress, December 13, 1776, Papers of the Continental Congress, Vol. 137, Appendix, 1.

[49] Henry Fisher to Pennsylvania Council of Safety, December 11, 1776 (second letter of that day), Hazard (comp.), *Pa. Arch.,* V, 100, 101.

[50] Richard Howe to Philip Stephens, December 12, 1776, British Admiralty, Secretary, In Letters, 487, Public Records Office, London.

[51] Robert Morris to Nicholas Biddle [December 13, 1776], Bank of North America Papers, Historical Society of Pennsylvania, Philadelphia.

[52] *Ibid.*

[53] Robert Morris to President of Congress, December 13, 1776, Papers of the Continental Congress, Vol. 137, Appendix, 1.

[54] Linn (comp.), *Pa. Arch.,* I, 340.

[55] Will of Joshua Fanning, December 14, 1776, Will Book R, 199, 214, Register of Wills, Philadelphia.

[56] Marine Committee to William Bingham, December 14, 1776, Marine Committee Letter Book, 47.

[57] Nicholas Biddle to James Read, December 17, 1776, Stan V. Henkels (comp.),

David N. Newbold Autograph Collection [Catalogue] (Philadelphia, 1928), 60.

[58] Robert Morris to President of Congress, December 17, 1776, Papers of the Continental Congress, Vol. 137, Appendix, 19.

[59] Id. to American Commissioners in France, December 21, 1776, Force, Fifth Series, III, 1331–37.

[60] Marine Committee to John Nicholson, December 25, 1776, Marine Committee Letter Book, 48.

[61] Robert Morris to George Washington, December 21, 1776, Force, Fifth Series, III, 1330, 1331; id. to John Hancock, December 23, 1776, Papers of the Continental Congress, Vol. 137, Appendix, 25.

[62] Committee to Transact Continental Business at Philadelphia to John Hancock, December 30, 1776, ibid., 49; William Duane (ed.), Extracts from the Diary of Christopher Marshall, December 30, 1776.

[63] Advertisement for deserters from the Randolph, Pennsylvania Evening Post, January 21, 1777.

[64] Committee to Transact Continental Business at Philadelphia to John Hancock, January 2, 1777, Papers of the Continental Congress, Vol. 137, Appendix, 57–60.

[65] Id. to George Washington, February 7, 1777, Committee to Transact Continental Business at Philadelphia Letter Book, 35–37, Library of Congress, Washington.

[66] Robert Morris to John Hancock, January 6, 1777, Pennsylvania Magazine of History and Biography, LXX (1946), 188–92.

Chapter XI

[1] Ford (ed.), Journal of Congress, December 21, 1776, VI, 1030–34.

[2] Letters from Philadelphia on strictly naval matters during the period of Congress' sojourn in Baltimore were generally signed by Robert Morris as vice-president of the Marine Committee, Marine Committee Letter Book, 48, 49, 52, 54, 55, 57–59.

[3] Committee to Transact Continental Business at Philadelphia to John Hancock, January 7, 1777, Papers of the Continental Congress, Vol. 137, Appendix, 77–80.

[4] Id. to id., January 10, 1777, Committee to Transact Continental Business at Philadelphia Letter Book, 42–46.

[5] "A just account of the treatment which Mr. Josiah, first Lieut. of the Continental brig And. Doria received while a prisoner," Pennsylvania Evening Post, April 29, 1777.

[6] Extracts from Muster Tables, H.M.S. Cerberus, November and December, 1776; "Captain's Log, H.M.S. Cerberus," November 17, 1776.

[7] "A just account of the treatment which Mr. Josiah, first Lieut. of the Continental brig And. Doria received while a prisoner," Pennsylvania Evening Post, April 29, 1777.

[8] Ford (ed.), Journal of Congress, October 10, 1776, VI, 860–66; "Commissioners of Naval Stores in account with the Ship Champion," Samuel W. Woodhouse Collection; Committee to Transact Continental Business at Philadelphia to George Washington, Washington Papers, Library of Congress.

[9] Extracts from Muster Tables, H.M.S. Cerberus, November and December, 1776.

[10] Advertisement for deserters from the *Randolph, Pennsylvania Evening Post,* January 21, 1777.

[11] Committee to Transact Continental Business at Philadelphia to John Hancock, January 16, 22, 1777, Papers of the Continental Congress, Vol. 137, Appendix, 88–91, 101, 102.

[12] Robert Morris to John Hancock, January 26, 1777, *ibid.,* 115–18.

[13] *Id.* to *id.,* January 28, 1777, *ibid.,* 123–26.

[14] *Id.* to Nicholas Biddle, January 30, 1777, Marine Committee Letter Book, 49.

[15] Marine Committee to Esek Hopkins, January 21, 1777, *ibid.,* 50.

[16] Robert Morris to Nicholas Biddle, January 30, 1777, *ibid.,* 49.

[17] "Account of Commissioners for Naval Stores with the Randolph," Samuel W. Woodhouse Collection.

[18] Will Book R, 181–83, 187, 188, 190, Register of Wills, Philadelphia.

[19] "Deposition of Joseph Frost," October 10, 1778, British Admiralty, Captains' Letters, Public Records Office, London, I, 1987.

[20] "Deposition of Joseph Berry," October 10, 1778, *ibid.*

[21] Committee to Transact Continental Business at Philadelphia to John Hancock, February 4, 1777, Papers of the Continental Congress, Vol. 137, Appendix, 136–41.

[22] Robert Morris to Nicholas Biddle, February 15, 1777, Marine Committee Letter Book, 55.

[23] Committee to Transact Continental Business at Philadelphia to John Hancock, February 10, 1777, Papers of the Continental Congress, Vol. 137, Appendix, 147–50; John Lloyd to Ralph Izard, March 22, 1777, Anne Izard Deas (ed.), *Correspondence of Mr. Ralph Izard of South Carolina* (New York, 1844), I, 264, 265.

[24] Marine Committee to Robert Morris, February 5, 1777, Marine Committee Letter Book, 59.

[25] Robert Morris to Nicholas Biddle, February 15, 1777, *ibid.,* 55.

[26] *Id.* to Thomas Albertson, February 18, 1777, *ibid.,* 58.

[27] *Id.* to Elisha Warner, February 15, 1777, *ibid.,* 57, 58.

[28] *Id.* to Committee of Secret Correspondence, February 19, 1777, Papers of the Continental Congress, Vol. 137, Appendix, 177–80.

[29] *Id.* to William Bingham, March 29, 1777, Marine Committee Letter Book, 64.

[30] Nicholas Biddle to James Biddle, March 11, 1777 (the letter is misdated February 11, 1777), "Edward Biddle Memoir."

[31] "Journal of Captain John Ferdinand Dalziel Smyth, of the Queen's Rangers," *Pennsylvania Magazine of History and Biography,* XXXIX (1915), 166, 167.

[32] New York *Gazette and Weekly Mercury,* February 24, 1777.

[33] John Lloyd to Ralph Izard, March 22, 1777, Deas (ed.), *Correspondence of Mr. Ralph Izard of South Carolina,* I, 264, 265.

[34] Marine Committee to Thomas Cushing, September 21, 1776, Marine Committee Letter Book, 21.

[35] Officers of the *Randolph* to Nicholas Biddle [September 1, 1777], Papers of the Continental Congress, Vol. 78, II, 245.

[36] Nicholas Biddle to James Biddle, March 11, 1777, "Edward Biddle Memoir."

[37] *"Port Folio* Biography."

[38] Esek Hopkins to the Marine Committee, February 28, 1777, Beck (ed.), *Hopkins' Letter Book,* 126, 127.

[39] *"Port Folio* Biography."

[40] *Ibid.*

[41] Nicholas Biddle to James Biddle, March 11, 1777, "Edward Biddle Memoir"; *ibid.,* Nicholas Biddle Letters.

[42] *Pennsylvania Evening Post,* March 29, 1777; *Pennsylvania Gazette,* April 2, 1777.

[43] Robert Morris to William Bingham, March 29, 1777, Marine Committee Letter Book, 64.

Chapter XII

[1] Nicholas Biddle to James Biddle, March 11, 1777, "Edward Biddle Memoir"; Marine Committee to Nicholas Biddle, April 26, 1777, Marine Committee Letter Book, 73, 74; *id.* to Livinus Clarkson and John Dorsius, April 26, 1777, *ibid.,* 75.

[2] Nicholas Biddle to Robert Morris, September 1, 1777, Papers of the Continental Congress, Vol. 78, II, 237.

[3] *Moultrie,* I, 191.

[4] "Minutes of the Navy Board of South Carolina," March 14, 1777, A. S. Salley, Jr. (ed.), *Journal of the Commissioners of the Navy of South Carolina, October 9, 1776–March 1, 1779* (Columbia, S.C., 1912), 51. This work is hereafter cited as *Journal of South Carolina Navy Board.*

[5] Samuel Nicholas to Silas Deane, August 11, 1777, Benjamin Franklin Papers, VI, 182, American Philosophical Society.

[6] "Depositions of Joseph Frost and Joseph Berry," October 10, 1778, British Admiralty, Captains' Letters, I, 1987.

[7] Marine Committee to Nicholas Biddle, April 26, 1777, Marine Committee Letter Book, 73, 74.

[8] George Logan to Samuel Lanford, April 7, 1777, British Admiralty, Class 5, 127, pp. 87–90.

[9] Marine Committee to Livinus Clarkson and John Dorsius, April 26, 1777, Marine Committee Letter Book, 75.

[10] *Id.* to Nicholas Biddle, April 26, 1777, *ibid.,* 73, 74.

[11] Nicholas Biddle to Robert Morris, September 1, 1777, Papers of the Continental Congress, Vol. 78, II, 237.

[12] Marine Committee to Nicholas Biddle, April 29, 1777, Marine Committee Letter Book, 77.

[13] *Id.* to *id.,* April 26, 1777, *ibid.,* 73, 74.

[14] *Id.* to Livinus Clarkson and John Dorsius, April 26, 1777, *ibid.,* 75.

[15] John Dorsius to the Marine Committee, August 26, 1777, Papers of the Continental Congress, Vol. 78, VII, 116.

[16] Biddle (ed.), *Charles Biddle's Autobiography,* 361.

[17] *"Port Folio* Biography."

[18] *South Carolina Historical and Genealogical Magazine* (Charleston), XX (1919), 22–26; XXI (1920), 112.

[19] Henry A. M. Smith, "The Baronies of South Carolina," *ibid.,* XV (1914), 1–17; "Genealogical Notes," *ibid.,* XVIII (1917), 37, 38; XXIV (1923), 63. Genealogical data supplied by Glen Drayton Grimke, from manuscripts in the collection of the late Mrs. John Drayton Grimke, Charleston.

[20] "Archdale Hall and the Bakers of Archdale," *ibid.,* VII (1906).

[21] *"Port Folio* Biography"; Will of Nicholas Biddle, January 12, 1778, Vol. 17, Book B, 815, Record of Wills, Charleston Free Library.

[22] From manuscripts in the collection of the late Mrs. John Drayton Grimke.

[23] Nicholas Biddle to Robert Morris, September 1, 1777, Papers of the Continental Congress, Vol. 78, II, 237.

[24] Edward Blake to Stephen Seymour, May 30, 1777, Salley (ed.), *Journal of South Carolina Navy Board,* 66.

[25] Officers of the *Randolph* to Nicholas Biddle [September 1, 1777], Papers of the Continental Congress, Vol. 78, II, 245.

[26] Biddle (ed.), *Charles Biddle's Autobiography,* 98–100.

[27] *Ibid.,* 148.

[28] News dispatch from Charlestown, June 12, 1777, *Pennsylvania Evening Post,* July 29, 1777.

[29] Biddle (ed.), *Charles Biddle's Autobiography,* 100, 101.

[30] News dispatch from Charlestown, July 7, 1777, *Pennsylvania Journal,* July 30, 1777.

[31] News dispatch from Charlestown, July 7, 1777, *Pennsylvania Evening Post,* July 29, 1777.

[32] Marine Committee to Nicholas Biddle, April 29, 1777, Marine Committee Letter Book, 73, 74.

[33] Resolutions of the Marine Committee, April 29, 1777, *ibid.,* 78.

[34] Nicholas Biddle to the Marine Committee, September 1, 1777, Papers of the Continental Congress, Vol. 78, II, 237.

[35] John Dorsius to the Marine Committee, August 26, 1777, *ibid.,* VII, 116.

[36] From the Marine Committee letters after the date of the series of resolutions of April 29, 1777, it is apparent that no other war vessels were ever assigned to the Abaco rendezvous. Marine Committee Letter Book, 81–100.

Chapter XIII

[1] John Dorsius to the Marine Committee, August 26, 1777, Papers of the Continental Congress, Vol. 78, VII, 116.

[2] News dispatch from New York, April 21, 1777, London *Public Advertiser,* June 7, 1777.

[3] John Dorsius to the Marine Committee, August 26, 1777, Papers of the Continental Congress, Vol. 78, VII, 116.

[4] Nicholas Biddle to Robert Morris, September 1, 1777, *ibid.,* II, 237.

[5] *"Port Folio* Biography."

[6] *Poor Richard's Almanack* (Philadelphia, 1753), American Philosophical Society.

[7] *"Port Folio* Biography."

[8] John Dorsius to the Marine Committee, August 26, 1777, Papers of the Continental Congress, Vol. 78, VII, 116.

[9] Nicholas Biddle to Robert Morris, September 1, 1777, *ibid.,* II, 237.

[10] *South Carolina and American General Gazette,* September 11, 1777; *North Carolina Gazette,* September 26, 1777.

[11] Nicholas Biddle to Robert Morris, September 1, 1777, Papers of the Continental Congress, Vol. 78, II, 237.

[12] John Dorsius to the Marine Committee, August 26, 1777, *ibid.,* VII, 116.

[13] Nicholas Biddle to Robert Morris, September 1, 1777, *ibid.*, II, 237.

[14] Officers of the *Randolph* to Nicholas Biddle [September 1, 1777], *ibid.*, II, 245.

[15] Nicholas Biddle to Robert Morris, September 1, 1777, *ibid.*, II, 237.

[16] John Dorsius to the Marine Committee, September 12, 1777, *ibid.*, VII, 127; Ford (ed.), *Journal of Congress*, October 3, 1777, V, 842–46.

[17] *South Carolina and American General Gazette*, September 11, 1777.

[18] Nicholas Biddle to Robert Morris, September 12, 1777, Papers of the Continental Congress, Vol. 78, II, 241.

[19] Biddle (ed.), *Charles Biddle's Autobiography*, 104.

[20] Pension application of John McPherson, Montgomery (comp.), *Pa. Arch.*, IV, 552. "Certificate of Service of John McPherson," Revolutionary Papers, XV, 33.

[21] Biddle (ed.), *Charles Biddle's Autobiography*, 103.

[22] Nicholas Biddle to the Marine Committee, September 12, 1777, Papers of the Continental Congress, Vol. 78, II, 241.

[23] *Gazette of the State of South Carolina* [Supplement], September 15, 1777.

[24] *South Carolina and American General Gazette*, September 11, 1777.

[25] *Gazette of the State of South Carolina*, September 15, 1777.

[26] Simeon Fanning to his mother, October 8, 1777, Fanning Papers, 64, Ferdinand J. Dreer Autograph Collection, Historical Society of Pennsylvania, Philadelphia.

[27] John Dorsius to the Marine Committee, September 12, 1777, Papers of the Continental Congress, Vol. 78, VII, 127.

[28] *Gazette of the State of South Carolina*, September 15, 1777.

[29] *South Carolina and American General Gazette*, September 11, 1777.

[30] *Gazette of the State of South Carolina*, September 15, 1777.

[31] John Dorsius to the Marine Committee, September 12, 1777, Papers of the Continental Congress, Vol. 78, VII, 127.

[32] Nicholas Biddle to Robert Morris, September 12, 1777, *ibid.*, II, 241.

[33] Clement Biddle to Timothy Matlack, January 18, 1778, Revolutionary Papers, XIX, 23.

[34] John Dorsius to the Marine Committee, September 12, 1777, Papers of the Continental Congress, Vol. 78, VII, 127.

[35] News dispatch from New York, November 3, 1777, *Pennsylvania Evening Post*, November 20, 1777; Nicholas Biddle to James Biddle, November 22, 1777, Nicholas Biddle Letters.

[36] Simeon Fanning to his mother, October 8, 1777, Fanning Papers, 64.

[37] John F. Watson to Thomas Forrest, February 15, 1821, *ibid.*, 27–30.

[38] *Johnson*, 117, 118.

[39] John Adams to Abigail Adams, September 30, 1777, Charles Francis Adams (ed.), *Letters of John Adams addressed to his wife* (Boston, 1841), I, 315; Boston *Independent Chronicle*, October 9, 1777.

Chapter XIV

[1] Robert Fanshawe to Richard Howe, February 12, 1778, British Admiralty, Captains' Letters, Class I, 488.

[2] Nicholas Biddle's letter of September 12, 1777, for example, reached York-

town, Pennsylvania, on October 3, 1777, Ford (ed.), *Journal of Congress,* October 3, 1777.

[3] Memorandum of Mrs. Mary Biddle, postscript added subsequent to 1778, Biddle (ed.), *Charles Biddle's Autobiography,* 242.

[4] *Moultrie,* I, 198.

[5] The South Carolina fleet consisted of the brigs *Comet* and *Notre Dame,* the schooner *Rattlesnake,* the sloop galley *Beaufort,* and the pilot boats *Tryall* and *Eagle.* Salley (ed.), *Journal of South Carolina Navy Board,* 102.

[6] *"Port Folio* Biography."

[7] Robert Fanshawe to Richard Howe, February 12, 1778, British Admiralty, Captains' Letters, Class I, 488.

[8] Nicholas Biddle to Robert Morris, November 23, 1777, Franklin Delano Roosevelt Collection, Hyde Park, New York.

[9] *South Carolina and American General Gazette,* November 20, 1777; Nicholas Biddle to James Biddle, November 22, 1777, Nicholas Biddle Letters.

[10] News dispatch from Charlestown, December 9, 1777, *Pennsylvania Gazette,* January 17, 1778.

[11] John Rutledge to Robert Howe, December 12, 1777, *Moultrie,* I, 192, 193; John Colcock to Edward Blake, December 12, 1777, Salley (ed.), *Journal of South Carolina Navy Board,* 113.

[12] Biddle (ed.), *Charles Biddle's Autobiography,* 104; *"Port Folio* Biography."

[13] John Colcock to Edward Blake, December 12, 1777, Salley (ed.), *Journal of South Carolina Navy Board,* 113.

[14] *Id.* to *id.,* December 12, 1777 (second letter), *ibid.,* 114.

[15] John Rutledge to Robert Howe, December 12, 1777, *Moultrie,* I, 192.

[16] Robert Howe to William Moultrie, December 13, 1777, *ibid.,* 194, 195.

[17] "Minutes of a Council of War," December 13, 1777, *ibid.,* 195.

[18] Robert Howe to William Moultrie, December 13, 1777, *ibid.,* 194, 195.

[19] *Ibid.,* 196.

[20] "Minutes of a Council of War," December 19, 1777, *ibid.*

[21] William Moultrie to Robert Howe, December 23, 1777, *ibid.,* 197.

[22] Robert Howe to William Moultrie, December 24, 1777, *ibid.,* 198.

[23] Salley (ed.), *Journal of South Carolina Navy Board,* December 13, 1777, pp. 114, 115.

[24] *Ibid.,* December 15, 1777, pp. 116, 117.

[25] *Ibid.,* 118.

[26] Resolution of Privy Council, December 17, 1777, *ibid.,* 118.

[27] John Colcock to Edward Blake, December 17, 1777, *ibid.,* 119.

[28] Navy Board of South Carolina to Hezekiah Anthony, December 17, 1777, *ibid.,* 119, 120; *id.* to Charles Morgan, December 22, 1777, *ibid.,* 123.

[29] John Colcock to Edward Blake, December 20, 1777, *ibid.,* 120, 121.

[30] *Ibid.,* 122.

[31] "Log Book on Board His Majesty's Ship Carysfort," December 24, 1777, British Admiralty, Class 52, No. 1642, Public Records Office, London.

[32] Robert Fanshawe to Richard Howe, February 13, 1778, British Admiralty, Captains' Letters, Class I, 448.

[33] Salley (ed.), *Journal of South Carolina Navy Board,* December 26, 1777, p. 124.

[34] Biddle (ed.), *Charles Biddle's Autobiography*, 104.

[35] Ford (ed.), *Journal of Congress*, October 3, 1777, V, 842–46.

[36] Members of the Marine Committee attending Congress at York at that time were Henry Marchant, Rhode Island; Richard Law, Connecticut; Richard Henry Lee, Virginia; Arthur Middleton, South Carolina; and George Walton, Georgia. Roll call of Congress, October 4, 1777, *ibid.*, IX, 765, 771.

[37] Committee of Foreign Affairs to American Commissioners in France, October 6, 1777, Francis Wharton (ed.), *The Revolutionary Diplomatic Correspondence of the United States* (Washington, 1889), II, 399.

[38] Marine Committee to Nicholas Biddle, October 24, 1777, Marine Committee Letter Book, 105.

[39] Biddle (ed.), *Charles Biddle's Autobiography*, 103.

[40] Ford (ed.), *Journal of Congress*, October 20, 1777, IX, 822–24.

[41] Nicholas Biddle to Robert Morris, November 23, 1777, Franklin Delano Roosevelt Collection.

[42] Biddle (ed.), *Charles Biddle's Autobiography*, 104.

[43] Salley (ed.), *Journal of South Carolina Navy Board*, December 27, 1777, p. 125.

[44] Biddle (ed.), *Charles Biddle's Autobiography*, 104.

[45] Salley (ed.), *Journal of South Carolina Navy Board*, December 27, 29, 1777, pp. 125, 126.

[46] Biddle (ed.), *Charles Biddle's Autobiography*, 105.

[47] John Colcock to Edward Blake, January 7, 1778, Salley (ed.), *Journal of South Carolina Navy Board*, 129.

[48] *Ibid.*, January 8, 1778, p. 130.

[49] *Ibid.*, January 8, 9, 1778, pp. 131, 132.

[50] "Trevett."

[51] Will of Nicholas Biddle, January 12, 1778, Vol. 17, Will Book B, 815, Record of Wills, Charleston Free Library.

[52] James Biddle to Nathaniel Shaw, Jr., August 25, 1778, Nathaniel Shaw Papers, Book 7, p. 29.

[53] Will of Nicholas Biddle, January 12, 1778, Vol. 17, Book B, 815, Record of Wills, Charleston Free Library.

[54] "Order Book of the South Carolina Line," January 11, 1778, *South Carolina Historical and Genealogical Magazine*, VII (1906), 139, 140.

[55] "*Port Folio* Biography."

[56] "Order Book of the South Carolina Line," January 11, 1777, *loc. cit.*, 139, 140.

[57] Wilmot G. DeSaussure (comp.), *The Names as far as can be ascertained of the officers who served in the South Carolina Regiments in the Revolution* (Charleston, 1886), 7–10; "*Port Folio* Biography."

[58] Salley (ed.), *Journal of South Carolina Navy Board*, January 13, 1778, p. 133.

[59] Edward Blake to Nicholas Biddle, January 13, 1778, *ibid.*, 134.

Chapter XV

[1] "A Journal of the Proceedings of His Majesty's Ship the Perseus," January 15, 1778, British Admiralty, Class 51, No. 688.

[2] "Journal of H.M.S. Carysfort," January 15, 1778, British Admiralty, Class 51, No. 168.

[3] *Moultrie,* I, 199.

[4] Biddle (ed.), *Charles Biddle's Autobiography,* 105.

[5] "Extract of a letter from Charlestown," January 16, 1778, *Pennsylvania Gazette,* March 14, 1778.

[6] Biddle (ed.), *Charles Biddle's Autobiography,* 105.

[7] News dispatch from Charlestown, January 29, 1778, *Pennsylvania Gazette,* March 21, 1778.

[8] *Moultrie,* I, 200.

[9] *Ibid.,* 201.

[10] Robert Fanshawe to Philip Stephens, January 25, 1778, British Admiralty, Captains' Letters, I, 488, p. 1790.

[11] Salley (ed.), *Journal of South Carolina Navy Board,* January 19, 1778, p. 135.

[12] *Moultrie,* I, 201.

[13] Biddle (ed.), *Charles Biddle's Autobiography,* 104.

[14] Salley (ed.), *Journal of South Carolina Navy Board,* January 21, 1778, p. 135.

[15] "Order Book of the South Carolina Line," January 21, 1778, *loc. cit.,* 139, 140.

[16] News dispatch from New York, April 1, 1778, *Pennsylvania Ledger,* April 25, 1778.

[17] "Order Book of the South Carolina Line," January 27, 1778, *loc. cit.,* 139, 140.

[18] Salley (ed.), *Journal of South Carolina Navy Board,* January 27, 1778, p. 136.

[19] *Ibid.,* February 5, 1778, p. 139.

[20] *Ibid.,* February 16, 1778, p. 140.

[21] *"Port Folio* Biography."

[22] Rawlins Lowndes to Henry Laurens, March 30, 1778, *South Carolina Historical and Genealogical Magazine,* X (1909), 171–73. This letter is hereafter cited as "Lowndes"; *"Port Folio* Biography."

[23] *Johnson,* 121. Affidavit of Richard Fordham, December 7, 1821, Fanning Papers, 63.

[24] "Autobiographical Sketch of the Life of Gen. John Burrows of Lycoming Co., Penna.," *Pennsylvania Magazine of History and Biography,* XXXIV (1910), 426.

[25] "Account of the Rebel Armed Vessels at Charlestown," December 23, 1777, British Admiralty, Captains' Letters, I, 488, pp. 423–26.

[26] *"Port Folio* Biography."

[27] Will of William Barnes, January 9, 1778, Will Book 19, 368, Charleston Free Library; Will of John McDougall, January 14, 1778, *ibid.,* 367.

[28] *"Port Folio* Biography."

[29] J. Blake to Thomas Hall, October 7, 1804, Charles Biddle Letter Book.

[30] John Rutledge to Henry Laurens, February 16, 1778, "Henry Laurens' Correspondence," Frank Moore, *Materials for History* (New York, 1861).

[31] J. Blake to Thomas Hall, October 7, 1804, Charles Biddle Letter Book.

[32] *Johnson,* 119.

[33] Robert Fanshawe to Richard Howe, February 13, 1778, British Admiralty, Captains' Letters, I, 488, p. 1790.

[34] *Id.* to *id.,* March 13, 1778, I, 488, pp. 445–47. "Master's Log, H.M.S. *Lizard,"* February 10–15, 1778, British Admiralty, Class 52, No. 1839, Public Records Office, London.

[35] J. Blake to Thomas Hall, October 7, 1804, Charles Biddle Letter Book.

36 *Port Folio* Biography."

37 J. Blake to Thomas Hall, October 7, 1804, Charles Biddle Letter Book.

38 *Ibid.;* "Lowndes."

39 *Pennsylvania Packet,* July 25, 1778.

40 Philip Treglohn to John Paul Jones, December 14, 1779, John Paul Jones Manuscripts.

41 "Facts procured by Mrs. Lucy Watson . . . respecting her brothers," Fanning Papers, 46.

42 "Incidents of the war and its calamities to a family—best known to the author," John Fanning Watson Manuscript Annals, 435; Charles Biddle to James Biddle, June 10, 1778, Nicholas Biddle Letters.

43 Affidavit of Alexander Robinson *et al.,* March 16, 1778, British Admiralty, Class 43, p. 23, Account General, Miscellanea, Head Money Vouchers.

44 Certificate of John Davis, August 21, 1801, Charles Biddle Letter Book.

45 "Lowndes."

46 Charles Biddle's Rough Draft.

47 Astronomical observations for March 7, 1778, supplied by the U.S. Naval Observatory, Washington.

48 *Port Folio* Biography."

49 "A Journal of the Proceedings of His Majesty's Ship the Yarmouth," March 8, 1778, British Admiralty, Class 51, No. 1091, Public Records Office, London. This is hereafter cited as *"Yarmouth* Journal."

50 "A remarkable instance of the lives of four men being providentially saved" [Broadside], New York Public Library. This broadside is hereafter cited as *"Yarmouth* Broadside."

51 "Lowndes."

52 J. Blake to Thomas Hall, October 7, 1804, Charles Biddle Letter Book.

53 "Lowndes."

54 J. Blake to Thomas Hall, October 7, 1804, Charles Biddle Letter Book; Nicholas Vincent to James Young, March 17, 1778, British Admiralty, Captains' Letters, I, 488, p. 310.

55 *"Yarmouth* Journal," March 8, 9, 1778.

56 Certificate of John Davis, August 21, 1801, Charles Biddle Letter Book.

57 William Moultrie to Robert Howe, April 18, 1778, quoting Captain Morgan, of the *Fair American, Moultrie,* I, 371, 372.

58 *"Yarmouth* Journal," March 8, 9, 1778.

59 J. Blake to Thomas Hall, October 7, 1804, Charles Biddle Letter Book.

60 "Lowndes."

61 William Moultrie to Robert Howe, April 18, 1778, *Moultrie,* I, 371, 372.

62 Biddle (ed.), *Charles Biddle's Autobiography,* 208, 209; "Port Folio Biography"; *Johnson,* 120.

Chapter XVI

1 Nicholas Vincent to James Young, British Admiralty, Captains' Letters, I, 488, p. 310; news dispatch from New York, April 13, 1778, *Pennsylvania Evening Post,* May 1, 1778.

2 *"Yarmouth* Journal," March 8, 9, 1778.

3 J. Blake to Thomas Hall, October 7, 1804, Charles Biddle Letter Book.

4 Biddle (ed.), *Charles Biddle's Autobiography,* 109.

[5] New London news dispatch, April 17, 1778, *Connecticut Courant,* April 21, 1778; *Pennsylvania Packet,* July 25, 1778.

[6] *"Yarmouth* Broadside."

[7] "Muster Table of His Majesty's Ship the Yarmouth," March–April, 1778, British Admiralty, Class 36, No. 8072, Public Records Office, London.

[8] *Westminster Journal and London Political Miscellany,* June 20, 1778; New York *Gazette and the Weekly Mercury,* April 20, 1778.

[9] *"Yarmouth* Broadside."

[10] *"Yarmouth* Journal," March 12, 1778.

[11] *"Yarmouth* Broadside."

[12] *"Yarmouth* Journal," March 12, 1778.

[13] "Muster Table of His Majesty's Ship the Yarmouth," March–April, 1778.

[14] *"Yarmouth* Broadside."

[15] Edward Hay to George Germain, March 27, 1778, British Colonial Office, Class 28, p. 57, Public Records Office, London.

[16] *"Yarmouth* Broadside."

[17] Affidavit of Alexander Robinson, *et al.,* March 16, 1778.

[18] "Bounty to the Yarmouth for destroying the Randolph, an American Privateer," October 22, 1778, British Admiralty, Class 43, p. 23, Account General, Miscellanea, Head Money Vouchers.

[19] "Extract of a letter from Charlestown," March 29, 1778, *Pennsylvania Packet,* July 25, 1778.

[20] William Moultrie to Robert Howe, April 18, 1778, *Moultrie,* I, pp. 371, 372.

[21] Marine Committee to John Bradford, April 28, 1778, Marine Committee Letter Book.

[22] "Lowndes."

[23] *South Carolina and American General Gazette,* April 16, 1778.

[24] William Moultrie to Robert Howe, April 18, 1778, *Moultrie,* I, 371, 372; Salley (ed.), *Journal of South Carolina Navy Board,* April 23, 1778, pp. 149, 150.

[25] Biddle (ed.), *Charles Biddle's Autobiography,* 107–109.

[26] *South Carolina and American General Gazette,* June 11, 18, 1778.

[27] John F. Watson to Daniel B. Cook, February 8, 1822, Fanning Papers, 55–57.

[28] Notes on death of Midshipman Simeon Fanning, *ibid.,* 64.

[29] New York *Gazette and Weekly Mercury,* April 20, 1778.

[30] *Pennsylvania Evening Post* [Supplement], April 20, 1778; *Pennsylvania Ledger,* April 22, 1778.

[31] William Ellery to William Vernon, April 25, 1778, "Papers of William Vernon and the Navy Board," *Rhode Island Historical Society Publications,* VIII (1900–1901), 239.

[32] Samuel Chase to Thomas Johnson, April 20, 1778, "Journal and Correspondence of the Council of Maryland, April 1, 1778–October 26, 1779," *Maryland Historical Society Publication, Archives of Maryland* (Baltimore), XXI (1901), 43.

[33] John Brown to Robert Morris, April 25, 1778, Stan V. Henkels (comp.), *The Confidential Correspondence of Robert Morris,* Catalogue No. 1183 (Philadelphia, 1917), 368.

[34] Memorandum of Mrs. Mary Biddle, undated, but with postscript added subsequent to 1778, Biddle (ed.), *Charles Biddle's Autobiography,* 242.

[35] Mrs. William Biddle to Mrs. George Lux, undated, *ibid.,* 3.

Index